Civil Engineering Quantities

Civil Engineering Quantities

IVOR H. SEELEY

and

GEORGE P. MURRAY
FRICS
Chartered Quantity Surveyor,
Formerly Napier University, Edinburgh

Sixth Edition

palgrave

First published 2001 by
PALGRAVE
Houndmills, Basingstoke, Hampshire RG21 6XS and
175 Fifth Avenue, New York, N.Y. 10010
Companies and representatives throughout the world

PALGRAVE is the new global academic imprint of St. Martin's Press LLC Scholarly and Reference Division and Palgrave Publishers Ltd (formerly Macmillan Press Ltd).

ISBN 0–333–80074–5

This book is printed on paper suitable for recycling and made from fully managed and sustained forest sources.

A catalogue record for this book is available from the British Library.

10 9 8 7 6 5 4 3 2 1
10 09 08 07 06 05 04 03 02 01

Printed in Great Britain by
Antony Rowe Ltd, Chippenham, Wiltshire

Contents

Part 2 – Worked Examples 117

Preface to Sixth Edition

This edition has been completely revised and overhauled to take the late Ivor Seeley's long established and popular standard text book into the twenty-first century. Apart from the necessary updating of the detailed information contained in the text, the principal change from the fifth edition is the separation of the explanatory material in Part 1 of the book from the 21 worked examples which are now contained in Part 2. This format was adopted because the majority of practical worked examples inevitably contain several work categories in their construction and therefore do not readily fit into any one particular explanatory chapter.

It is considered that this change makes accessing of material simpler, with all chapters being cross-referenced to the appropriate worked examples while all the worked examples are equally cross-referenced back to the appropriate chapters and other relevant worked examples. This layout permits readers wishing to study a particular classification of civil engineering to start either with the text or with a worked example as suits their needs.

Another important change which makes accessing material simpler is the re-ordering of the chapters of Part 1 of the book to follow the Work Classification order of Section 8 of CESMM3. These two significant changes in format should make the book much more user-friendly.

CESMM3 has an ethos of cost significance throughout the various rules and measurement conventions, and an important aim of this book is to highlight such cost-sensitive features so that bill compilers can actively improve the quality of bill information conveyed to tendering contractors. Method-related charges represent an area where CESMM3 provides an optional means of pricing the significance of non-permanent work and plant utilised in executing contract works. These charges are given full coverage along with considerable emphasis on the cost significance of location and the effect of bodies of water on work. In addition, in Part 2 of the book, there are five worked examples where bodies of water are involved and demonstrate the operation of these rules.

It is intended that this new edition should serve the requirements of practising civil engineers and quantity surveyors and students of these disciplines in the preparation of bills of quantities. In order to study the measurement of civil engineering successfully, readers should have a copy of CESMM3 to hand for reference when referring to this book.

Edinburgh George P. Murray

Acknowledgements

The authors express their thanks to The Institution of Civil Engineers for kind permission to quote from the *Civil Engineering Standard Method of Measurement* (Third Edition) and the *General Conditions of Contract for use in connection with Works of Civil Engineering Construction* (Sixth Edition).

The authors are deeply indebted to Dr Martin Barnes for his kind permission to refer to his authoritative work, *The CESMM3 Handbook* (Thomas Telford, London, 1992) which comprehensively amplifies the third edition of the *Civil Engineering Standard Method of Measurement.*

Grateful thanks are due to Mr Nicholas Hudson, Manager, Education and Training, The Royal Institution of Chartered Surveyors for permission to make use of past RICS examination papers as some of the Worked Examples in Part 2 of the book.

Hints on Referring to this Book

The book comprises two parts:
Part 1 – Measurement Theory and Practice
Ethos of CESMM3 and the detailed rules of each Work Classification.
Part 2 – Worked Examples
Practical examples with detailed measurements to illustrate the rules of CESMM3.

There are various ways in which this book may be accessed:

Firstly and obviously, the traditional approach of reading the volume right through would be appropriate for a student requiring to study all or most types of billing of civil engineering work under CESMM3.

Secondly, readers only requiring guidance or revision of a particular Work Classification can find the relevant chapter very quickly, as all chapters in Part 1 follow the same order as the Work Classifications in CESMM3. Appropriate Worked Examples of various complexities are then cross-referenced at the end of each chapter.

Thirdly, readers requiring guidance on billing a particular form of construction can access an appropriate Worked Example from the contents of Part 2 or the Index. The relevant explanatory chapters and all other related Worked Examples are cross-referenced in each Worked Example should further study be required.

To gain the most benefit from this book, readers are advised to have a copy of CESMM3 at hand for cross-reference.

PART 1

Measurement Theory and Practice

CHAPTER 1

Scope and Context of Civil Engineering Measurement

Introduction

Civil engineering measurement is a fundamental requirement for the evaluation of the cost of proposed works and the calculation of the final accounts for work executed. Formal agreement to standardise the method of preparing such measurements within the civil engineering industry occurred much later than in the building sector but the current code, *Civil Engineering Standard Method of Measurement – Third Edition* (or 'CESMM3'), is an excellent document with an innovative tabular layout which makes reference to the rules very convenient.

It should be noted that access to a copy of CESMM3 is strongly recommended during any study of this book as frequent references to that document will be made throughout the text.

Civil engineering contracts may involve very large works both in scale and cost and it follows that the method of measurement should reflect this in its ethos and approach. Under CESMM the engineer or surveyor preparing the bill has to consider not only the tangible finished construction but the adverse conditions under which some of the work may be executed, and to allow the tendering contractor to include the cost of temporary works or plant not forming part of the final measured work.

Some engineers were critical of this approach to measurement when it was first introduced in 1976 in the first edition of CESMM as they felt they were being expected to take on some of the risk by pointing out special difficulties on site such as bodies of water and other special circumstances. They felt these risk factors were strictly up to the contractor to spot and for the contractor to decide on how to overcome such difficulties on site. However they rather missed the point, which is that a truly useful bill of quantities should reflect the nature of the work proposed and the circumstances under which it will be executed. There is no intention of absorbing any associated risk within the bill of quantities and taking risk away from contractors; rather the bill can be viewed as providing additional cost-significant information which contractors may use to formulate their tender prices. In this respect bills should not impose or suggest methods of executing the work unless there is no choice because the engineer requires a particular constructional method to be adopted – in which case this material fact should be made quite clear.

There are several ways in which CESMM3 reflects the ethos of cost significance of location and method. Although these features will be dealt with in more detail later, it is worthwhile to give some instances here:

(1) CESMM3, rule 2.5 may be summarised as 'work should be itemised in the bill of quantities in sufficient detail to distinguish between different classes of work, and between work of the same nature in different locations or any other circumstance which may affect cost'.

(2) One of the innovative features of CESMM3 is the incorporation of method-related options allowing for pricing elements of cost not necessarily directly proportional to finished work. Civil engineering frequently involves the use of costly plant or sophisticated temporary works which are not obvious in the final structures but nevertheless represent very significant cost. Contractors are permitted to insert their own items into the bills to cover for method-related charges both as fixed and time-related costs.

A major criticism of some earlier building methods of measurement was that 80 per cent of the cost was contained in 20 per cent of the items – thus 80 per cent of the items were effectively a waste of time and effort in producing them. CESMM3 has largely addressed this aspect in that the measured items represent the main cost elements of the work while the ancillary labours and the like are frequently deemed to be included. The contractor can readily value these ancillary elements from the contract drawings and specifications and incorporate them in the costings for the all-inclusive main item.

Development of Civil Engineering Codes of Measurement

The Institution of Civil Engineers published a report of a committee dealing with engineering quantities in 1933, and thus provided for the first time a standard procedure for drafting bills of quantities for civil engineering work. Prior to the introduction of this document there was no uniformity of practice in the measurement of civil engineering quantities, and engineers responsible for the preparation of civil engineering bills of quantities largely worked up their own systems of measurement as they thought fit. The order and nature of the billed items, the units of measurement and even the method of tabulating the information in specific columns – usually referred to as 'ruling' – which was adopted for the bills of quantities, varied considerably.

It will be appreciated that this lack of uniformity in the preparation of civil engineering bills of quantities made the task of civil engineering contractors in pricing them far more difficult than it is today, now that a more uniform method of measurement has been generally adopted.

In 1953, after much deliberation and consultation, a revised document, entitled *Standard Method of Measurement of Civil Engineering Quantities*, was issued by the Institution of Civil Engineers, and this was reissued with slight amendments in 1963 and a metric addendum in 1968. This amended the previous (1933) report to meet the changing needs of civil engineers and contractors, and tied up with the provisions of the General Conditions of Contract for use in connection with Works of Civil Engineering Construction. Certain sections of the 1933 report were simplified, particularly those dealing with concrete and pipe lines. New sections covering site investigation and site clearance were added and provision was made for the measurement of prestressed concrete.

In 1967 the Construction Industry Research and Information Association (CIRIA) established a working party to identify research needs aimed at improving contract procedure. One of the projects that followed aimed at developing and testing an improved form of bill of quantities for civil engineering contracts, and the results were summarised in CIRIA report 34. This study sought to define the needs of the industry and to propose means of making the information in the bill more useful, and so to reduce the high administrative cost of measurement. The investigations incorporated the use of experimental features of bills of quantities on live civil engineering contracts. The dominant conclusion in the report is that civil engineering bills of quantities, apart from scheduling the components of the contemplated work, should also contain charges related to the method and timing of the contractor's operations.

Following the publication of the CIRIA Report a steering committee was appointed by the Institution of Civil Engineers to undertake a detailed reappraisal of the civil engineering code of measurement. The steering committee spent five years formulating its proposals and throughout this period consulted extensively with the construction industry and other relevant bodies and persons. The resulting *Civil Engineering Standard Method of Measurement* was published in 1976.

The principal changes introduced by the CESMM were as follows:

(1) Greater standardisation of format, both in the component items and in the way they are described. A reduction of the previous variety that frequently arose from house styles and often led to unnecessary confusion to tendering contractors.

(2) It introduced various levels of classification or pigeon holes from which descriptions can be developed. There are also coding arrangements, which have no contractual significance, although they will assist where computers are used and form a useful basis for cost analysis.

(3) Use of method-related charges to represent more clearly site construction costs, such as the cost of setting up and operating plant, labour teams and the like. In these cases the best cost parameter is not the finished physical work but what the contractor has to do on site.

(4) A large number of small changes to detailed rules of measurement, resulting in the removal of anomalies and differences in interpretation. Cost is very much influenced by the location of work, and although it was not found practicable to frame rules to cover this, engineers or surveyors preparing bills can reflect this in the way they prepare the information and describe the items. It was claimed that bills prepared in accordance with the CESMM would be easier to compile, be of greater use to the contractor, better reflect the costs involved and more effectively serve other purposes, such as programming, cost control and management.

The second edition of *Civil Engineering Standard Method of Measurement* (CESMM2) was published in 1985, following two years of preparation work. The measurement notes were retitled 'rules' and expanded, rearranged and classified to make reference and interpretation easier. Additional items were inserted to keep pace with new technology, particularly in site investigation and geotechnical processes. A new section was included to cover sewer renovation. Bills produced under CESMM2 were more comprehensive and problem areas in the first edition suitably clarified. Furthermore, an attempt was made to secure greater compatability with building measurement practice, with the introduction of SMM7.

The third edition of *Civil Engineering Standard Method of Measurement* (CESMM3) updated the code, brought it into alignment with the sixth edition of the *ICE Conditions of Contract*, and new sections were introduced on water mains renovation and simple building works incidental to civil engineering works.

Scope of Civil Engineering Works

Before comparing the methods adopted for the measurement of civil engineering work with those used for building work, some consideration should be given to the nature and scope of civil engineering works, to appreciate fully and understand the need for a different and separate mode of measurement to operate in respect of these latter works. This comparison is included primarily for the use and guidance of quantity surveyors, many of whom are mainly concerned with the measurement of building works.

Civil engineering works encompass a wide range of different projects, some of which are of great magnitude. Vast cuttings and embankments, mass and reinforced concrete structures, large structural steel construction, reservoirs, sewage schemes, piling for heavy foundations, harbour works, dry docks, roads, canals and railways, all form the subject matter of civil engineering contracts.

These works require considerable skill, ingenuity and technical knowledge in both their design and construction. The use of new materials and techniques is continually changing the nature and methods of construction used in these projects, and the increasing size and complexity of these works demand a greater knowledge and skill for their measurement and valuation.

Some works involve elements of uncertainty, as for example the excavation work for extensive deep foundations or the laying of underground services under very variable site conditions. Many civil engineering projects are carried out on the banks of rivers or on the sea coast, and on low-lying marshy land, thus making the operations that are involved even more difficult and exacting. For these reasons it is essential that a code of measurement specially applicable to this class of work should be used.

Owing to the magnitude of most civil engineering works, it is advisable that the code of measurement adopted should be relatively simple, to avoid the separate measurement of labours and small items, some of which were dealt with separately when measuring building work, prior to the introduction of SMM7. Furthermore, owing to the very nature of the works, there is a great deal more uncertainty than on building works, and the method of measurement needs to be more flexible to allow for variations in the methods of construction used and changes effected during the course of the constructional work made necessary by site conditions. The main function of a bill of quantities is to enable prices to be obtained for the project on a uniform basis and precise dimensions cannot always be prepared at the 'taking-off' stage. The quantities should always be as accurate as the drawings and other data permit but they will be adjusted following the remeasurement of the completed work on the site and the work, as executed, valued at billed or comparable rates, on what is often termed a 'measure and value contract'.

Extensive temporary works are likely to be required during the construction of civil engineering works and the contractor will need to cover the cost of these works in some part of the bill of quantities.

Civil Engineering Contracts Generally

In the simplest of terms a contract can be defined as a legally binding agreement between parties. In the case of civil engineering works the contract is normally an agreement to have work done in return for a specified sum of money. The client commissioning the work is legally known as the 'employer' while the party carrying out the work is legally known as the 'contractor'. It is important that the extent of the proposed work is clearly specified while the timing and method of payments for the work also are clearly stipulated.

In practice, within the UK, the majority of civil engineering contracts will be based on one of the standard ICE conditions of contract issued by agreement between the Institution of Civil Engineers, the Association of Consulting Engineers and the Federation of Civil Engineering Contractors. There is a wide choice of procurement routes available to clients, varying from the 'traditional' based on a design by consultant engineers and a prepared bill of quantities, through to design and construct where the contractor is responsible for the structural integrity of the finished works. There are ICE standard forms of contract to suit these varying circumstances but as this book is primarily concerned with civil engineering measurement, the form of contract will be assumed to be the traditional approach based on the *ICE Condition of Contract*, 6th edition, drawings, specification and bills of quantities. Should the ICE 6th edition be adopted there is provision in clause 57 for the use of CESMM3 as the rules of measurement within the contract.

The foregoing deals with the concept of civil engineering contracts only in the most simple of terms but it is prudent to draw attention to legislation enacted in the 1990s which has affected construction contracts in the UK. The two Acts which have affected virtually all work with very few exceptions are:

(1) The Construction (Design and Management) Regulations 1994; usually referred to as the 'CDM Regulations'.

(2) The Housing Grants, Construction and Regeneration Act 1996; usually referred to as the 'Construction Act'.

The first is concerned with safety throughout the total life of any construction through the design stage, construction phase, occupancy or use and the ultimate demolition or decommissioning of the works. The second is concerned with fair payment terms and dispute resolution within construction contracts for clients, contractors and sub-contractors.

These Acts apply irrespective of the contract conditions chosen by a client but have been fully implemented by amendments in the appropriate ICE standard conditions.

Contract Documentation

Assuming the traditional procurement route with ICE 6th edition form of contract and a bill of quantities then the contract documents in order of importance are as follows:

(1) *Conditions of Contract*
As detailed above, the conditions of contract represent the legally binding agreement between the parties and cover such important elements as expected completion date of the work, methods and timing of payments, access to the works, sequence of construction, storage areas available to the contractor etc.

(2) *Contract Drawings*
These indicate the location, scope and design complexity of the works and show graphically the full extent of what is required to be constructed.

(3) *Specification*
The specification details the quality required in the works. The contract drawings indicate locational information but cannot readily represent quality – they therefore have cross-references to specification clauses which fully describe the expected quality of each element. Quality may be specified by prescriptive or performance criteria.

(4) *Bill of Quantities*
The definition used in rule 1.7 of CESMM3 is as follows: 'Bill of Quantities means a list of items giving brief identifying descriptions and estimated quantities of the work comprised in a Contract'. This definition rightly infers that the bill should be brief and should not unnecessarily repeat information contained elsewhere on the drawings or the specification. Because of the uncertain nature of much of civil engineering work at the billing stage the quantities are correctly defined as 'estimated', and in the majority of contracts the works will be remeasured on site to reflect the true quantities actually required.

It should be noted that bills of quantities, while desirable, are not essential contract documents. However the other three documents are essential in order to fully detail what is contractually required.

Reasons for Bills of Quantities

Although not essential to form a contract, bills are nevertheless commonly prepared for civil engineering contracts in the UK. The reasons for the popularity of bills of quantities can be summarised as follows:

(1) All tendering contractors base their prices on the same information and therefore tenders are strictly comparable (even if an error exists in the bill).

(2) Contractors are saved the costly exercise of each having to take off quantities for themselves. Should there be an error in their own quantities the result would be that the tender figure is too high or too low irrespective of their intended rates for items of work.

(3) Bills provide a fair basis for valuing variations and adjustments for the final account.

(4) Bills may provide a convenient basis for valuation of certificated stage payments during the contract, before the accurate remeasurement figures are available.

(5) Bills provide an approximate checklist for the contractor to order materials and other resources.

(6) Bills can provide data for cost analyses for use in cost planning of future projects.

Some clients, in recent years, have been attracted to the 'design and construct' procurement route which transfers more risk to the contractor. This has not lead to the demise of bills of quantities as the majority of contractors still prefer to build up their tenders using a traditional bill to price with unit rates. Contractors will either prepare these bills in house or commission them along with the project design from outside consultants.

Comparison of Civil Engineering and Building Methods of Measurement

There are two separate and distinct practices of measurement operating for civil engineering and building works. There is, however, considerable common ground as regards the general approach, units of measurement employed and items of work that can be measured under both codes.

As previously stated, civil engineering work should be measured in accordance with *Civil Engineering Standard Method of Measurement* prepared by the Institution of Civil Engineers and the Federation of Civil Engineering Contractors. Building works are generally measured in accordance with *Standard Method of Measurement of Building Works*, issued by the Royal Institution of Chartered Surveyors and the Building Employers Confederation.

The details of building works are usually in a far more precise stage at the time of preparing the bill of quantities than is the case with civil engineering works. Furthermore, building work normally covers more works sections, and is in consequence subject to more detailed measurement. For instance, in building work, backfilling trenches, compacting trench bottoms and earthwork support are each measured separately, whereas in civil engineering work most of these items are included in the excavation rates. In the absence of variations in design, most building work with the exception of sub-structural, drainage and external works, will not be subject to remeasurement and the contractor will be paid for the quantities of work incorporated in the bill of quantities.

In contrast, in civil engineering, most of the work will be subject to remeasurement and the bill quantities are merely considered as estimated. The items under CESMM3 rules are generally quite brief and the bill is much less of a stand-alone document than is the case with building bills, thus the tendering contractor will require to refer frequently to the drawings and specification in order to amplify the bill items for pricing purposes. There is often more locational and method-related information presented in civil engineering bills and contractors require to consider these factors in assessing their rates for the work. Furthermore as a greater proportion of the work is often below ground level, there is a consequently increased risk in tendering for civil engineering work owing to such variable factors as nature of the ground, ground water and weather.

CESMM3 avoids the expression 'measured extra over' in the various rules. However the concept does exist in the method of measurement in some Work Classifications, but the arguably ambiguous phrase 'extra over' is eliminated. One example of this would be in Class I: Pipework – Pipes, where measurement rule M3 states that the measured lengths of pipes in trenches shall include the lengths occupied by fittings and valves. The fittings and valves are measured by number in Class J: Pipework – Fittings and Valves but separately identified as within trenches (additional description rules A4). Fittings and valves in trenches are therefore effectively extra over the pipes in which they occur but not so stated in the Bill of Quantities.

In some of the larger civil engineering contracts there is also some building work. With these contracts the question often arises as to how the works as a whole are to be measured.

Take, for example, a large power station contract. The best procedure would appear to be to measure the main superstructure, the ancillary buildings and possibly the chimneys in accordance with *Standard Method of Measurement of Building Works*. The structural steel frameworks could be measured under either code of measurement. The remainder of the power station contract, comprising heavy foundations, piling, wharves and jetties, railway sidings, cooling towers, circulating water ducts, roads, sewers and water mains, are all essentially civil engineering work, and are best measured in accordance with *Civil Engineering Standard Method of Measurement*.

When CESMM was published in 1976 it introduced a different approach to measurement and pricing with three divisions of measurement in each work class with consequently greater uniformity in bill descriptions, and the use of method-related charges to permit the separation of items that are not proportional to the quantities of permanent work. SMM7 adopted a similar approach for building work and hence increased the amount of commonality in the approach adopted in the two measuring codes, which was also extended into some of the detailed measuring procedures, such as structural metalwork/steelwork.

Readers requiring further information on building measurement are referred to *Building Quantities Explained* by Ivor H. Seeley and Roger Winfield (Macmillan – now Palgrave, 1998).

Effect of CESMM3 on Pricing

CESMM3 permits greater standardisation in the format of bills of quantities and this assists contractors in pricing. The drafting committee believe that bills prepared under CESMM3 are more consistent, with work adequately itemised and described to include cost-significant items with a consistent level of detail. It is also stated that the coding system permits estimating, valuation, purchasing and cost control to use the same numerical references and that these will also simplify computerised data processing.

General Items and Method-Related Charges

Where the general items have been satisfactorily listed and priced and full use made by the contractor of method-related charges, then the pricing of measured work is simpler. In theory all services and facilities that are not proportional to the quantities of permanent work will have been separated for pricing purposes. In practice all sorts of permutations are possible.

One contractor may not insert any method-related charge items, while another could include for each and every type of plant, as encouraged to do by Class A3, which, for instance, lists earth compaction plant and concrete mixing plant. Both of these types of plant involve some fixed costs in transporting plant and off-loading together with the subsequent transporting to a depot or another site. In-between these fixed events the plant is operated and maintained and these can be regarded as time-related charges. On the other hand they could be considered as essential components of the earth compaction or concrete production, and hence could be included in the measured work unit rates.

These possible variations in approach in dealing with the pricing of plant could result in considerable differences in measured rates and general items. Hence the analysis, checking and comparison of priced bills by quantity surveyors and engineers may require considerable care before making any recommendations to clients regarding acceptance of particular lenders.

However the majority of contractors, engineers and quantity surveyors now find the detailed rules within the various Work Classifications to be good, practical and workable requirements both at the pre-tender and post-tender stages of projects.

CHAPTER 2

Fundamental Principles of CESMM3

Introduction

Civil Engineering Standard Method of Measurement, third edition (CESMM3) defines a 'Bill of Quantities' as a list of items giving brief identifying descriptions and estimated quantities of the work comprised in a Contract (1.7). (Perhaps the word 'concise' would be better substituted for 'brief'.) All references in brackets refer to paragraphs in *Civil Engineering Standard Method of Measurement* (paragraphs being the terminology used in CESMM3).

A civil engineering bill is not intended to describe fully the nature and extent of the work in a contract, and in this respect differs fundamentally from a bill for building work. The descriptions of civil engineering billed items merely *identify* the work and the estimator pricing the bill will need to obtain most of the information required for estimating from the Drawings and Specification.

Martin Barnes in *CESMM3 Handbook* (Telford, 1992) has described how the need for civil engineering contract financial control arises from the difficulty experienced by Employers in clearly identifying to Contractors their exact requirements and the difficulty of Contractors in assessing accurately the probable cost of the work. To achieve effective control a Bill of Quantities must be prepared with the object of limiting these difficulties as far as is practicable.

One of the ways of limiting these difficulties was the recognition in CESMM that site costs are not necessarily solely represented by measurements of completed pieces of work, rather some means of indicating location, nature or importance should be incorporated where appropriate. The paragraphs in CESMM3 which refer to this important aspect are (2.5), (5.8), (5.10) and (5.20). These requirements may be summarised as:

(2.5) Although Bills of Quantities should be kept as brief and simple as possible, work should be itemised in sufficient detail to distinguish between different classes of work, and between work of the same nature carried out in differing circumstances and locations.

(5.8) Bills may be arranged in separately numbered parts to distinguish between work affected by differences in nature, location, access, sequence, timing or other special characteristic.

(5.10) Work is normally itemised and described in accordance with the rules in the various Work Classifications – but further itemisation and additional description may be provided if the nature, location, importance or any other special characteristic is thought likely to give rise to special methods or costs.

(5.20) Where existing bodies of open water (not groundwater) are on site or bound the site, each body of water is to be identified in the preambles to the bill. Reference is to be given to Drawings showing the boundaries of such water and any anticipated fluctuation in water levels.

Another feature introduced in CESMM to assist contractors to assess the price of work in a more practical manner is 'method-related charges'. These charges may be of benefit where costs are not strictly in proportion to the quantities of work executed and contractors can opt to use them in their tender if they so desire. Method-related charges are detailed in Section 7 of CESMM3 and are fully explained later in this chapter.

Definitions (CESMM3; Section 1)

A number of definitions are contained in Section 1 of CESMM3 and the more important are now stated and examined.

The term *work* (1.5) differs from *Works* in the ICE Conditions of Contract, having a wider coverage to embrace everything that the Contractor has to do and includes all such liabilities, obligations and risks.

The expression *expressly required* (1.6) is used extensively in CESMM3, and appears in Bills of Quantities to indicate that specific requirements will be shown on the Drawings, described in the Specification or ordered by the Engineer. Typical examples of its use in CESMM3 are rule A2 of Class B relating to trial pits and trenches involving hand excavation, rule M13 of Class E relating to the double handling of excavated material and rule M15 of Class E covering timber or metal supports left in excavations. In these cases, the work will only be measured and paid for when ordered by the Engineer. It is important that agreement should be reached between the Contractor and the Engineer's Representative as to the extent of the express requirement, and that this shall be recorded before work is started.

Daywork (1.8) is the method of valuing work on the basis of time spent by operatives, materials used and plant employed, with an allowance to cover oncosts and profit. This basis of valuation is considered in more detail later in this chapter and may be used where billed or adjusted rates would be inappropriate.

CESMM3 contains four surface definitions to be used in excavation and associated work, with the object of avoiding uncertainty in the excavation level descriptions. *Original Surface* (1.10) denotes the original surface of the ground before any work is carried out. As work proceeds the Contractor is likely to excavate to lower surfaces, eventually producing the *Final Surface* (1.11) as shown on the Drawings, and being the surface that will normally receive the permanent work. There may also be intermediate stages, as for instance first to excavate to formation or base level of a road, below which excavation is needed over certain areas for catchpits and other features. The reduced or formation level constitutes the *Excavated Surface* (1.13) for the main excavation and the *Commencing Surface* (1.12) for the lower excavation, while the lowest excavated surface (base of catchpit) constitutes both the *Final Surface* (1.11) and the *Excavated Surface* (1.13) for the lower pocket of excavation. The substitution of the term 'surface' for 'level' stems from the fact that all excavated and original surfaces are not necessarily level.

Paragraph 1.14 enables ranges of dimensions in billed descriptions to be reduced in length and ensures uniformity of presentation and interpretation. For example, general excavation could be billed with a maximum depth range of 2–5 m, signifying that the excavation is to depths exceeding 2 m but not exceeding 5 m.

General Principles (CESMM3; Section 2)

CESMM3 is concerned with the measurement of civil engineering work, but where some complex building, mechanical engineering, electrical engineering, or other work is included in a civil engineering contract, then this work should be adequately itemised and described and the method of measurement stated in the Preamble to the Bill of Quantities (2.2 and 5.4). Large civil engineering contracts often include some items of relatively simple building work, such as the superstructure to a pumphouse on a sewage treatment works. In these circumstances, the work will be classified as simple building works incidental to civil engineering works and measured in accordance with Class Z of CESMM3.

Maintenance and repair work, and alterations to existing work are not generally mentioned in CESMM3. As a general rule itemisation and description of such work should follow the principles prescribed for the relevant class of new work. Reference to extraction or removal will need to be given in billed descriptions or headings. The principal exceptions relate to sewer and water main renovation and ancillary works which are covered in Class Y and illustrated in examples in Part 2 of this book.

Occasionally it will be necessary to deal with components which are not covered in CESMM3 and non-standard items should be inserted in the bill which adequately describe the work and its location. Paragraph 2.5 emphasises the principle of providing for the inclusion of possible cost differentials arising from changes in location or any other aspects, by giving the Contractor the opportunity to make allowance for these cost differences in rates and prices.

The importance of locational information may be illustrated by considering the cost-significant factors involved in pipe trench excavation, such as the practicability of battering the sides of trenches, the existence or otherwise of boulders, adequacy of working space and related matters. For this reason lengths of pipelaying are billed separately with locations indicated by reference to the Drawings as rule A1 of Class I. The probable impact of construction costs must be considered and the work suitably subdivided in the bill to indicate the likely influence of location on cost.

In some instances CESMM3 states that certain procedures *may* or *should* be employed as against the more positive direction used in other parts of the Method incorporating the word *shall*. In the former instances there is no infringement of the CESMM if the procedure is not followed and this is intentional. For example, paragraph 4.3 indicates that code numbers may be used to number items in Bills of Quantities and 5.22 recommends that Bills should be set out on A4 size paper – both relate to bill layout and arrangement and have no contractual significance. Paragraph 5.8 suggests that priceable items in the Bill of Quantities may be arranged into numbered parts, while 5.10 recommends that the inclusion of further itemisation and additional description may be provided to incorporate factors which could give rise to special methods of construction or cost considerations. In the latter instances the person preparing the bill has to exercise judgement on likely cost-significant factors, and it would be quite unrealistic to adopt more positive terminology, which could entitle the Contractor to a Bill amendment.

Application of the Work Classification (CESMM3; Section 3)

The Work Classification provides the basic framework of CESMM3 constituting, as it does, a list of the commonly occurring components of civil engineering work. It will assist with Contractor's cost control, recording of prices as a basis for pre-contract estimating, computer processing and specification preparation.

There are 26 main classes of work, with each class made up of three divisions, which classify work at successive levels of detail. Each division contains a list of up to eight descriptive features of work. Each item description in the Bill of Quantities will incorporate one feature from each division of the relevant class (3.1). For example, Class H (precast concrete) contains three divisions – the first classifies different types of precast concrete units (beams, columns, slabs and the like), the second classifies the different units by their dimensions (lengths and areas) and the third classifies them by their mass (weight). With pipes (Class I) the classification is pipe material, nominal bore, and depth at which laid.

The entries in the divisions are termed 'descriptive features' as when three are linked together (one from each division), they normally provide a reasonably comprehensive description of a billed item. However many items will require further description either because of paragraph (5.13) which requires additional description where special considerations are present, or because of the four other reqirements in the Work Classifications as now explained.

Each class contains a set of measurement, definition, coverage and additional description rules, which amplify and clarify the preceding information. It is vital to read these notes in conjunction with the preceding measurement particulars, since they may make reference to factors that have to be included in the price of the measured item without the need for specific mention, or give matters that have to be inserted in the description of the measured item in the Bill.

Billed item descriptions are not required to follow precisely the wording in the work classification, although in many instances it will be advisable to do so. In measuring a joint in concrete made up of a rubber waterstop 175 mm wide, the billed description can state exactly that without the need to mention that the waterstop is 'plastics or rubber; width not exceeding 150–200 mm' as G652. On occasions an additional description rule accompanying the work classification will require more descriptive detail than is given in the classified lists, for instance the sizes and types of marker posts shall be stated in item descriptions (Class K; additional description rule A11).

The various rules override the tabulated classifications and it is better to simplify the wording of the work classification rather than to duplicate information, although the classification list will still provide the code number for the item where it is required. For example, the item description of a carriageway slab of DTp specified paving quality concrete, 150 mm deep, will not require the inclusion of concrete pavement from the first division of Class R, since it would be superfluous, nor would the addition of depth, 100–150 mm, be appropriate when the actual depth of the slab is required in additional description rule A1 (Class R), and to accord with the procedure described in 3.10.

Lists of up to eight different descriptive features are given in work classifications to cover the most commonly encountered items in the class, but they cannot encompass every conceivable alternative, hence subdivision 9 is left vacant to accommodate some other type or category.

The assembly of a description based on the three divisions of tabulated classification may not always be adequate, having regard to Section 5 of the CESMM3 and rules accompanying work classifications. It is helpful to separate the standard description from the additional information by a semicolon.

Billed descriptions of components for Permanent Works shall be concise and shall not include the processes of production or constructional techniques. An item of fabric reinforcement could read 'Mild steel fabric reinforcement type A252 to BS 4483, nominal mass: 3.95 kg/m^2', but certainly not as 'Supply, deliver, cut and fix mild steel fabric reinforcement type A252 to BS 4483, nominal mass: 3.95 kg/m^2'. However carefully such an item is drafted, there is a risk that an operation may be omitted, such as cleaning the reinforcement, and for which the Contractor might subsequently claim. It is more satisfactory to rely on the wording of the Specification, Drawings and Conditions of Contract together to provide the complete contractual requirements. Workmanship requirements should be written into the Specification and not the Bill of Quantities.

No billed item may contain more than one component from each division of a work classification list (3.4). Taking Earthworks (Class E) as an example, a single billed item cannot incorporate excavation for foundations, filling and disposal of excavated material, nor can it include both topsoil and rock in the same item, nor a combination of maximum depth ranges. A similar principle applies to the use of additional descriptions, which often stem from additional description rules accompanying the CESMM3 work classification. For instance in Class I (Pipework – Pipes) additional description rule A2 requires materials, joint types, nominal bores and lining requirements of pipes to be stated in item descriptions. Hence variations in any of these components will result in separate billed items. This highlights the importance of rules in the work classifications – they are not merely explanatory comments and the rules of measurement, definition, coverage and additional description must be read very closely in conjunction with the tabulated classification lists. The measurement rules (3.6) identify any variation from the normal measurement approach described in rule 5.18; definition rules (3.7) clarify the meaning of terms used in the work classification; coverage rules (3.8) amplify the extent of the work to be priced in bill items; and the additional description rules (3.9 and 3.10) make provision for further descriptions and subdivisions of billed items. Some believe that the work classification is unduly inhibiting, but it does at least ensure a good measure of uniformity in bill descriptions.

The CESMM3 Work Classification is confined to Permanent Works and the rates inserted against these items in the Bill of Quantities with cover the costs that are proportional to the quantities of measured work. For instance, there is no item of measured work for bringing plant to and from the site. Where the cost of this activity is significant the Contractor could advantageously enter it as a method-related charge.

The Work Classification prescribes the unit of measurement to be used for each billed item, ranging from stated sums and numbered items, linear items in metres, areas in square metres (hectares for general site clearance), volumes in cubic metres and weight (mass) in tonnes.

Coding and Numbering of Items (CESMM3; Section 4)

Section 4 of CESMM3 describes the coding system adopted in the Work Classification and how it can be used in the Bill of Quantities for numbering billed items.

Each item in the Work Classification has been assigned a code number consisting of a letter and not more than three digits. The letter corresponds to the Work Class, such as E for Earthworks, and the digits relate to the relevant components in the first, second and third divisions of the class. An example will serve to illustrate its application.

Code H445 identifies an item as:

class	H	precast concrete
first division	4	column
second division	4	length 10–15 m
third division	5	mass 2–5 t

In practice the description of this item will need amplifying to include the position in the Works, concrete specification, cross-section and principal dimensions, mark or type number and mass of the particular unit, as required by rules A1, A2, A4 and A6 of Class H.

The symbol * is used in the rules to the Work Classification to indicate all the numbers in the appropriate division, such as H44* representing the group of code numbers from H441 to H448 inclusive.

As a general rule billed items will be listed in order of ascending code number (4.3). The code numbers have no contractual significance (4.4).

Where a component of an item is not listed in the Work Classification, the digit 9 shall be used (4.5). The digit 0 can be used for divisions that are not applicable or where fewer than three divisions of classification are given (4.6). Suffix numbers can follow the code to cover varying additional descriptions of the type described earlier for precast concrete columns, when the code numbers would be H445.1, H445.2, H445.3 etc.

Although the coding system is not compulsory, there are distinct advantages to tendering Contractors in having bills coded in accordance with Section 4 of CESMM3. In addition to the convenience of bills being set out in a uniform sequence, estimators are greatly assisted by the codes themselves as they can be used as shorthand references to their own files of cost data. Estimators quickly become fluent in codes and would recognise E424 as 'General excavation, material other than topsoil, rock or artificial hard material, maximum depth 1–2 m'. It should be noted that this item would most likely be considerably shortened in the Bill of Quantities by using the Class E Definition rule D1, to become: 'General excavation, maximum depth 1–2 m'. Thus the coding system is of value in defining the whole item although the second division description is 'deemed' and is not required to be stated in the Bill item description.

Bills may be subdivided into parts covering different phases or sections of the work, such as the component parts of a sewage treatment works, and items with the same code number may be repeated in different parts of the bill. The different parts of the bill can be numbered and the part number can prefix the item number. Thus an item K152 in Part 6 of the bill would become 6.K152.

Preparation of the Bill of Quantities (CESMM3; Section 5)

Measurement of Completed Work (5.1)

The rules prescribed in Section 5 for the preparation of Bills of Quantities will also apply to the measurement of completed work (5.1).

Sections of the Bill of Quantities (5.2)

Paragraph 5.2 prescribes a standard format for civil engineering Bills of Quantities to ensure uniformity of presentation. For example, a Bill of Quantities for a riverworks contract for a new power station might contain the following:

Section A	List of principal quantities	
Section B	Preamble	
Section C	Daywork schedule	
Section D	Work items	
	Part 1	General items
	Part 2	Demolition and siteworks
	Part 3	Access roads
	Part 4	Pipework
	Part 5	Dredging
	Part 6	Pump chambers

	Part 7 Circulating water ducts
	Part 8 Wharf wall
	Part 9 Jetty
Section E	Grand summary

The sections are identified by letters to distinguish them from the locational or cost-significant parts of the Works, which have reference numbers.

List of Principal Quantities (5.3)

Paragraph 5.3 advocates the inclusion of a list of principal quantities, being the main components of the Works, with their approximate estimated quantities, so that tenderers obtain an overall picture of the general scale and character of the proposed Works at the outset. It is expressly given *solely* for this purpose with the intention of avoiding any possible claims on account of divergences between the list of principal quantities, or the impression given thereby, and the detailed contents of the Bill of Quantities. Nevertheless, some Quantity Surveyors feel that the inclusion of such a list on a remeasure type of Contract may be of limited value and could be contentious. However, this list will assist the Contractor in determining whether he has the resources to carry out the work.

The list can be kept relatively brief and should not usually exceed one page in length. It is best prepared from the draft bill, although it is not essential to subdivide the list into the bill parts. The amount of detail given will vary with the type and size of contract.

A list of principal quantities relating to a reservoir follows:

Part		
1	General Items	
	Provisional Sums	£20 000
	PC Items	£76 000
2	Reservoir	
	excavation	15 000 m^3
	concrete	12 500 m^3
	formwork	6 600 m^2
	steel reinforcement	150 t
3	Pipework	
	pipelines	850 m
	valves	22 nr
4	Embankment	
	filling	12 000 m^3
5	Access Road	
	concrete road slab	1 800 m^2
6	Fencing	
	mild steel fence	1 400 m

Preamble (5.4 and 5.5)

The preamble in a civil engineering bill of quantities is to indicate to tendering contractors whether methods of measurement other than CESMM3 have been used for any part of the Works and whether any modifications have been made in applying CESMM3 to meet special needs where there are important practical reasons for adopting a different procedure (5.4). Circumstances in which a different procedure may be used include the introduction of performance specifications resulting in less detailed measurement, and the use of permitted alternatives, as sometimes adopted for highway and tunnelling contracts, and contractor-designed work, and possibly involving the use of non-standard rules for measurements. Wherever practicable the unamended CESMM3 should be used in the interests of uniformity.

The majority of civil engineering contracts include work below ground in general excavation, trenching for pipes, boring or driving, and in other ways. Paragraph 5.5 requires a definition of rock to be included in the Preamble in these circumstances, and it is usually related to geological strata as in the DTp *Specification for Highway Works*. Alternative or complementary approaches include prescribing a minimum size of boulder (0.20 m^3 in the DTp Specification and 1 m^3 in rule M8 of Class E of CESMM3, except that the minimum volume shall be 0.25 m^3 where the net width of excavation is less than 2 m), and strata which necessitate the use of blasting or approved pneumatic tools for their removal. This definition can be of considerable significance in determining whether or not additional payments shall be made for excavation, boring or driving work.

Daywork Schedule (5.6 and 5.7)

It is necessary to make provision for a daywork evaluation of work which cannot be assessed at bill rates or rates analogous thereto. CESMM3 provides three alternative procedures (5.6 and 5.7):

(1) A list of the various classes of labour, material and plant for which daywork rates or prices are to be inserted by the tenderer.

(2) Provision for payment at the rates and prices and percentage additions contained in the current Federation of Civil Engineering Contractors Schedules of Dayworks, adjusted by the Contractor's percentage additions or deductions for labour, materials, plant and supplementary charges.

(3) The insertion of provisional sums in Class A of the bill of quantities for work executed on a daywork basis comprising separate items for labour, materials, plant and supplementary charges, and applying the appropriate percentage addition or deduction, as prescribed in the second method, to each provisional sum.

The third method is felt by the authors to offer the most advantages, since it directly influences the Tender Total, thus maintaining an element of competition, at the same time providing a widely known and accepted basis of computation which is easily implemented.

Work Items

Division into Parts (5.8)

The Bill of Quantities is divided into sections in accordance with paragraph 5.2 and Section (d) contains work items which may be arranged into numbered parts, and which will differ from one bill to another. The division into parts is mainly determined by the main components of the project, locational considerations, limitations on the timing or sequence of the work, and it enables the person preparing the bill to distinguish between parts of the work which are thought likely to give rise to different methods of construction or considerations of cost (5.8). This form of division will extend the usefulness of the Bill for estimating purposes and in the subsequent financial control of the contract. Sound division into parts requires knowledge of the factors influencing the Contractor's costs and may assist in promoting more positive working relationships between the Engineer and the Contractor.

It should be noted that paragraph (5.8) states that bills 'may' be divided into parts and therefore this is not obligatory, but it is worthwhile where appropriate for the benefits noted above. Where bills are split into parts, items shall be arranged in the general order of the Work Classification (5.8).

However General Items (Class A) may be grouped as a separate part of the bill to cover all the general matters for the whole of the works, thus avoiding the repetition of such general items in each division of the bill. This arrangement is permitted by paragraph (5.8) and is likely to be the most appropriate bill layout in the vast majority of contracts. In contrast should a sizable contract comprise two or more very different working conditions – for example, part wholly on dry land and part in estuary waters – it might be useful to provide Tenderers with Class A Work Classifications separately for both distinct parts of the work because of the very diverse nature of the risks involved.

Headings and Sub-headings (5.9)

Paragraph 5.9 prescribes that each part of the bill shall be given a heading and that each part may be further subdivided by sub-headings, all inserted as part of item descriptions. For the sake of clarity, a line shall be drawn across the item description column below the last item to which the heading or sub-heading applies, and headings and sub-headings shall be repeated at the start of each new page listing appropriate items (5.9).

Itemisation and Description (5.10)

All work shall be itemised in the bill with the descriptions framed in accordance with the Work Classification. However, paragraph 5.10 states that item descriptions may be extended or work subdivided into a larger number of separate items than required by CESMM3 if it is thought likely that the work will give rise to special methods of construction or considerations of cost. The word 'may' is used to prevent the Contractor having a basis of claim for extra payment if the previous assumptions proved incorrect, and to permit flexibility of approach in the preparation of bills.

The cost of similar work in different locations can vary considerably, and in these circumstances locational details should be inserted in the bill items to permit the Contractor to adjust his rates accordingly. For instance, reinforced concrete of the same mix to be laid in the base of a pump sump, in a floor slab at ground level, or in the tank base to a water tower, are all similar forms of construction but carried out under entirely different conditions, resulting in considerably different costs and creating the need for additional descriptive information in the bill items.

Paragraph 5.10 represents one of the important changes in ethos which CESMM introduced in 1976 and leads to much more useful Bills of Quantities being produced. For example, when considering work affected by tidal water, it is sensible to split the measured items up depending on whether they are affected by water at all times, only affected between tides, or if above high tide. It should be noted that this provision of separate items is in addition to the provisions of (5.20) which draws the Tendering Contractor's attention to the existence of bodies of water in a more general way. It should be further noted that the fact that work is 'above high tide' will not necessarily mean that the works will be free of water, as high tide is usually quoted as the mean (that is, average) high tide and should storm conditions exist then considerably higher water may occur on occasions. It is therefore important that this heading of items is given so that contractors may include for any relevant risk factors in their pricing.

Descriptions (5.11–5.13)

Item descriptions only *identify* work whose nature and extent is defined by the contract documents as a whole, including the Drawings, Specification and Conditions of Contract (5.11). This policy encourages the complete design of work prior to inviting tenders, and the cost of civil engineering work frequently depends extensively on the shape, complexity and location of the work and the nature of the terrain; this information is best extracted from the Drawings. To assist in the process of identification CESMM3 often requires the inclusion of information on location or other physical features (5.13). Paragraph 5.12 extends this approach by stating that any descriptive information required by the Work Classification may be replaced by reference to the appropriate Drawings or Specification clauses.

The use of measurement procedures at variance with those prescribed in CESMM3 without express exclusions might possibly be construed as 'errors' and treated as variations in accordance with clause 55(2) of the ICE Conditions of Contract. Hence it is important that the requirements of CESMM3 should be closely followed in drafting civil engineering bills of quantities. Situations will arise where no guidance is given by CESMM3 and a suitable non-standard item should be drafted. In such circumstances it would be good practice to insert an appropriate explanatory note in the Bill of Quantities regarding the basis of the non-standard measurement.

Ranges of Dimensions (5.14)

Where the Work Classification prescribes a range of dimensions for a component, but the component in question is of one dimension, this dimension may be stated in the item description in place of the prescribed range (5.14). For instance, the placing of *in situ* concrete suspended slabs in Class F have four ranges of thickness listed in the third division. When measuring slabs all having a thickness of 200 mm, the thickness given in the item description may optionally be stated as 200 mm in place of the CESMM3 range of 150–300 mm (exceeding 150 mm and not exceeding 300 mm).

Prime Cost Items (5.15 and 5.16)

Prime Cost (PC) Items shall be inserted in a Bill of Quantities under General Items (Class A) to cover work carried out by Nominated Sub-contractors and each prime cost is to be followed by two further items:

(1) Labours in connection therewith including site services provided by main Contractors for their own use and which they also make available for use by the Nominated Sub-contractor and which are listed in CESMM3 (5.15), such as temporary roads, scaffolding, hoists, messrooms, sanitary accommodation and welfare facilities, working space, disposal of rubbish and provision of light and water. Where the Nominated Sub-contractor is not to carry out work on the site, the item shall include unloading, storing and hoisting materials supplied and the return of packing materials (5.15).

(2) A further item expressed as a percentage of the PC Item to cover all other charges and profit (5.15).

This procedure follows closely the arrangements detailed in the ICE Conditions of Contract (clauses 58 and 59). Any special labours beyond those specified in paragraph 5.15(a) must be included in item descriptions. Where substantial special attendance facilities are envisaged but cannot be assessed precisely, these should be incorporated in Provisional Sums.

Where a bill item incorporates goods, materials or services supplied by a Nominated Sub-contractor, that item should be appropriately cross-referenced with the Prime Cost item for their supply (paragraph 5.16).

Provisional Sums (5.17)

Provisional Sums shall be used to cover contingencies of various types and they can be entered in various sections of the Bill of Quantities for subsequent adjustment. Items for specific contingencies are to be included in the General Items (Class A – 4.2), while other items may be included in other classes to cover, for instance, possible extensions of work (5.17). A general contingency sum shall be entered in the Grand Summary in accordance with paragraph 5.25.

The omission of provisional quantities means that the quantities in the Bill are to be measured accurately from the Drawings and are to be the best possible forecast of the nature and extent of the work which will actually be required, including such items as excavation of soft spots and hours of pumping plant.

The ICE Conditions of Contract [56(2)] provides for bill rates to be increased or decreased if they are rendered unreasonable or inapplicable as a result of the actual quantities being greater or less than those stated in the bill. It will be appreciated that the cost of one billed item frequently depends on its relationship to others, and the cost of the whole work can change substantially if the relative proportions of the quantities are varied.

The inclusion of Provisional Sums to cover possible additional work will result in appropriate rates for the work subsequently having to be negotiated.

Quantities (5.18)

Paragraph 5.18 prescribes that 'quantities shall be computed net from the Drawings'. The billed quantities will be the lengths, areas, volumes and masses of the finished work which the Contractor is required to produce, with no allowance for bulking, shrinkage or waste. The only exceptions are where CESMM3 or the Contract contain conventions for measurement in special cases, such as the volume of concrete is to include that occupied by reinforcement and other metal sections (rule M1 of Class F).

In the original *Standard Method of Measurement of Civil Engineering Quantities* some items were measured 'extra over' others – that is, the price for the second item covered only additional costs over the first. For example, facings and fair-faced brickwork were measured as extra over the cost of ordinary brickwork, thus eliminating the need to deduct the ordinary brickwork, displaced by faced work. Similarly bends, junctions and other fittings were measured extra over pipe sewers and drains. The three editions of the CESMM discontinued this practice. Brickwork faced on one face will be measured as a composite item, while pipe lengths are measured along their centre lines and shall include lengths occupied by fittings and valves (rule M3 of Class I), but the fittings and valves are not measured extra over, although the estimator will need to deduct the costs of the lengths of displaced pipe when estimating the rates for the enumerated fittings and valves (Class J).

Quantities are usually rounded up or down (half a unit or more up and less than half a unit down) to avoid the use of fractional quantities in the bill. Where fractional quantities are used, because of the high unit cost of the item, they should be restricted to one place of decimals (5.18).

Units of Measurement (5.19)

Paragraph 5.19 lists the units of measurement used in civil engineering bills of quantities with their standard abbreviations. Square metres are abbreviated to m^2 or m2 and not sq m, and cubic metres to m^3 or m3 and not cu m. Number is represented by 'nr' and not 'no'. The term 'sum' is used where there is no quantity entered against an item. The abbreviations are restricted to not more than three characters, contain no capital initials and are not followed by a full stop.

Work affected by Water (5.20)

Paragraph 5.20 prescribes that where an existing body of open water (other than groundwater) such as a river, stream, canal, lake or body of tidal water is either on the site or bounds the site, each body of water shall be identified in the preamble to the Bill of Quantities. A reference shall also be given to a drawing indicating the boundaries and surface level of each body of water or, where the boundaries and surface levels fluctuate, their anticipated ranges of fluctuation.

A typical preamble clause could be 'The Site is bounded by the Beeston Canal whose location is shown on Drawing BSDW 12B. The width of the canal is constant and it is anticipated that the surface level may fluctuate between 85.30 and 86.00 AOD'.

Paragraph 5.20 provides the very necessary overall warning to contractors of the existence of bodies of water on or bounding the site, and the possible attendant associated risks to the works in general. CESMM3 also provides for the pricing of more specific risks owing to the presence of water affecting individual items or groups of items by the provisions of paragraphs 5.8, 5.10 and 5.13. These clauses require additional information to be given where work by its nature, location, importance or any other special characteristic is likely to lead to special methods of construction or considerations of cost. One such reason for additional description in items of work is where the work is likely to be affected by water. An example of work of this nature would be the foundations and piers for a bridge which are in the water course of a river. It is obvious that the piers in the river bed are going to be more difficult and expensive to execute than any similar piers which are founded entirely on dry land.

In CESMM3 – Class E, Earthworks there are some specific rules regarding water affecting excavation. Where excavation work occurs below a body of open water, rules A2 and M7 of Class E require a suitable reference to a preamble created to satisfy paragraph 5.20. This requirement allows the contractor to identify the body of water concerned and assess any risks involved.

In order to comply with the spirit as well as the letter of the various CESMM3 requirements regarding work affected by water, the bill compiler has to make a judgement as to the level of detail which is justified by the particular circumstances. In a straightforward case all that may be necessary is a note or heading drawing attention to the body of water. However in a more complex and cost-significant circumstance it may be necessary to give locational information regarding the water to each individual section or item of work.

There are several Worked Examples in Part 2 of this book which demonstrate the principles of compliance with the above rules, namely Worked Examples 8, 12, 14, 15 and 16.

Ground and Excavation Levels (5.21)

With excavation, boring or driving work, it is necessary to define the 'Commencing Surface' where it is not also the 'Original Surface', and the 'Excavated Surface' where it is not also the 'Final Surface' (5.21). Quite often, however, these intermediate surfaces will not be mentioned in the descriptions, and it will then be assumed that the item covers the full depth from the 'Original Surface' (before any work in the Contract is commenced) to the 'Final Surface' (when all work shown on the drawings has been executed).

The definitions of these terms are given in paragraphs 1.10–1.13 inclusive. The surfaces do not have to be identified by a level, as for instance above Ordnance Survey Datum; provided the descriptions are clear and practical they are satisfactory. For instance, such descriptions as '300 mm below Original Surface' and '150 mm above formation' are acceptable.

The rules use the term 'surface' rather than level as in many cases, on the site, the surface may not be level. For example, for an excavation item which quotes an excavated surface to be 'a certain depth below original surface', that surface would not necessarily be level as it would follow the contours of the original ground.

The final sentence of (5.21) intends that excavation work should not be split into horizontal bands of depth categories but should be categorised by the total overall depth of the item. This can be explained more readily by reference to Diagram 1 (overleaf). The diagram represents a section through a typical piece of general excavation and the bill item should read as follows:

Item A E426 General excavation, maximum depth: 5–10 m .... m^3

The contractor will choose the most appropriate excavation plant based on the maximum depth at which it will be expected to operate and thus in the vast majority of cases that single most suitable piece of plant will perform the whole volume of the excavation required. It follows that splitting items up into any further depth category is normally not worthwhile and may even be confusing.

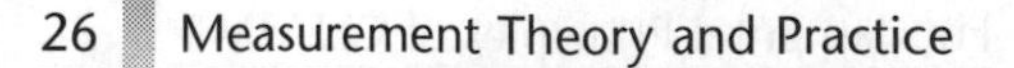

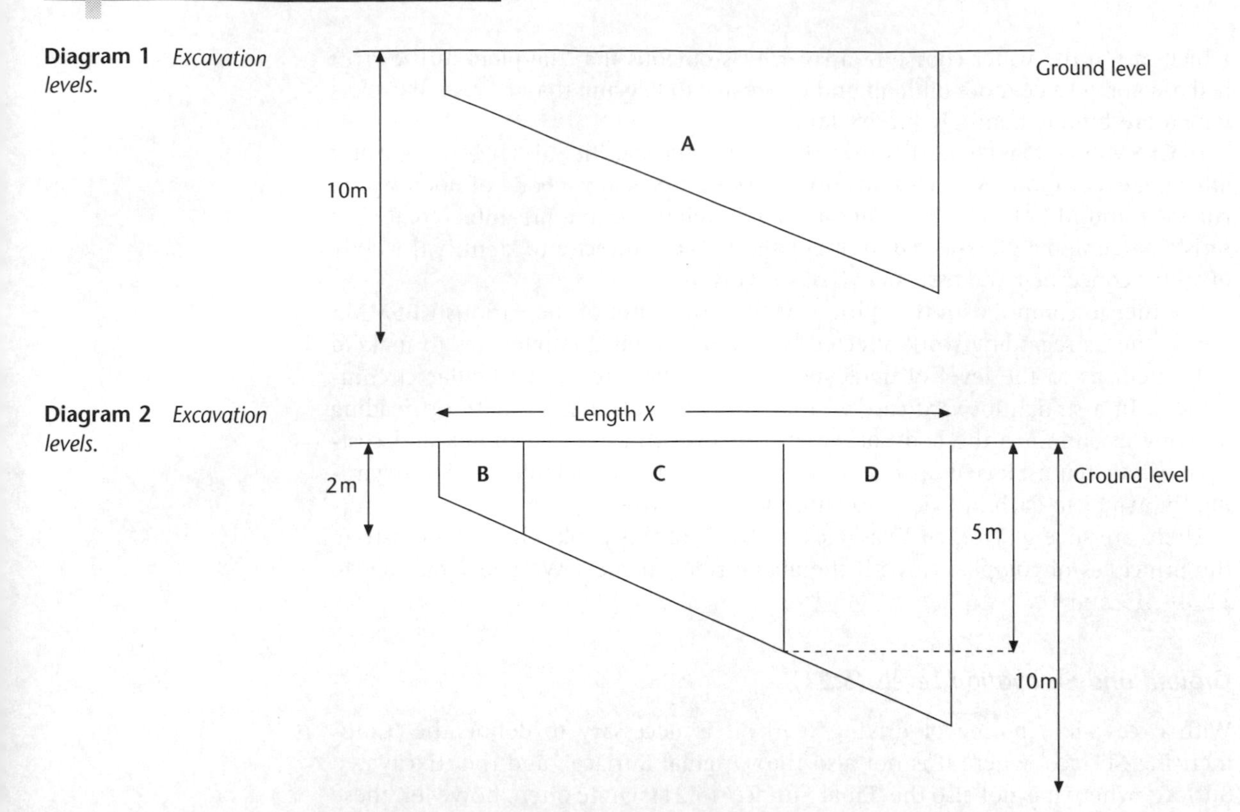

Diagram 1 *Excavation levels.*

Diagram 2 *Excavation levels.*

Diagram 2 shows the same cross-sectional shape of an excavation where the work has been split vertically into the depth categories in the Third Division of Class E: Earthworks. This would give three volumes of general excavation represented by items B, C and D. This is not to be recommended in practice for the reasons stated above and the inference of paragraph 5.21. Such an approach might only be justified where 'Length *X*' is exceptionally large and the compiler of the bill is convinced that different types of plant may be used effectively within the different categories of depth on such a large project.

Form, Setting and Grand Summary (5.22–5.27)

The Bill of Quantities should desirably have the format on A4 size paper described in paragraph 5.22 and as illustrated below (the quantity, rate and amount: £ columns shall each have a capacity of ten million less one, and a binding margin should be provided):

Number	*Item Description*	*Unit*	*Quantity*	*Rate*	*Amount* £	*Amount* p
20	90	10	20	20	20	8
widths (in mm)						
				Page total		

The amounts on each page shall be totalled and these totals carried to a summary at the end of each part of the bill. The total of each part is transferred to the Grand Summary (5.23 and 5.24). The Part Summaries are normally followed by the *General Contingency Allowance,* which is a Provisional Sum inserted to cover unforeseen work (5.25), an *Adjustment Item* (5.26) and finally the Grand Total (total of the priced bill of quantities) (5.27).

Where Bills of Quantities are produced by established quantity surveying practices they will be quite likely to retain their own standard approach to bill stationery and layout, which should in any case conform to the principles recommended in CESMM3.

Completion, Pricing and Use of the Bill of Quantities (CESMM3; Section 6)

Paragraph 6.1 prescribes that rates and prices shall be inserted in the rate column in pounds sterling with pence entered as decimal fractions of one pound. The generally accepted practice is to regard figures in the 'rate' column as rates and those in the 'amount' column as prices on the supposition that quantity × rate = price.

The prices in each part are totalled and transferred to the Grand Summary in the manner previously described, paragraph 6.2.

An *Adjustment Item* is included in the Grand Summary as a convenient place where the tenderer can make an adjustment without having to alter rates or amounts against work items. The final tender adjudication is normally undertaken by senior estimating and management staff, who are particularly concerned with assessment of the risk involved and pricing levels. Previously such adjustments were often made to some of the larger prices entered against preliminary or general items in the Bill. The inclusion of the Adjustment Item to incorporate a lump sum addition or deduction as the last item in the Grand Summary is a much more satisfactory arrangement for both Contractor and Employer (6.3).

The Adjustment Item is a fixed lump sum and the sum entered against this item is not adjustable for variations in the Contract Sum, although it is subject to adjustment when the Baxter adjustment formula is incorporated to deal with labour and material price fluctuations (6.5). The Baxter formula superimposes price fluctuation resulting from index movement over adjustments in the Contract Sum assessed under the ordinary Contract Conditions.

Payment of the Adjustment Item shall be made by instalments in interim certificates in the proportion that the value of certified permanent and temporary works [sub-clause 60(2)(a) of the ICE Conditions of Contract] bears to the total of the Bill of Quantities, before the addition or deduction of the Adjustment Item, and with no retention money deducted, and a statement to this effect shall appear in the Preamble. These payments shall not exceed in aggregate the amount of the Adjustment Item and any final balance due is certified in the next certificate prepared after the issue of the Certificate of Substantial Completion for the whole of the Works under clause 48 of the Conditions of Contract (6.4).

Method-Related Charges (CESMM3; Section 7)

Underlying Philosophy

The valuation of variations and agreement to the cost of delays have generally been the main causes of dispute on civil engineering contracts. Contractors frequently claim that the measured quantities of permanent work priced at billed rates do not represent the true value of constructional work where significant variations have occurred. Engineers, on the other hand, generally believe that the priced bill of quantities represents a shopping list of items, and on completion of construction the work can be remeasured and valued at the billed rates. That the latter is unsatisfactory is evidenced by the large claims settlements agreed on many projects, where variations and unforeseen physical conditions or artificial obstructions occur.

Many of the costs arising from civil engineering operations are not proportional to the quantity of the resulting permanent work. It cannot really be a sound approach to recover the cost of bringing a tower crane on to the site and its hire, operation and subsequent removal by hidden costs in the 'preliminaries', where provided, or in the cost per cubic metre of the various work sections for which the crane was used. It is believed by the drafting committee that method-related charges provide a better way of representing the Contractor's site operation costs, such as the provision of site accommodation and temporary works, and the setting up of supervision and labour, sometimes described as 'site mobilisation'.

Objectives

Accepting that expertise in design rests with the Engineer, it seems equally evident that expertise in construction methods lies with the Contractor. It is accordingly logical that the Contractor should be able to decide the method of carrying out the works. A blank section in the Bill of Quantities will permit the Contractor to list, describe and price these items.

CESMM3 does not make the use of method-related charges compulsory but the sponsors see great merit in their use through easier evaluation of variations, a more stable and realistic cash flow to the Contractor and by directing the Engineer's attention to the basis of construction costs, to lead to more rational designs.

The extent of temporary works on a civil engineering contract is often enormous and to spread their costs over unit rates must be unsatisfactory, since so few of them are proportional to the quantities of permanent work. Hence it is believed by the sponsors to be beneficial to all parties for the Contractor to have the opportunity to insert these costs, properly itemised in a separate part of the bill.

Division into Time-Related and Fixed Charges

There are two basic types of method-related charge: time-related charges and fixed charges (7.1). The cost of bringing an item of plant on to a site and its subsequent removal is a fixed charge and its running cost is a time-related charge. The tenderer is requested to distinguish between these charges and must fully describe them so that the coverage of the items entered is positively identified. The fixed costs are not related to quantity or time. With time-related items, the Contractor is to enter full descriptions of the items and their cost, but not the timing or

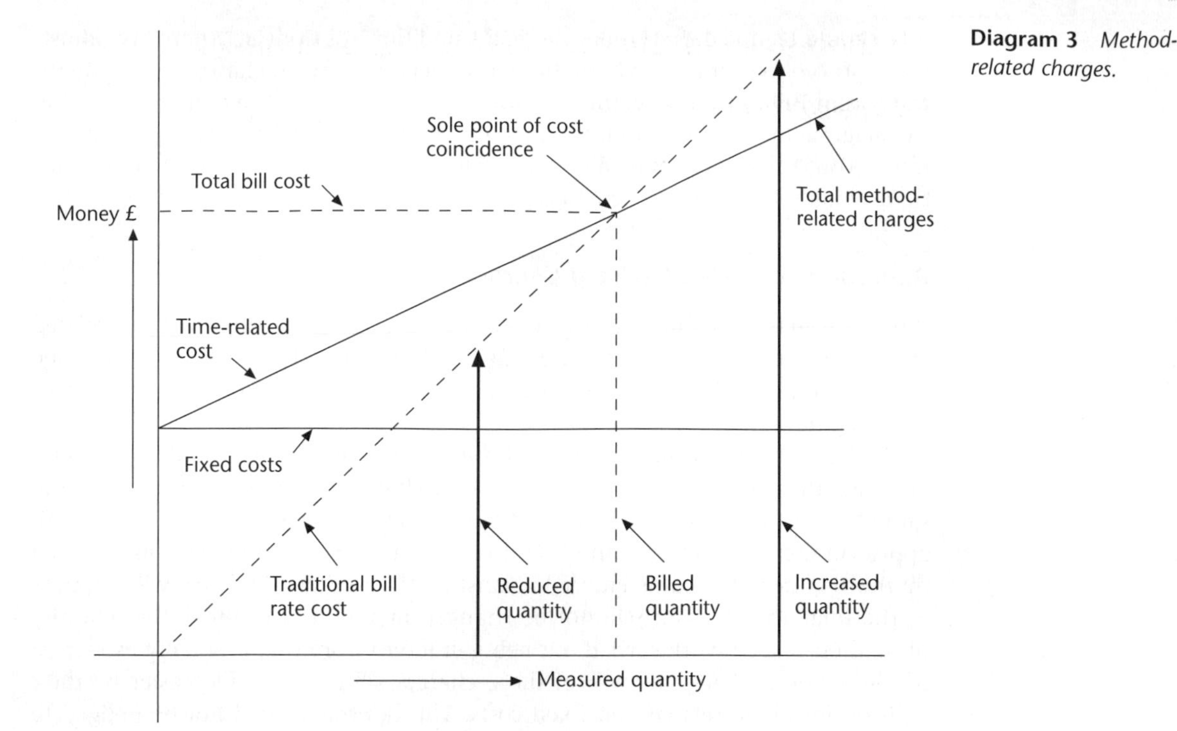

Diagram 3 *Method-related charges.*

duration, as they will not be charged at weekly or monthly rates. The Quantity Surveyor or Engineer preparing the bill will provide adequate blank space and the Contractor will enter the particulars in the description column, preferably using the order of classification and descriptions adopted in Class A (7.3). Typical Bill entries covering both types of method-related charge are given in Chapter 4.

The concept of the relationship between fixed and time-related costs versus unit rate-related costs is illustrated graphically in Diagram 3. In the diagram the straight-line graph of the traditional bill rate cost is shown as a broken line, as are the related billed quantity and the total bill cost. The total method-related charges (shown as full lines) are made up of two components: firstly the fixed costs which could represent the costs of transporting, setting up and ultimate removal of a piece of plant or a piece of temporary work; secondly the time-related costs which could represent the running costs, hire charges, fuel costs etc. which are directly associated with the time spent on site. Lastly, shown as bold lines, are the possible reduced or increased quantities which might result on site and be confirmed by remeasurement.

It is worth stressing that there is only one point of convergence between the two systems of costing which tends to reinforce the arguments in favour of adopting the more flexible method-related charge approach. The diagram demonstrates that, under the traditional quantity/unit rate system, should the quantity decrease in the remeasurement of the actual work executed, then the Contractor may not gain a full recovery of the costs. On the other hand, should the quantities increase, then the Contractor may recover more than is due in costs incurred.

Conversely, the diagram illustrates that under the method-related charge system, should the quantities vary significantly from those estimated in the Bill, then the Contractor should always be paid an appropriate and fair reimbursement for the work.

It should be noted that under the ICE Conditions of Contract there are adjustment procedures for rates where there have been significant changes in the quantities from Bill to Final Account, but any such adjustments have been ignored in the diagram for simplicity. In this regard the method-related system of pricing contracts would almost certainly allow for easier resolution of such contractual claims than would otherwise be the case.

Application of Method-Related Charges

Problems may arise in practice where Contractors entering method-related charges in a bill fail to identify them as fixed or time-related, or fail to describe them adequately. This will involve the Quantity Surveyor or Engineer in constant checking of entries.

The items entered as method-related charges are not subject to admeasurement, although the Contractor will be paid for these charges in interim valuations in the same way as he is paid for measured work, and a statement to this effect shall appear in the Preamble (7.6 and 7.7). Hence, in the absence of variations ordered by the Engineer, the sums entered against method-related charges will reappear in the final account, and will not be changed merely as a result of the quantity of method-related work carried out being different from that originally estimated by the tenderer. The valuation of these charges should be made easier by their division into time-related and fixed costs. The Contractor will not be obliged to construct the works using the methods or techniques listed in his method-related charges, but he will nevertheless be paid as though the techniques indicated had been adopted (7.8). For example, if the Contractor inserted charges for a concrete batching plant and subsequently used ready-mixed concrete, the appropriate interim payments will be distributed over the quantity of concrete placed. If, however, changes in techniques are instructed by the Engineer, then these changes will be paid for as variations. Method-related charges shall, however, like the Adjustment Item, be subject to Baxter formula price adjustment.

The introduction of method-related charges thus enables the Contractor optionally to enter separately in the tender such non-quantity proportional charges as considered will have a significant influence on the cost of the work, and for which no allowance has been made in the rates and prices for other items (7.2). Where the Contractor omits to enter any method-related charges and merely prices the contract as a traditional Bill of Quantities, these charges will be deemed to have been included in the pricing of other items and the tender will not be invalidated. If the Contractor enters a method-related charge for an item that cannot be performed or if the cost is obviously incorrect, the Engineer should draw the attention of the Contractor to the mistake and give him the opportunity to withdraw his tender.

All method-related charges must be fully described (7.4), including the resources expected to be used and the particular items of Permanent or Temporary Works to which the item relates, although a method can be changed subsequently (7.5). It is in the Contractor's interest to be explicit in his descriptions to secure prompt payment. Martin Barnes postulates in *CESMM3 Handbook* (Telford, 1992) that where activities on the site resemble those described in the method-related charges, payment can be made promptly, otherwise the Engineer may have grounds for withholding payment until the related permanent work is complete.

Alongside the description of each method-related charge the tenderer will enter whether it is fixed or time-related. In interim valuations, payment of fixed charge items will be made when the operation so described, such as erection of site offices, has been completed. Time-related charges for items such as maintaining a temporary access road will be paid monthly, according to the Engineer's assessment of the proportion of total time that has elapsed at the date of assessment. If the Contractor enters the operation of a tower crane for 22 weeks as a time-related charge and then proceeds to use it on the site for 28 weeks, no additional payment or adjustment will necessarily follow. Conversely, as described by Barnes, if a method-related charge covered de-watering plant be subsequently rendered unnecessary by a drought, the Contractor is still eligible for the payment because he bore the risk of having to do an indeterminate amount of work, the payment being *pro rata* to the proportion of associated Permanent Work completed. Only in the case of variations will the price be subject to adjustment. If a variation increases work volume or causes delay, and thereby results in an increase in the cost of method-related charges, these can be adjusted within the terms of the Contract, without the necessity of a claim. On occasions a variation deleting work could result in a reduction in a charge. Much depends on whether the variation actually extends or shortens the time for which the resources are required.

Class A shows specified requirements that the Engineer or Quantity Surveyor may insert in the bill, followed by a list of items which the Contractor may enter, but is not compelled to do so. He will choose to do so if he considers that it provides a more realistic basis for pricing. The danger is that he could enter almost any items except materials and so abuse the arrangements. In practice, site accommodation, services and temporary works have been the items most commonly inserted and plant to a lesser extent. Multi-purpose types of plant like tower cranes, derrick systems and ropeways are very suitable items, since they are used for hoisting a variety of materials and involve both fixed and time-related charges.

With the payment of time-related charges the Engineer is not tied to the dates shown on the programme and will have regard to the date when the items were actually provided on the site. Interim payments for time-related charges should be proportional to the extent of satisfactory completion of the particular activity, and the Engineer will need to assess the total period over which the charge should be spread. The Contractor should ensure that the descriptions and durations of time-related charges match the information given in the contract programme, thus assisting in substantiating the Engineer's assessment of a reasonable proportion for payment. In the event of variations, time-related charges require adjustment if rendered unreasonable or inapplicable; the more precise the descriptions, the more realistic the adjustments.

Advantages and Disadvantages of Method-Related Charges Approach

The use of method-related charges should remove substantial sums of construction costs, which do not vary in proportion to the volume of permanent works executed, from the pricing of these permanent works and so reduce likely claims. If used effectively they should enable the Contractor to recover in monthly valuations the cost of items other than permanent work on an equitable basis, either in the event of work proceeding largely as planned at tender stage or in the event of substantial variations.

In either case the Contractor will be able to recover these non-quantity proportional items on a monthly basis and not be obliged to wait until the end of the contract, or at least the later stages, to submit claims to recover costs.

The Employer should have the benefit of a more accurate valuation of variations with improved monitoring of the financial position of the contract. He will also be aware of the level of expenditure at an earlier stage, which will help him to plan his cash flow and budget for his ultimate level of financial commitments. It is interesting to note that in the majority of contracts, incorporating method-related charges, their use proved beneficial.

It is claimed that, although there can still be different approaches to the pricing of bills, by introducing method-related charges the different bases for computation and approach are more clearly identified. The Employer thus gains by the use of a cost structure that is better suited to deal with variations and changes, while the Contractor receives more prompt and equitable payment. No significant problems have occurred with final account preparation, and this approach assists the Contractor in making claims and the Engineer in settling them on a more realistic basis with less argument and conflict. When method-related charges are not used, differing policies for pricing and allocating indirect costs are hidden within the wide variation in measured work unit rates.

The success of the method-related charges approach is largely dependent on its sensible use by both Contractor and Engineer. If Contractors refuse to enter method-related charges and Quantity Surveyors and Engineers are slow in authorising payment of them under sub-clause 60(i)(d) of the ICE Conditions of Contract, then little will be achieved, particularly in easing the Contractor's cash flow problems.

Some of the more traditionally minded consultant Engineers and Quantity Surveyors fear that method-related charges will be used by Contractors to build in high early payments into the contract to improve their cash flow at the beginning of the works. This is not a sustainable argument as the method-related charge should only become payable when it is actually required on site. The method-related charge should be clearly defined in the Bill and therefore no doubt should exist about when costs have actually been expended. Many schemes of front loading tenders have in any case been attempted by Contractors over the years long before the introduction of method-related charges.

Anyone wishing to study the use of method-related charges in more detail is directed to the very full coverage of this subject in Martin Barnes' book *CESMM3 Handbook* (Telford, 1992).

On the whole the use of method-related charges, although not without their dangers, can lead to improved design, estimating, tender selection, contract administration and cost control techniques, with better cash flow to the Contractor.

CHAPTER 3

Measurement Practice and Bill Production

Introduction

In the first two chapters the scope and context of civil engineering measurement and the fundamental principles of CESMM3 have been addressed. Before proceeding to detailed discussions of the individual work classifications of CESMM3, it is considered appropriate at this point to explain the background techniques adopted by Quantity Surveyors and Engineers towards measurement practice and bill production. These techniques have been developed and refined over a history of 350 years of measuring civil and military construction projects. The earliest measurements were made post construction on a measure-and-value basis to agree a fair final account for the works, but by the mid-nineteenth century Bills of Quantities were being produced based on measurements from the plans of proposed works. Large investments in works of civil engineering infrastructure in Victorian times for sewerage, water schemes and railways lead to many very large contracts being let with the consequent desire to exercise appropriate cost control, particularly when public funding was involved. This situation led to Bills of Quantities in the civil engineering sector becoming common practice as bills provided a fair and transparent basis for awarding contracts and adjusting final accounts.

Measurement and Billing Techniques Generally

Bills of Quantities comprise two main elements which complement each other, namely *items* and *quantities*. To produce accurate and useful bills, both elements must be carefully prepared in a logical sequence to avoid missing anything of importance. Good item writing requires the skills of interpreting drawings, understanding how the work will be carried out including the operative skills and plant involved, communication in concise technical language and knowledge of the applicable rules of CESMM3. Many items under CESMM3 will represent standard situations where the description is generated simply by following the three divisions of the measurement rules, but skill and experience are essential in order to identify the non-standard and unusual situations which demand additional description or itemisation indicated by paragraphs 2.5, 5.8, 5.10 and 5.20 of CESMM3. Calculation of the quantities for items requires the skills of mensuration, spatial concept of three dimensions from a two-dimensional drawing and a logical noting system to record the data for future use.

Two main methods of bill production have developed within the quantity surveying profession which are now detailed.

Direct Billing

This is the traditional approach, tracing its roots back to the original trade-by-trade measuring of completed building work. The surveyor takes off one work classification at a time and works steadily through the work, producing a draft bill usually with fully developed items and headings as well as the quantities. Once this document is calculated and checked the bill can be typed directly from this draft. Larger projects are split between several Quantity Surveyors on a work classification basis, each preparing draft bills. In practice certain works must by their nature be taken off and billed direct, for example general items and works of alteration and renovation. The major advantage of direct billing is the simplicity of only dealing with the concept of one work classification at a time. On the other hand great care is necessary to prevent duplication or omission when several surveyors are employed in taking off one project.

Group System

The group system is a sophisticated development of the direct system, mainly applicable to building works rather than civil engineering. It is most effective for taking off quantities for whole elements of construction involving several trades or work classifications. Examples of such elements are sub-structures, walling, finishes, roofs and components such as doors and windows, complete with the adjustments in the structure for their openings. The group system can be used to some advantage in measuring civil engineering earthworks and foundation construction. The benefits of the system are the multiple use of quantities and the clear division of taking off tasks among a team of surveyors working on the same project. The main disadvantage of the group system is its three-stage approach involving separately taking off, abstracting and billing, which can lead to errors in transferring data from stage to stage. The group system was mechanised during the 1960s with the 'cut and shuffle' approach and now tends to be computerised, several excellent software packages being available on desk top computers.

The system has few advantages in the billing of many of the CESMM3 work classifications which by their nature are unique and not readily grouped, but as the system is still commonly adopted by Quantity Surveyors it is further explained later in this chapter.

Measurement Processes

Dimensions Paper

All dimensions and mathematical calculations should be entered on separate sheets of dimensions paper or in dimensions books. These entries are to be carefully made so that they can be readily checked by another person without any possible chance of confusion arising.

The normal ruling of 'dimensions paper' on which the dimensions (scaled or taken direct from drawings) are entered, is indicated below:

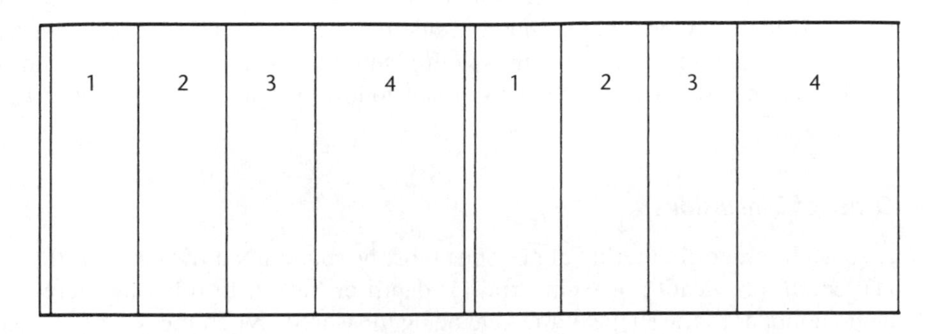

Each dimension sheet is split into two identically ruled parts, each consisting of four columns. The purpose of each column will now be indicated for the benefit of those readers who are unfamiliar with the use of this type of paper.

Column 1 is termed the 'timesing column' in which multiplying figures are entered when there is more than one of the particular item being measured.

Column 2 is termed the 'dimension column' in which the actual dimensions, as scaled or taken direct from the drawings, are entered. There may be one, two or three lines of dimensions in an item depending on whether it is linear, square or cubic.

Column 3 is termed the 'squaring column' in which the length, area or volume, obtained by multiplying together the figures in columns 1 and 2, is recorded, ready for transfer to the abstract or bill.

Column 4 is known as the 'description column' in which the written description of each item is entered. The right-hand side of this wider column is frequently used to accommodate preliminary calculations and other basic information needed in building up the dimensions and references to the location of the work, and is referred to as 'waste'.

In the worked examples that are contained in Part 2 of this book the reader will notice that one set of columns only is used on each dimension sheet with the remainder used for explanatory notes, but in practice both sets of columns would be used for 'taking-off'.

Spacing of Items

Ample space should be left between all items on the dimension sheets so that it is possible to follow the dimensions with ease and to enable any items, which may have been omitted when the dimensions were first taken-off, to be subsequently inserted, without cramping up the dimensions unduly.

Waste

The use of the right-hand side of the description column for preliminary calculations, build-up of lengths, explanatory notes and related matters should not be overlooked. All steps that have been taken in arriving at dimensions, no matter how elementary or trivial they may appear, should be entered in the waste section of the description column. Following this procedure will do much to prevent doubts and misunderstandings concerning dimensions arising at some future date.

Side notes of a locational nature are particularly important as these more than anything can justify why a size has been measured. The human memory is of very short duration and trying to follow one's own taking off even after a few days or weeks without any waste build-ups and side notes is a very difficult task. Therefore it is even more important that noting should always be undertaken in a careful manner so that another person can follow the take off logically in the future.

Order of Dimensions

A constant order of entering dimensions must be maintained throughout, that is (1) length, (2) breadth or width, and (3) depth or height. In this way there can be no doubt as to the shape of the item being measured. When measuring a cubic item of concrete 10 m long, 5 m wide and 0.50 m deep, the entry in the dimension column would be as follows:

	10.00 5.00 0.50		Provision of conc. – designed mix grade C10, ct. to BS 12, 20 mm agg. to BS 882; min. ct. content 250 kg/m³. & Placing mass conc. in base, thickness: 300–500 mm.

It will be noted that dimensions are usually recorded in metres to two places of decimals with a dot between the metres and fractions and a line drawn across the dimension column under each set of figures. Where the dimensions apply to more than one descriptive item, a bracket should be inserted as illustrated.

Timesing

If there were three such items, then this dimension would be multiplied by three in the timesing column as shown below:

3/	10.00 5.00 0.50		Provision of conc. – designed mix grade C10, ct. to BS 12, 20 mm agg. to BS 882; min. ct. content 250 kg/m³. & Placing mass conc. in base, thickness: 300–500 mm.

If it was subsequently found that a fourth bed was to be provided, then a further one can be added in the timesing column by the process known as 'dotting on', as indicated below:

3/ 1.	10.00 5.00 0.50		Descriptions as previous items

Where there are a number of units of the same item, all multiplying factors should appear in the timesing column. Taking, for instance, 30 rows of piles with 4 piles in each row, entries on the dimension sheet would be:

30/4/	1		Number of preformed conc. piles, grade C25, 300 × 300 mm, len. 10.6 m; m.s. drivg. heads & shoes.
30/4/	10.00		Depth driven.

Care should be taken when writing the 'slash' symbols for multiplication that the slash is not capable of being confused with the denominator line of a vulgar fraction. For example, 3/4/ means 12 times but if noted carelessly could easily be mistaken for three over four or three-quarters times – giving a very large margin of error in the computed quantity for that item.

Abbreviations

Many of the words entered in the description column are abbreviated to save space and time spent in entering the items by highly skilled technical staff. Many abbreviations have become almost standard and are of general application; for this reason a list of the more common abbreviations is given in Appendix 1. A considerable number of abbreviations are obtained merely by shortening the particular words, such as the use of 'fwk.' in place of 'formwork', 'rad.' for 'radius' and 'conc.' for 'concrete'. The author also believes that it would be permissible to omit the metric symbols in billed item descriptions, but has included them in the examples, following the practice adopted in *CESMM3 Handbook* (Telford, 1992).

Grouping of Dimensions

Where more than one set of dimensions relates to the same description, the dimensions should be suitably bracketed so that this shall be made perfectly clear. The following example illustrates this point:

	148.00		Clay pipes to BS 65 w.s. & s flex. jts. nom. bore 225 mm in trs, between mhs 8 & 12, depth: 2–2.5 m.
	246.00		
	132.00		
	56.00		

Where the same dimensions apply to more than one item, the best procedure is to segregate each of the separate descriptions by an '&' sign as illustrated below, and to insert the customary bracket:

	260.00 16.00 3.20		Excavn. for cuttgs. max. depth 2–5 m; Excvtd. Surf. 0.30 m above Final Surf. & Fillg. embankts. selected excvtd. mat. other than topsoil or rock.

Deductions

After measuring an item of construction it is sometimes necessary to deduct for voids or openings in the main area or volume. This is normally performed by following the main item by a deduction item as shown in the following example:

	11.80 10.35 0.20		Placg. mass conc. a.b. in ground slab; thickness 150–300 mm.
	1.60 1.45 0.20		Ddt. ditto. (opgs).

The above advice only applies to the group system of take off where a negative item is required to effect a deduction at the abstract stage of the billing process. However in the 'cut and shuffle' and direct billing systems, deductions can be effected directly within the dimensions of an item.

Figured Dimensions

When taking off it is most desirable to use figured dimensions on the drawings in preference to scaling, since the drawings are almost invariably in the form of prints, which are not always true to scale. It is sometimes necessary to build up overall dimensions from a series of figured dimensions and this work is best set down in waste, on the right-hand side of the description column.

Numbering and Titles of Dimension Sheets

Each dimension sheet should be suitably headed with the title and section of the project at the head of each sheet and with each sheet numbered consecutively at the bottom. Some prefer to number each set of columns on each dimension sheet separately. The entering of page numbers on each dimension sheet ensures the early discovery of a missing sheet and that the sheets are in the correct sequence.

At the top of the first dimension sheet for each main section of the work should be entered a list of the drawings from which the measurements have been taken, with the precise drawing number of each contract drawing carefully recorded. A typical example of such a list follows:

NORTH CREAKE OUTFALL SEWER SHEET NR 1

Drawings
NC/SEW/1/10A (Layout Plan)
NC/SEW/1/5A (Sewer Sections)
NC/SEW/1/6B (Sewer Sections)
NC/SEW/1/7B (Sewer Sections)
NC/SEW/1/12A (Manhole Details)

The importance of listing the contract drawings from which the dimensions have been obtained in this way, is that in the event of changes being made to the work as originally planned resulting in the issue of amended drawings, it will clearly be seen that these changes occurred after the Bill of Quantities was prepared and that variations to the quantities can be expected.

It is good practice to punch all dimension sheets at their top left-hand corner and fasten them together with Treasury tags.

Take Off Lists

Where the work contained in a project is complex or fragmented, it is good practice to prepare a take off list at the outset listing the main components in the order that they will be measured. This enables the person measuring the work to look at the project in its entirety, to reduce the risk of omission of items and to provide a checklist as the detailed measurement proceeds.

Query Sheets

It is good practice to enter any queries that may arise during the taking-off on technical matters on query sheets, which are normally subdivided vertically into two parts. The first column contains details of the matters on which clarification or amplification are required and the second column is used for the Engineer's reply.

Use of Schedules

When measuring a number of items with similar general characteristics but of varying components, it is often desirable to use schedules as a means of setting down all the relevant information in tabulated form. This assists with the taking off process and reducing the risk of error, and is particularly appropriate for the measurement of a considerable number of manholes as illustrated in the Sewer example (Worked Example 9) in Part 2 of this book.

Abstracting

When the items on the dimension sheets after squaring cannot conveniently be transferred direct to the appropriate section of the bill, they may be grouped in an abstract, where they will be suitably classified and reduced to the recognised units of measurement preparatory to transfer to the bill. The various phases of abstracting are described below.

Group System Bill Production

Working-up

This chapter is concerned with the final stages leading up to the preparation of bills of quantities for civil engineering work, after the dimensions have been taken off. The term 'working-up' is applied to all the various operations collectively and can comprise the following processes:

(1) Squaring the dimensions and entering the resultant lengths, areas, volumes and weights in the third or squaring column on the dimensions paper.

(2) Transferring the squared dimensions to the abstract, where they are written in a recognised order, ready for billing, under the appropriate section headings, and are subsequently totalled and reduced to the recognised units of measurement in readiness for transfer to the bill.

(3) In the bill of quantities, the various items of work making up the project are then listed under appropriate section headings, with descriptions printed in full and quantities given in the recognised units of measurement, as laid down in *Civil Engineering Standard Method of Measurement* (CESMM3). The bill also contains rate and price columns for pricing by contractors when tendering for the project.

An example of an abstract and resulting bill is illustrated at the end of this chapter. This example is based on the detailed take off of the Stone Faced Sea Wall illustrated in Worked Example 8 in Part 2 of this book. Readers therefore have a sample where they may follow all three stages of the production of a Bill of Quantities under the group system of taking off.

Squaring the Dimensions

The term 'squaring the dimensions' refers to the calculation of the numbers, lengths, areas and volumes and their entry in the third or squaring column on the dimensions paper. The following example illustrates the squaring of typical dimensions on dimensions paper:

Dimensions				Notes
7/2/	15.20	212.8	Fwk. fair fin. hor. width: 0.1–0.2 m.	Linear item: Total length is 212.80 m or 212 metres, 800 millimetres (14 × 15.20 m)
	90.00 10.00	900.0	Fwk. fair fin. vertical.	Square or superficial item: area is 900 m²
	90.00 2.40 1.00	216.0	Placing of mass conc. in bases & grd. slabs, thickness ex. 500 mm.	Cubic item: Volume of concrete is 321 m³. Note method of casting up a series of dimensions relating to the same item with the total entered in the description column and the use of the bracket. Deductions following the main items can be dealt with in a similar manner.
	50.00 2.10 1.00	105.0		
			321.0	

The squaring must be checked by another person to eliminate any possibility of errors occurring. All squared dimensions and waste calculations should be ticked in coloured ink or pencil on checking and any alterations made in a similar manner. Amended figures need a further check. Where, as is frequently the case, calculating machines are used for squaring purposes a check should still be made.

Abstracting

An example showing typical completed abstract sheets is given later in this chapter, and the items will subsequently be produced in bill form. The abstract covers the dimensions for the Stone Faced Sea Wall taken-off in Worked Example 8 in Part 2 of this book, where the dimensions have been squared in readiness for abstracting. As each item is transferred to the abstract the description of the appropriate dimension item is crossed through with a vertical line on the dimension sheet, with short horizontal lines at each end of the vertical line, so that there shall be no doubt as to what has been transferred.

The abstract sheets are ruled with a series of vertical lines spaced about 25 mm apart and are usually on A3 paper.

Each abstract sheet is headed with the project reference, sheet number and section of the work, and possibly the sub-section of the work, to which the abstracted dimensions refer. The section headings normally follow those given in *Civil Engineering Standard Method of Measurement* (CESMM3) and are usually produced in the same order.

Entries in the abstract should be well spaced and it is necessary for the worker-up to look through the dimension sheets, before starting to abstract, in order to determine, as closely as possible, how many abstract sheets will be required. They should not be any closer than shown in the example.

The items will be entered in the abstract in the same order as they will appear in the bill, as far as is practicable, since the primary function of the abstract is to classify and group the various items preparatory to billing, and to reduce the dimensions to the recognised units of measurement. Descriptions are usually spread over two columns with the appropriate dimension(s) in the first column and any deductions in the second column. The total quantity of each item is reduced to the recognised unit of measurement such as kilogrammes to tonnes.

It is good practice to precede each description in the abstract with the prefix C, S, L or Nr, denoting that the item is cubic, square, linear or enumerated to reduce the risk of errors arising with regard to units or quantities.

Where it is necessary to abstract a number of similar items but of different sizes, the best procedure is to group these items under a single heading with each size entered in a separate column, as shown in the following example:

Cast (spun) iron s & s pipes to BS 1211 (class B) w. caulked lead jts. in trenches, depth ne 1.5 m

150 mm dia.	225 mm dia.	300 mm dia.	375 mm dia.
154.00 (6) 186.00 (9) 218.00 (10)	104.00 (7) 192.00 (8) 184.00 (9)	226.00 (10) 176.00 (11)	204.00 (11) 142.00 (12)

The number entered in brackets after the dimension represents the page number of the dimension sheet from which the dimension has been extracted, for ease of reference.

All squaring and abstracting work and the transfer of the abstract items to the bill must be checked by a second person to verify their accuracy.

Billing

The example given later in this chapter, incorporates the billed items for the Stone Faced Sea Wall, based on the entries in the abstract example. As each item is transferred to the bill it is crossed through on the abstract to prevent any possibility of errors occurring during the transfer stage.

The order of billed items will be the same as in the abstract, as far as is practicable, and they will be grouped under suitable section headings and specification preambles as appropriate.

Each item in the bill is indexed, usually by the numbering of items in the first column and preferably incorporating CESMM3 coding. It will be noticed that all words in the billed descriptions are inserted in full without any abbreviations and this procedure should always be followed to avoid any possible confusion.

Provision is usually made for the total sum on each page of the bill relating to a given section of work to be transferred to a collection at the end of the section. The total of each of the collections is transferred to a Grand Summary, the total of which will constitute the tender total. This procedure is preferable to carrying forward the total from one page to another in each section, since the subsequent rectification of errors in pricing may necessitate alterations to a considerable number of pages.

Billed descriptions should conform to the requirements of CESMM3, follow in a logical sequence and be concise, yet must not, at the same time, omit any matters which will be needed by the Contractor to be able realistically to assess the price for each item.

The first bill is likely to cover General Items incorporating Specified Requirements and Method-related Charges, where the Contractor can price items that are not proportional to the quantities of Permanent Works.

Other Methods of Bill Preparation

Direct Billing

As explained in the Introduction to this chapter, direct billing is a one-stage approach to bill preparation as the draft bill is produced when the quantities are taken off, thus eliminating the need for the abstracting and billing stages of the group system. In the case of larger projects using direct billing it is common to have only one item per page of take off, thus avoiding possible cramming of dimensions should more of the same item need to be added later, but more importantly allowing items of the draft bill to be shuffled readily into the ultimate bill order. Care obviously needs to be taken to number sheets in a way that avoids loss and omission of any sheets of take off.

Direct billing can be used to advantage in several CESMM3 work classifications including demolition and site clearance, structural metalwork, timber, piling, rail track and sewer and water main renovation.

A typical example of a page of direct billing is illustrated overleaf. The example is based on the same project as Worked Example 8, Stone Faced Sea Wall from Part 2 of this book, so that the two approaches to bill noting may be compared.

'Cut and Shuffle'

The system of 'cut and shuffle' was developed in the early 1960s and by the late 1970s was probably the most widely used method of entering dimensions and descriptions. It has been aptly described as a rationalised traditional approach. Unlike abstracting and billing there is no universally accepted format and many different paper rulings and methods of implementation are used in different offices.

However, the following criteria apply to most systems:

(1) Dimensions paper is subdivided into four or five separate sections which can subsequently be split into individual sections.

(2) Only one description with its associated dimensions is written on each section.

(3) Dimension sheets are subsequently split into separate slips and sorted into bill work sections and eventually into bill order.

(4) Following the intermediate processes of calculation and editing, the slips form the draft for producing the final bill of quantities.

Typical example of direct billing

WORKED EXAMPLE 8 Stone Faced Sea Wall			SHEET NR	F/1
Commentary*	Item Nr.	Description	Unit	Qty
Note: Commentary only for purposes of explanation and would not be part of normal stationery for direct billing.		**Class F: *In situ* Concrete** Provision of Concrete		
The quantities for this item would be transferred from the placing items.	F224	Designed mix, grade C25, cement to BS 12, 40 mm aggregate to BS 882 Qty of item F544.1 = 884.13 Qty of item F544.2 = 73.80	m^3	958
Additional description given as para. 5.10 of CESMM3.		Placing of Concrete, Mass walls thickness: exceeding 500 mm; backing to masonry		
Para. 5.20 of CESMM3. Deducts taken at same time. Deduction of cast in masonry.	F544.1	Below high water level base 60.00 × 4.00 × 2.00 Dt. taper 0.5/60.00 × 4.00 × 0.35 Dt. toe top 60.00 × 0.35 × 0.35 middle section 60.00 × 2.96 × 2.00 upper section 60.00 × 2.10 × 1.80 Dt. ashlar 60.00 × 0.51 × 4.20	m^3	884
	F544.2	Above high water level Average 60.00 × 1.85 × 0.60 next coping stone 60.00 × 0.75 × 0.48 Dt. ashlar 60.00 × 0.40 × 0.60	m^3	74

The cut and shuffle method is designed to eliminate the preparation and checking of the abstract and the draft bill. Hence there is only one major written operation, namely taking off, compared with the three entailed with abstracting and billing.

One method of carrying out the technique is now described:

(1) Taking off is carried out on A4 sheets of dimensions paper, ruled vertically into four columns, and thus accommodating four items per sheet. Dimensions are entered on one side only of each sheet and each column is generally stamped with the project reference and numbered consecutively. 'Ditto.' items must include a reference to the column number of the main item, where full particulars can be found.

(2) As sections of the taking off are completed, the side casts are checked and repeat dimensions calculated.

(3) When the taking off is complete, each column is marked with the taking off section number, work section reference and column number. A copy of each dimension sheet is obtained, generally either by using NCR (no carbon required) paper or by photocopying. However, some systems operate without the need to produce a copy.

(4) The taker off retains the copy and the original sheet is cut into four slips, each containing one item. Some quantity surveyors use sheets that are already perforated.

(5) The slips are shuffled or sorted into sections, such as Earthworks, *In situ* Concrete, Concrete Ancillaries and Precast Concrete. Similar items are collected together and the whole of the slips placed, as near as possible, in bill order.

(6) When all the slips for an individual work section have been sorted, they are edited to form the draft bill, with further slips being inserted as necessary to provide headings, collections and other relevant items. The correct unit is entered on the 'parent' or primary item slip and the 'children' or repeat item slips are marked 'a.b.' (as before). As each section is edited it is passed to a calculator operator for squaring.

(7) The calculator operator squares, casts, reduces and inserts the reduced quantity on the parent item slip. This operation is double checked.

(8) Parent and children slips are separated. The parent slips form the draft bill and are ready for processing.

(9) Any further checks on the draft bill are then carried out and final copies made and duplicated.

(10) The children slips are then replaced to provide an abstract in bill order for reference purposes during the post-contract period.

Computers and Bill Production

An increasing use is being made of desk top computers for the preparation of bills of quantities, resulting from the reducing cost of hardware (equipment) and the improved range and efficiency of software. Computer-aided bill production systems provide the facility to check accuracy, but care is needed in the coding of dimensions and entry of data. The coding can be double checked, although a random check may be considered adequate.

The use of computer-aided bill of quantities production packages eliminates the reducing, abstracting and billing operations by converting coded dimension sheets into bills of quantities. Codes are frequently based on the CESMM3 reference codes to form a standard library of descriptions. Items not covered by the standard library are termed rogue items but these are unlikely to be very extensive. The rogue items are suitably coded and entered into either the standard library or the particular project library. The computer normally prints a master copy of the bill of quantities which can be photocopied on to ruled paper to give a high standard of presentation.

Range of Computer Programs

Desk top computers can be used to advantage in many activities associated with civil engineering projects and the following selection gives an indication of their wide range and scope, stemming from their extensive storage capacity, and ease of retrieval of data and monitoring of progress:

(1) bills of quantities production
(2) automatic measurement of some civil engineering works
(3) materials scheduling, possibly linked with computer-aided design (CAD)
(4) steel reinforcement calculations
(5) earthwork calculations (cut and fill, and mass haul)
(6) specification production
(7) feasibility studies and cost control
(8) cost reporting
(9) estimating and tendering
(10) tender analysis
(11) budgetary controls
(12) valuations
(13) formula price adjustment
(14) variations and final accounts
(15) fee management
(16) quotations and enquiries
(17) cash flow forecasting
(18) capital programming
(19) project planning and control
(20) progress statements
(21) resource analysis
(22) sub-contractors' payments
(23) maintenance scheduling
(24) plant and equipment scheduling.

ICEPAC

The leading software system for civil engineering bill preparation and contract administration is the ICEPAC (Telford) System. This incorporates the CESMM3 Standard Library, operates on a wide range of hardware, has direct access to the CESMM3 Price Database, links to CAD and the Moss Drainage System, and has digitiser input and many other facilities.

CESMM3 Library of Item Descriptions

The CESMM3 Library of Item Descriptions (Telford, 1991) interprets the relevant rules and allows the user to select appropriate information for addition to the basic description derived from CESMM3. The aim is to provide sufficient information whereby a user can build up complete item descriptions in 90 per cent of cases by direct reference to the library.

The library will enhance the manual preparation of civil engineering bills using traditional methods by eliminating the need to refer regularly to other sources to produce complete item descriptions. The library has been compiled with computer usage in mind and hence its adaptation to the needs of computer systems is relatively simple. The library is available in several commercially available software packages, of which the leading one is ICEPAC as previously described.

STONE FACED SEA WALL

ABSTRACT OF DIMENSIONS OBTAINED FROM WORKED EXAMPLE 8

EARTHWORKS 1

Excavn.

C/Gen. excavn., max. depth: 0.25–0.5 m.
E422

23.4 (7)

= 23 m^3

C/Gen. excavn., max. depth: 1–2 m excvtd. surf. hwl.
E424

91.1 (1)

= 91 m^3

C/Gen. excavn., max. depth: 5–10 m; Commg. Surf. hwl.
E426

1085.8 (1)

= 1086 m^3

Excavn. Ancillaries

S/Prepn. of excvtd. surfs. below hwl.
E522.1

240.0 (3)

= 240 m^2

S/Prepn. of excvtd. surfs. above hwl.
E522.2

78.0 (7)

= 78 m^2

Fillg. Ancillaries

S/Prepn. of filled surfs.
E722

54.0 (3)

= 54 m^2

C/Disposal of excvtd. mat.
E532

	Ddt.
1176.9 (2)	
23.4 (7)	253.5 (2)
1200.3	
253.5	
946.8	

= 947 m^3

C/Fillg. to structures.
E613

253.5 (2)

= 254 m^3

Note: The deductions are crossed through after transfer.

STONE FACED SEA WALL

IN SITU CONCRETE 2

C/Provsn. of conc. designed mix, grade C25, ct to BS 12, 40 mm agg. to BS 882.	F224	C/Placg. of conc. mass walls thickness: ex. 500 mm; backg. to masonry below hwl.	F544.1	Conc. Ancillaries S/Fwk. ro.fin.slopg; width: 0.2–0.4 m; below hwl.	G123
1012.6 (3)	Ddt.	1012.6 (3)	Ddt.	21.0 (4)	
88.2 (4)	128.5 (5)	128.5	128.5 (5)		
1100.8	14.4 (6)	884.1		= 21 m^2	
142.9	142.9				
957.9		= 884 m^3			
				S/Fwk. ro. fin. vert. width: 0.4–1.22 m; below hwl.	G144.1
= 958 m^3				36.0 (4)	
				= 36 m^2	
				S/Fwk. ro. fin. vert. width: 0.4–1.22 m; above hwl.	G144.2
		C/Ditto. above hwl.	F544.2		
				66.0 (5)	
		88.2 (4)	Ddt.		
		14.4	14.4 (6)	= 66 m^2	
		73.8			
		= 74 m^3			
				S/Fwk. ro. fin. vert; below hwl.	G145
				348.0 (4)	
				= 348 m^2	

Note: C denotes cubic items, S superficial ones, L linear ones and Nr are enumerated items.
Numbers in brackets denote dimension sheet page numbers.
In a straightforward project like this with a restricted number of items and where the quantities can be totalled on the dimension sheets, it is quite feasible to omit the abstract and transfer the quantities direct from the dimension sheets to the bill.

STONE FACED SEA WALL

PILES | LIGHT DUTY PAVEMENT 3

		Interlockg steel piles type 2N, setn. modulus 1150 cm^3/m, grade 43A to BS4360. S/Driven area. P832
225.0 (3) = 225 m^2		
		S/Area of piles of len: n.e. 14 m; treated w. 2cts. bit. paint. P833
225.0 (3) = 225 m^2		

		S/Granular base, depth: 75 mm. R713
180.0 (7) = 180 m^2		
		S/Red precast conc. flgs. to BS7263 type D; thickness: 50 mm. R782
180.0 (7) = 180 m^2		

STONE FACED SEA WALL

MASONRY 4

Ashlar masonry, granite flush ptd. w. mortar type M3.

S/Vert. st. wall; thickness: 300 mm, fair faced b.s.
U731

27.0 (6)

= 27 m^2

S/Battered fcg. to conc; thickness: nom. 400 mm above hwl.
U736

42.0 (5)

= 42 m^2

S/Ditto. thickness: nom. 600 & 400 mm in alt. cos. av. 514 mm, below hwl.
U746

252.0 (5)

= 252 m^2

L/Copg. 1125 × 600 mm rdd. w. sinkgs. as Dwg. WE8.
U771.1

60.0 (6)

= 60 m

L/Copg. 450 × 225 mm 2^{ce} wethd. & 2^{ce} thro. as Dwg. WE8.
U771.2

60.0 (6)

= 60 m

L/Plinth 525 × 600 mm 2^{ce} splyd. as Dwg. WE8
U777

60.0 (6)

= 60 m

L/Dpc; width: 300 mm, 2 cos of slates, ld. bkg. jt. in mortar type M3.
U782

60.0 (7)

= 60 m

Worked Example 8 Bill of Quantities for Stone Faced Sea Wall (prepared from Abstract on previous pages)

Number	*Item Description*	*Unit*	*Quantity*	*Rate*	*Amount*	
					£	*p*
	CLASS E: EARTHWORKS					
	General Excavation					
E422	Maximum depth 0.25–0.5 m.	m^3	23			
E424	Maximum depth 1–2 m, excavated surface high water level.	m^3	91			
E426	Maximum depth 5–10 m; Commencing Surface: high water level.	m^3	1086			
	Excavation Ancillaries					
E522.1	Preparation of excavated surfaces below high water level.	m^2	240			
E522.2	Preparation of excavated surfaces above high water level.	m^2	78			
E532	Disposal of excavated material.	m^3	947			
	Filling					
E613	Filling to structures.	m^3	254			
	Filling Ancillaries					
E722	Preparation of filled surfaces.	m^2	54			
			Page total			

Bill of Quantities (contd.) Stone Faced Sea Wall

Number	Item Description	Unit	Quantity	Rate	Amount £	p
	CLASS F: IN SITU *CONCRETE*					
	Provision of Concrete					
F224	Designed mix, grade C25, cement to BS 12, 40 mm aggregate to BS 882.	m^3	958			
	Placing of Concrete, Mass walls thickness: exceeding 500 mm; backing to masonry					
F544.1	Below high water level.	m^3	884			
F544.2	Above high water level.	m^3	74			
	CLASS G: CONCRETE ANCILLARIES					
	Formwork rough finish					
G123	Sloping, width: 0.2–0.4 m; below high water level.	m^2	21			
G144.1	Vertical, width: 0.4–1.22 m; below high water level.	m^2	36			
G144.2	Vertical, width: 0.4–1.22 m; above high water level.	m^2	66			
G145	Vertical; below high water level.	m^2	348			
			Page total			

Bill of Quantities (contd.) Stone Faced Sea Wall

Number	*Item Description*	*Unit*	*Quantity*	*Rate*	*Amount*	
					£	*p*
	CLASS P: PILES					
	Interlocking steel piles type 2N, section modulus 1150 cm³/m, grade 43A to BS 4360.					
P832	Driven area.	m²	225			
P833	Area of piles of length: not exceeding 14 m; treated with two coats of bitumen paint.	m²	225			
			Total			
	CLASS R: PAVINGS					
	Light duty pavement					
R713	Granular base, depth: 75 mm.	m²	180			
R782	Red precast concrete flags to BS 7263 type D; thickness: 50 mm.	m²	180			
			Total			
	Note: Two different classes have been inserted on the same page because of the small number of items involved. Hence it is necessary to have two totals for transfer to the Grand Summary.					
			Page total			

Bill of Quantities (contd.) Stone Faced Sea Wall

Number	*Item Description*	*Unit*	*Quantity*	*Rate*	*Amount*	
					£	*p*
	CLASS U: MASONRY *Ashlar masonry granite flush pointed with mortar type M3*					
U731	Vertical stone wall; thickness: 300 mm, fair faced both sides.	m^2	27			
U736	Battered facing to concrete; thickness; nominal 400 mm, above high water level.	m^2	42			
U746	Ditto., thickness: nominal 600 and 400 mm, in alternate courses, average 514 mm, below high water level.	m^2	252			
U771.1	Coping 1125 × 600 mm rounded with sinkings as Drawing 10.	m	60			
U771.2	Coping 450 × 225 mm, twice weathered and twice throated as Drawing WE8.	m	60			
U777	Plinth 525 × 600 mm, twice splayed as Drawing WE8	m	60			
U782	Damp-proof course; width: 300 mm, two courses of slates laid breaking joint in mortar type M3.	m	60			
			Page total			

CHAPTER 4

CESMM3: Classes A–D

Contract and Preparatory Site Matters

Class A: General Items
Class B: Ground Investigation
Class C: Geotechnical and Other Specialist Processes
Class D: Demolition and Site Clearance

Introduction

This chapter is concerned with two quite distinct matters, firstly the General Items which are largely concerned with contractual obligations covered in Class A, and secondly with the measurement of preparatory site operations covered in Classes B to D which include site investigation, geotechnics, demolitions and site clearance.

General Items frequently cover matters which are incidental or non-permanent but which may nevertheless represent quite large proportions of any project's cost.

The preparatory works in Classes B, C and D may in some cases be issued as contracts in their own right rather than being part of the main works contract. This could be due to the work having to be completed before the true nature of the permanent works can be determined or it may be used as a time-saving exercise where, for example, the demolitions can be progressed while the designs for the new works are being completed.

Class A: General Items

General Items represent three broad categories of project cost:

(1) Costs associated with elements incidental to the permanent work such as insurances, services, temporary accommodation and other temporary works, which the Contractor is specifically required to provide as obligations under the contract.

(2) Costs which the Contractor chooses to include as Method-related charges. Typically some of these costs will cover elements which are imposed by legislation such as safety, health and welfare requirements, others will cover plant and other temporary works which the Contractor opts to price under this heading.

(3) Provisional Sums for work which cannot be fully defined at the tender stage and Prime Cost Items for Nominated Sub-contracts.

Class A: General Items is unique within Section 8 in not specifying any required units of measurement within the three divisions of rules. However, measurement rule M1 states that the unit of measurement for general items shall be a sum of money except where another unit is used in accordance with measurement rule M2. (In practice, rule M1 is also modified by measurement rules M4, M5 and M6.) Rule M2 requires that a quantity shall be given where the value is to be subject to admeasurement under ICE Conditions, clause 56(1) and the unit of measurement stated.

Additional description rule D2 requires that specified requirements shall distinguish between establishment and removal of services and facilities and their continuing operation or maintenance. This could activate rule M2 in regard to admeasurement as the following sample items illustrate:

A211.1 Specified requirements; accommodation for Engineer's staff; offices as Specification clause 123, establishment and removal — sum

A211.2 Specified requirements; accommodation for Engineer's staff; offices as Specification clause 123, maintenance — sum

A211.3 Specified requirements; accommodation for Engineer's staff; offices as Specification clause 123, maintenance after issue of Substantial Completion Certificate — wk 15

The sum required to price item A211.1 is in effect a fixed cost while that of item A211.2 is a time-related cost. As the relevant time is the duration of the works, which is under the control of the Contractor, it is still priced as a sum and would not normally be adjusted for the actual duration taken. However the time that the offices are required to be kept after the Substantial Completion date is entirely at the discretion of the Engineer and is therefore measured on a time basis. In addition the quantity could be subject to admeasurement as the actual time could be a longer or shorter period than envisaged at the billing stage and a per week basis makes adjustment for the final account very straightforward.

Contractual requirements, A1**, comprise bonds and insurances which the contact conditions stipulate and these items provide an appropriate place for the Contractor to include the cost. Performance bonds (A110) are bonds taken out by the Contractor with a bank or insurance company to provide the client with certain financial guarantees should the Contractor default through bankruptcy or otherwise. The insurances in A120 and A130 include insurance of the works, constructional plant and third parties, and are contractual requirements under the ICE Conditions of Contract, clauses 21 and 23.

A2** covers requirements specified by the Engineer which the Contractor is bound to meet, whereas the method-related charges entered under A3** are items which the tendering Contractor chooses to insert. Rule D1 of Class A defines 'specified requirements' as all work, other than the Permanent Works, which is expressly stated in the Contract (Specification or other contract document) to be carried out by the Contractor and of which the nature and extent is defined. This ensures that the attention of tendering Contractors is drawn to contractual requirements which in other circumstances might be a matter for their own decision. Taking pumping and de-watering as examples, these appear under 'Specified requirements' A276 and A277 where the Engineer has decided that these procedures will be carried out under the contract. However pumping and de-watering appear again under A356 and A357 as Method-related charges, in order that a Contractor may include for these costs should that method of working be chosen where it is not a contractual requirement. Another prime example of this would be work in a tidal estuary where a number of options are possible:

(1) The Engineer had no fixed requirements as to method of construction; no items would be generated under A275 for cofferdams.

(2) The Contractor may decide to work between the tides: allows for reduced productivity in the unit rates and has no requirement for a Method-related charge.

(3) The Contractor decides to adopt a cofferdam as the constructional method and includes for this as Method-related charge items.

(4) The Engineer decides that a cofferdam is the only method of construction which will satisfy the particular situation and makes provision of the cofferdam a specified requirement – therefore items required under A275 (conforming to rule A2).

Testing of materials or the works is provided for in items A250 and A260 which should include the particulars of sampling and methods of testing. It should be noted that some testing is included separately in other classes of the Work Classification, for example P8** Pile tests. Should the works require substantial testing facilities then it would be prudent to provide items to cover the establishment, removal and maintenance of suitable facilities. In any case the contractor would be free to insert an allowance for such facilities under 'Method-related charges' if this was considered necessary.

Another function of specified requirements items is to obtain a price which can be adjusted in the event of a variation. Otherwise, if for instance the Engineer is to change the details of accommodation for the Engineer's Staff, in the absence of a specific item, adjustment of an undisclosed price could prove difficult.

The Method-related charges division of Class A lists a number of the more common items, but these do not restrict the Contractor in any way. The Contractor can insert, in the space provided in the General Items part of the Bill, other items which will not be proportional to the quantities of the Permanent Works, distinguishing between time-related and fixed charges. Some typical entries are illustrated at the end of this section of this chapter.

The time element of time-related charges can be expressed in various ways, but such expressions as 'the duration of construction' or 'completion of the wharf' are generally more useful than stated lengths of time which are not related to site activities and which may prove more difficult to apply to changed conditions.

It should be noted that although the provision of space for Method-related items to be inserted by contractors is provided under Class A: General Items, the principles of their use are defined under Section 7 of CESMM3. These principles have been explained in Chapter 2 of this book.

While most of Class A: General Items thus far have been concerned with non-permanent cost elements, the remainder of the Class covers permanent work which is either not defined or will be carried out under Nominated Sub-contracts.

Provisional sums for daywork are given under A41* and the items detailed in accordance with measurement rule M5 which refers back to clause 5.6 of CESMM3. Clause 5.6 allows two approaches to daywork: 5.6(a) which requires a list of the various classes of labour, materials and plant to be priced by the tenderer together with a statement of the conditions under which the contractor will be paid; or the more popular 5.6(b) which is based on the 'Schedules of Dayworks carried out incidental to Contract Work' issued by the Federation of Civil Engineering Contractors with provision for percentage adjustments to be made by the tenderer.

Other provisional sums are covered by A420 and would be sums for items which cannot be foreseen at the time of tendering. An example of a relatively small cost item which is often dealt with by provisional sum is the cost of telephone calls by the Engineers. Items under A222 would cover the installation, removal and rental of the telephones specified but it would be rather unfair to expect the Contractor to quote a binding rate for the cost of the calls by parties outside the Contractor's control. Another reason for provisional sums is uncertainty, for example for work which can only be assessed once the ground has been opened up and the nature of existing construction determined.

Prime Cost Items are included for work under Nominated Sub-contracts which can be of two types: A5*0 for Nominated Sub-contracts which include work on site and A6*0 for Nominated Sub-contracts which do not include work on site. Measurement rule M6 states that labours under A520 or A620 are only those defined in paragraph 5.15. Any other required labour would be specified as Special labours and included as A530 or A630; and furthermore under additional description rule A6 the nature of the labour shall be stated. 'Special Labours' in this context are sometimes referred to as Special Attendance.

There now follows an example of a typical bill of quantities for Class A: General Items, containing many of the items discussed in this section of this chapter.

Number	Item Description	Unit	Quantity	Rate	Amount £	Amount p
	CLASS A: GENERAL ITEMS					
	Contractual requirements					
A110	Performance bond.	sum				
A120	Insurance of the Works.	sum				
A130	Third party insurance.	sum				
	Specified requirements					
	Accommodation for Engineer's staff					
A211.1	Establishment and removal of office for the Engineer's staff, as Specification clause A25.	sum				
A211.2	Maintenance of offices for the Engineer's staff.	sum				
A211.3	Maintenance of offices for the Engineer's staff after the issue of the Completion Certificate.	wk	15			
	Attendance upon Engineer's staff					
A242	Attendance upon the Engineer's staff; chainmen.	wk	80			
	Testing of materials					
A250	Testing of materials; concrete test cubes as Specification clause C86.	nr	300			
	1/1		Page total			

Class A: General Items

Number	Item Description	Unit	Quantity	Rate	Amount £	Amount p
	Specified requirements					
	Testing of the Works					
A260.1	Clay pipes, nominal bore 150 mm, length 1380 m, as Specification clause 121.1.	sum				
A260.2	Clay pipes, nominal bore 225 mm, length 2540 m, as Specification clause 121.2.	sum				
A260.3	Clay pipes, nominal bore 300 mm, length 1170 m, as Specification clause 121.3.	sum				
	Temporary Works					
A272.1	Traffic regulation: establishment and removal as Specification clause A37.	sum				
A272.2	Traffic regulation: continuing operation and maintenance as Specification clause A37.	wk	80			
A276.1	Pumping plant: establishment and removal as Specification clause A52.	sum				
A276.2	Pumping plant: operation and maintenance as Specification clause A52.	h	600			
	1/2	Page total				

Class A: General Items
(Blank pages in Bill of Quantities – entries of method-related charges made by tendering Contractor)

Number	Item Description	Unit	Quantity	Rate	Amount £	Amount p
	Method-related charges					
	Accommodation and buildings					
A311.1	Establish offices: fixed.	sum				
A311.2	Maintain offices for duration of construction: time-related.	sum				
A311.3	Remove offices: fixed.	sum				
	Services					
A321.1	Establish electricity supply and standby generator: fixed.	sum				
A321.2	Provision of electricity for duration of construction: time-related.	sum				
	Plant					
	30 t crane for excavation and concreting of settling tanks					
A.331.1	Bring to site: fixed.	sum				
A.331.2	Operate and maintain: time-related.	sum				
A.331.3	Remove: fixed.	sum				
	Temporary works					
	Compressed air for tunnelling from access shaft 7 to access shaft 10					
A358.1	Establish compressed air plant: fixed.	sum				
A358.2	Compressed air supply: time-related.	sum				
A358.3	Remove compressed air plant: fixed.	sum				
	Supervision and labour					
A371	Management and supervision for duration of construction: time-related.	sum				
A373	Labour for maintenance of plant and site services for duration of construction: time-related.	sum				
	1/3			Page total		

Class A: General Items

Number	Item Description	Unit	Quantity	Rate	Amount £	p
	Provisional Sums					
	Daywork					
A411	Labour.	sum			60000	00
A412	Percentage adjustment to Provisional Sum for Daywork labour.	%				
A413	Materials.	sum			30000	00
A414	Percentage adjustment to Provisional Sum for Daywork materials.	%				
A415	Plant.	sum			30000	00
A416	Percentage adjustment to Provisional Sum for Daywork plant.	%				
A417	Supplementary charges.	sum			5000	00
A418	Percentage adjustment to Provisional Sum for Daywork supplementary charges.	%				
	Other Provisional Sums					
A420.1	Permanent diversion or support of existing services.	sum			18000	00
A420.2	Repairs to existing structures and plant.	sum			25000	00
	Nominated Sub-contracts which include work on the Site					
A510.1	Mechanical plant.	sum			30000	00
A520.1	Labours.	sum				
A530	Special labours, attendance as Specification clause A105	sum				
A540.1	Other charges and profit.	%				
A510.2	Lighting installation.	sum			13000	00
A520.2	Labours.	sum				
A540.2	Other charges and profit.	%				
	Nominated Sub-contracts which do not include work on the Site					
A610.1	Bollards to wharf (20 nr).	sum			10000	00
A620.1	Labours.	sum				
A640.1	Other charges and profit.	%				
A610.2	Rubber buffers to fender piles (200 nr).	sum			5000	00
A620.2	Labours.	sum				
A640.2	Other charges and profit.	%				
	1/4		Page total			

Class B: Ground Investigation

Ground investigation is a highly specialised procedure which is intended to provide prior details of the ground conditions so that projects may be appropriately designed. As this procedure could influence the whole design ethos of any project and have significant effect on the cost, there are implications of legal liability. Should the advice given prove to have been substantially wrong then the client may well consider litigation to recover damages.

Class B of CESMM3 can be conveniently split between the more practical tasks of obtaining the site samples and the professionally skilled practice of taking readings and interpreting the results. Thus it may be convenient to seek tenders for items under B1** to B4**, trial pits and trenches, boreholes and samples from a specialist contractor; but negotiate a separate professional service contract for the analysis of the samples (work covered under B5** to B8**) site tests, instrumental observations, laboratory tests and professional services. This split could clarify the legal responsibilities alluded to previously. The latter section of Class B is quite specialised and readers requiring more details on these aspects are referred to Martin Barnes' *CESMM3 Handbook* (Telford, 1992).

Work under Class B may be included with a construction contract along with the other Work Classes, but where the ground investigation information is required before any meaningful design work can proceed it is likely that this work will be let as a separate contract to be executed early enough to allow the essential design processes to be completed within programme.

The measurement of trial pits, trenches and boreholes is classified in CESMM3 B1** to B3**, amplified by some important additional description rules. Each group of pits, trenches and boreholes generates at least two bill items, namely the number of holes and the aggregate depth measured in metres, under various classifications. This approach enables costs that are proportional to the number of holes, such as moving boring rigs, to be kept separate from costs related to the depths of holes. Separate items are required for excavation in rock, support to excavations and backfilling if required. Removal of obstructions and pumping are measured by the hour which reflects the fairest way of paying for such imponderables.

Rule A1 of Class B requires item descriptions for the number and depth of trial pits and trenches to state the minimum plan area at the bottom of the pit or trench or where the work is undertaken to locate services, the maximum length of the trench. However rule A2 requires item descriptions for the number and depth of trial pits and trenches (B11* to B14*) to identify separately those expressly required to be excavated by hand because of the higher costs entailed. The items for both light cable percussion and rotary drilled boreholes shall state the nominal diameter. The diameters of rotary drilled boreholes are related to core sizes. For instance a core size of 11 mm requires a hole size of 18 mm, and a core of 25 mm a hole of 32 mm; core sizes range from 11 to 150 mm.

Samples and tests are numbered with the descriptions, covering size, type and class in accordance with BS 5930 (*Code of practice for site investigations*). With samples a distinction is made between (1) 'undisturbed' (normally a solid core placed in an airtight tube) and 'disturbed' (loose excavated soil); (2) soft material and rock; (3) samples taken from 'trial pits or trenches or sources at surface' and those from 'boreholes'.

Rule C1 of Class B stipulates that items for ground investigation shall be deemed to include the preparation and submission of the records and results. However any analysis and interpretation of the results would be included under B8** Professional Services (rule M2).

There now follows examples of typical bill items for a selection of ground investigation works.

Number	Item Description	Unit	Quantity	Rate	Amount £	Amount p
	CLASS B: GROUND INVESTIGATION					
	Trial pits					
B114	Number in material other than rock, maximum depth 3–5 m; minimum plan area at bottom of pit: 2.25 m^2.	nr	34			
B130	Depth in material other than rock; minimum plan area at bottom of pit: 2.25 m^2.	m	136			
B160	Depth backfilled with excavated material.	m	136			
B170	Removal of obstructions.	h	15			
B180	Pumping at a minimum extraction rate of 8000 l/h.	h	30			
	Rotary drilled boreholes (nominal minimum core diameter: 100 mm)					
B310	Number.	nr	14			
B342	Depth with core recovery in holes of maximum depth 5–10 m.	m	112			
B360	Depth backfilled with cement grout.	m	112			
B370	Core boxes, 3 m long.	nr	28			
	Samples					
B412	Disturbed samples of soft material from the surface or from trial pits: minimum 5 kg; Class 3.	nr	102			
B421	Open tube samples from boreholes; 100 mm diameter × 600 mm long, undisturbed sample; Class 1.	nr	56			

Class C: Geotechnical and Other Specialist Processes

Class C covers the rather sophisticated techniques of altering the nature and properties of soils and rocks, processes which are usually carried out by specialist subcontractors. These specialist operations are quite likely to generate method-related charges for the required plant.

Before looking in any detail at the measurement rules for the various specialist processes it is worth drawing attention to some general rules which apply to the whole section as appropriate: namely rule M1 – adoption of commencing surface (see also paragraph 5.21 for the basic rule on commencing surfaces); rule C1 deems coverage to include disposal of excavated material and dead services; and rule D1 which conveniently assumes drilling and excavation shall be carried out in normal soil unless otherwise stated.

The measurement of grouting is split into two sections: C1** to C4** dealing with forming the holes for the grouting; and C5** dealing with the materials and injection of the grout. Drilling or driving the holes are measured by metres classified by inclination and depth bands (C1** to C3**). The grout holes are also enumerated to cover the number of holes, the number of stages and the number of water pressure tests (C4*0). The measurement of the holes by length and also by number in CESMM3 appears to be a double measurement but is a facility to allow the contractor to price for the number of locations and relocations of the specialised plant on site in addition to the total length of drilling or driving required. In a similar manner the tonnage of dry grout materials is given under C51* and also again as the tonnage of injection materials under C522 to C525. As the mass of grout materials in both cases excludes the mixing water (rules M5 and M7), the total mass quoted for the dry materials will equal the total mass of all injected grout in the Bill of Quantities.

The measurement of diaphragm walls is covered by C6** which includes the excavation, concrete, reinforcement, waterproof joints and guide walls. Note that the items are deemed to include preparation and upholding sides of excavation (rule C2), trimming faces and preparing tops of the concrete walls (rule C3), supporting reinforcement and preparing protruding reinforcement to receive other work (rule C4). It is worth noting that while the measurement of diaphragm walls under SMM7 for Building Work – Section D40 Embedded Retaining Walls is very similar to the CESMM3 approach, there are some subtle differences.

The measurement of ground anchors (C7) and sand, band and wick drains (C8) comprise both enumerated items to cover such activities as the moving of plant from one location to another, and linear items to cover the cost of materials that are proportional to length, such as tendons and sand.

Readers requiring more detailed information on the measurement of these specialist techniques are referred to Barnes, *CESMM3 Handbook* (Telford, 1992).

Class D: Demolition and Site Clearance

Class D embraces the demolition and removal of objects above the original surface of the ground and tree roots below it. Other items below ground, such as basements and base slabs, will normally be measured under Class E.

The work is described and itemised briefly, since it is assumed that tenderers will have to inspect the site to assess the working conditions, items to be removed and their likely saleable value, if any.

General clearance embraces shrubs and trees with a girth not exceeding 500 mm (trunk measured at 1 m above ground), tree stumps not exceeding 150 mm diameter, hedges and undergrowth, and pipelines above ground not exceeding 100 mm nominal bore. It is measured in hectares (D100), with clear identification of the particular area, preferably delineated on a tender drawing. Larger trees and stumps are enumerated in their respective girth and diameter ranges (D210 to D250 and D310 to D330).

Buildings and other structures also need to be clearly identified, possibly by reference numbers or letters or names on a tender drawing. The bill description must include the predominant materials and the total volume above ground within the external faces of enclosing walls and roof. Items for demolition and site clearance shall be deemed to include disposal of the materials arising from the works (rule C1 of Class D). Separate items are required for any materials or components which are to remain the property of the Employer.

Demolition of pipelines above ground exceeding 100 mm nominal bore and those within buildings, exceeding 300 mm nominal bore, are measured by length in metres. Prices include the demolition and removal of supports (rule C4).

It should be noted that if any of the existing materials involved in Class D be toxic or hazardous, where precautions are required under any of the health and safety regulations, then these elements should be described and itemised separately. This is because of the additional care and much greater costs involved in dealing with and disposing of such materials and would invoke the requirements of CESMM3, paragraph 5.10.

Worked Example (in Part 2 of this book)

As an illustration of Class D: Demolition and Site Clearance:

WE1 Demolition and Site Clearance

CHAPTER 5

CESMM3: Class E Excavation, Filling and Landscaping

Class E: Earthworks

Measurement of Earthworks

Earthworks form a major part of most civil engineering contracts. The pricing of this work is made difficult by its relatively uncertain nature and extent and the effects of weather and water. The measurement rules attempt to recognise these factors and to permit the tenderer to make allowance for them.

The three divisions of basic rules in Class E are accompanied by extensive measurement, definition, coverage and additional description rules, all of which must be considered when itemising earthworks measurements. The requirements of paragraph 5.21 regarding ground and excavation levels must also be taken into consideration as discussed below.

Basic volumes of excavation are itemised by type of excavation in the First Division (E1** to E4**); by nature of the excavated material in the Second Division; and in the case of foundations and general excavation only (E3** and E4**) by the classification of maximum depth in the Third Division. Separate items for each stage of excavations are only given where separate stages are expressly required in the conduct of the works (rule M5). The requirement to include 'commencing' or 'excavated' surfaces in item descriptions is covered by rule A4 and paragraph 5.21. The terminology used to define the various surfaces encountered in excavations is explained in paragraphs 1.10–1.13.

The easiest way to explain this rather complex set of interrelated rules and conditions is to take typical examples of excavation items. Firstly, take a very basic example: 'E424 – General excavation, maximum depth 1–2 m .... m^3'. This item, by not stating any levels in its description, would represent excavation commencing at 'original' surface and finishing at 'final' surface in accordance with rule A4. The phrase generated by '2' in the Second Division of the code 'Material other than topsoil, rock or artificial hard material' is conveniently deemed to be that unless otherwise stated (rule D1), thus saving much repetitious wording. It is worth noting that by using the coding system in bills of quantities (Section 4 of CESMM3), the estimator can quickly see from the 2 in the code that the excavation material is ordinary, even though it is not quoted in the item description.

Secondly, take a slightly more involved example: 'E412 – General excavation, topsoil, maximum depth 0.25–0.5 m, excavated surface underside of topsoil .... m^3'. This item could be where the client has a definite requirement for the topsoil and would thus constitute a stage in the excavation in accordance with rule M5. Because a stage has been generated, there is the requirement to state the excavated surface which is not a final surface in this case.

The following item could be 'E425 – General excavation, maximum depth 2–5 m, commencing surface underside of topsoil, excavated surface 0.3 m above final surface .... m^3'. This item represents the bulk of the general excavation below the topsoil but is halted under the terms of the specification to leave 300 mm of protection to the final formation surface which would only be stripped out immediately prior to the placing of concrete. This specification requirement generates a stage in the excavation, hence the defining of the excavated surface. The work did not commence at the original surface as per item E412 and thus the commencing surface must also be stated.

The final item for this example of general excavation would be 'E422 – General excavation, maximum depth 0.25–0.5 m, commencing surface 0.3 m above final surface .... m^3'. This item represents the final stage of general excavation in accordance with the specification and under rule A4 requires the commencing surface to be identified, but as the excavated surface is also the final surface this need not be stated.

The last three sample items assume that the three stages in the excavation have been expressly required in the conduct of the works, otherwise a different approach may be adopted by the compiler of the bill. If it is assumed that there are no specified stage requirements in the conduct of the excavations then the following items could be billed:

E415 – General excavation, topsoil, maximum depth 2–5 m .... m^3
E425 – General excavation, maximum depth 2–5 m .... m^3
E435 – General excavation, rock, maximum depth 2–5 m .... m^3

There is no set stage between the ordinary excavations and the topsoil so there is no requirement to separate the items into stages, thus the apparently impossibly thick topsoil at 2–5 m thick. However common sense prevails and tendering contractors would realise that the topsoil will be the upper layer within these items. Presumably there is no particular requirement by the client for the topsoil in this instance, otherwise it would be preferable to treat it as a stage in the conduct of the work as in the first example of topsoil above.

The rock is also not further defined and could exist anywhere within the range 2–5 m maximum depth. This appears at first reading to be a rather ill-defined item description but it means that the rock and ordinary material can occur at any depth in the excavation, in layers or lumps. The definitions in paragraphs 1.12 and 1.13 allow the commencing and the excavated surfaces to apply to groups of items (as well as to single items), as is the case with the group of three items above.

Not all compilers of civil engineering Bills of Quantities would agree with the less detailed approach adopted in the last sample group of items. Some would wish to separate layers of differing materials from each other, particularly where it is considered that different plant may be used for the different excavation materials encountered – thus invoking paragraph 5.10 which requires separation of items if different considerations of cost are thought likely. This approach may be favoured if there were two or more quite distinctly different materials in the works, say sandy soil and hard rock. However on the other side of the argument, it should be remembered that the tendering contractors would normally have access to the full details of any site investigation report on the likely ground conditions expected in the works. Thus they would be in possession of much more detail when preparing their prices than the less detailed items appear to provide.

Further discussion of this contentious issue in favour of the less detailed approach is given by Barnes in '*CESMM3 Handbook*' (Telford, 1992). The author of this book is, on balance, more inclined towards the more traditional approach of (for example) separating the layers of topsoil from ordinary materials and from rock. However in the end, the compilers of Bills of Quantities will make up their own minds on the best way of presenting the work to tendering Contractors, bearing in mind the nature, complexity and other relevant details of the particular project. In this respect paragraphs 2.5, 5.10 and 5.11 should also be kept in mind:

Paragraphs 2.5 and 5.10 say that itemisation should reflect differences in the cost of work due to particular circumstances consistent with brevity.

Paragraph 5.11 says that descriptions shall identify the work covered by the items but the exact nature and extent of the work is to be ascertained from the drawings, specification and conditions of contract.

As mentioned above, rule D1 of Class E prescribes that where material is not defined in the bill items, it is deemed to be normally occurring soft natural material (other than topsoil, rock or artificial hard material). Some special categories of excavated material such as running sand are not listed, as this operation is akin to dealing with groundwater and constitutes a Contractor's contractual obligation. Rule M8 prescribes that an isolated volume of artificial hard material or rock occurring within other material to be excavated shall not be measured separately unless its volume exceeds $1\,m^3$, except that the minimum volume shall be $0.25\,m^3$ where the net width of excavation is less than 2 m.

Rule C1 provides that excavation items are deemed to include additional excavation to provide working space, upholding the sides of excavations and removal of dead services. Tenderers should allow for these items in excavation rates or in method-related charges. This straightforward approach to earthwork support and working space renders these elements, in effect, risk factors which Contractors can price based on their own experience and assessment of the particular features of the works. The same approach would presumably apply to underpinning work (which is not mentioned in CESMM3), where the rather wider and more complex working space requirements would still be solely a matter of judgement for the contractor, possibly to price as a method-related charge. This mature approach to these costs is in contrast to the mechanistic and arbitrary measurements of such features in building methods of measurement.

With regard to the measurable volume of excavations to accept structures or foundations; rule M6 states that the volume shall only be that occupied by or vertically above any part of the structure or foundation. This is in effect the smallest hole in the ground into which (hypothetically) the structure could be lowered by a crane. This rule exactly complies with the rules which quantity surveyors are familiar with when measuring building work excavations.

Excavation below a body of open water, such as a river, stream, canal, lake or body of tidal water, is measured separately in accordance with rule M7, at the highest applicable water level. In the case of tidal waters, and in particular regarding work near the shore edge, compilers of Bills of Quantities may consider further itemisation to reflect the differences in cost between work between tides and work wholly below tides. Such further detail could be justified under paragraph 5.10 to reflect the nature and location of the work in these circumstances. The detail reflected in Bills of Quantities is subject to individual assessment of the particular nature of the works and the individual interpretation of paragraphs such as 2.5, 5.8, 5.10 and 5.20.

Rule M4 indicates that dredging is normally measured from soundings taken before and after the work is done. Where hopper or barge measurements are permissible this must be stated in a preamble to the Bill of Quantities, clearly identifying the circumstances in which the alternative method can be adopted. Dredging to remove silt is measured only where it is expressly required that silt which accumulates after the final surface has been reached shall be removed (rule M14). This reflects the reality of such work in water where the contractor may have completed the work to the contractual levels, only for a storm or flood to deposit silt into the already dredged areas. This risk does not normally rest on the contractor and the engineer would usually issue an instruction so that the work becomes 'expressly required' and is therefore measurable.

Extra payment for double handling of excavated material is limited to that expressly required by rule M13. If the Contractor stockpiles without being instructed to do so he will not be entitled to additional payment, even although it might have been difficult to avoid it, as with excavated material to be subsequently used as fill. Excavation within borrow pits is classed as general excavation and shall be the net volume measured for filling, and is deemed to include the removal and replacement of overburden and unsuitable materials.

The quantities of material excavated or used as filling are measured net using dimensions from the drawings, with no allowance for bulking, shrinkage or waste (rule M1), with the exception of additional filling resulting from settlement or penetration into underlying material in excess of 75 mm in depth (rule M18) – a difficult provision to apply in practice.

Filling items are deemed to include compaction (rule C3) and filling material shall be deemed to be non-selected excavated material other than topsoil and rock unless otherwise stated (rule D6). These convenient rules save on much repetitive wording in bill items.

Bulk filling is measured by volume and is classified as filling to structures, embankments and general, while filling to stated depth or thickness is measured by area. In the case of the latter, items must distinguish surfaces which are inclined to angles over 10° from horizontal in three categories of inclination (rule A14). Work to stated depth or thickness is defined as where filling material is provided in a uniform total compacted depth or thickness such as drainage blankets, top-soiling, pitching and beaching (rule D8).

Filling to structures shall only be measured to the extent that the volume filled is also measured as excavation in accordance with rule M6 (rule M16). This rule effectively prevents any measurement of backfilling to working space which, in any case, is itself deemed to be included (rule C1).

Under rule D7 the Contractor may use excavated rock as filling where the Specification permits, but he will only be paid at the rates for filling with excavated rock in locations where this is expressly required. Rules M20 and M21 requiring the measurement of the volume of rock fill in transport vehicles at the place of deposition in the case of soft areas and below water are often difficult to implement in practice.

The volume of disposal of excavated material measured shall be the difference between the total net volume of excavation and the net volume used for filling (rule M12). Disposal of excavated material shall be deemed to be disposal off the site unless otherwise stated in item descriptions (rule D4), and where disposal on site is required, the location shall be stated in the item description (rule A9).

Trimming and preparation of both excavated surfaces and filled surfaces, as governed by rules M10, M11, M22 and M23, have a number of common factors to consider and are therefore discussed together. Trimming is measured to surfaces which are to receive no permanent works whether or not trimming is expressly required in the contract. Thus a surface of excavation or filling, left permanently exposed at the end of the contract, will require to have an item for trimming measured in the bill (M10 and M22). In a similar manner excavated surfaces and filled surfaces which are to receive permanent works (other than filling, landscaping or where formwork is also measured) will require an item for preparation, whether or not preparation is expressly required (M11 and M23).

The effect of rules M11 and M23 is that no preparation is measurable if the surface concerned is to receive further Class E works (filling or landscaping) or where formwork for concrete work is also measured. Thus vertical preparation to the sides of excavations is quite rare and would only apply if, for example, concrete was designed to be cast directly against the side of the excavation or brickwork or masonry walling was built directly against the soil. In most cases vertical concrete surfaces will require formwork and built walling will have filling to structures between it and the vertical excavated face, both situations being exceptions to the requirement to measure preparation.

Landscaping (E8**) comprises turfing, seeding and planting only, as the provision and deposition of soil is covered under 'filling to stated depth or thickness' (E64*). It should be noted that fertilising and any trimming and preparation of surfaces shall be deemed to be included with landscaping items. Turfing and seeding are measured in square metres separately identifying work to surfaces at an angle exceeding 10° to the horizontal (rule A18). Plants, shrubs and trees are enumerated stating the species and size, while hedges are measured in metres stating the species, size and spacing, and distinguishing between single and double rows.

Mensuration of Volumes of Earthwork

Various methods can be used to calculate the volume of excavation and/or filling required as part of civil engineering works. The method used is often largely determined by the type of work involved. Accuracy and speed of operation are the main factors to consider when selecting the method of approach.

A very common volume calculation required in civil engineering is that for cuttings and embankments to accommodate road and railway works. With the almost universal use of computers, there are several packages available which calculate the required volumes often as an adjunct to the land surveying package used in the design of the works. Although most work will be calculated in this way, it is considered that some background knowledge of the manual methods of calculation is still of value to compilers of bills of quantities. It should be noted that all methods of calculating such complex volumes are approximations but the accuracy achieved, either manually or electronically, will normally be more than satisfactory in most practical applications. To manually calculate the volumes of cuttings and embankments there are two inter-related formulae commonly used, both of which require to use the areas of cross-sections through the construction.

In simpler cases involving three cross-sections only, the prismoidal formula may be used, whereby:

$$\text{volume} = \frac{1}{6} \times \begin{matrix}\text{total}\\\text{length}\end{matrix} \times \left\{ \begin{matrix}\text{area of}\\\text{first section}\end{matrix} + \begin{matrix}\text{4 times area of}\\\text{middle section}\end{matrix} + \begin{matrix}\text{area of last}\\\text{section}\end{matrix} \right\}$$

Most transportation schemes will be much longer than three cross-sections and in these cases the appropriate formula is known as Simpson's rule. This formula is in effect many prismoidal formulae combined end to end. Using Simpson's rule the areas at intermediate even cross-sections (nrs. 2, 4, 6, etc.) are each multiplied by 4, the areas at intermediate uneven cross-sections (nrs. 3, 5, 7, etc.) are each multiplied by 2 and the end cross-sections taken once only. The sum of these areas is multiplied by one-third of the distance between the cross-sections to give the total volume. To use this formula it is essential that the cross-sections are taken at the same fixed distance apart and that there is an odd number of cross-sections (even number of spaces between cross-sections).

For instance, taking a cutting to be excavated for a road, 300 m in length and 40 m in width, to an even gradient, with mean depths calculated at 50 m intervals as indicated below and side slopes 2 to 1, and assuming that stripping of topsoil has already been taken.

Cross-section	1	2	3	4	5	6	7
Mean depth (m)	4	10	16	20	18	12	6

The width at the top of the cutting can be found by taking the width at the base, that is, 40 m and adding 2/2/the depth to give the horizontal spread of the banks (the width of each bank being twice the depth with a side slope of 2 to 1). The average width of the cutting relevant to the depth of each cross-section can be calculated in a tabular format as follows:

Cross-section	*Depth (m)*	*Width at Top of Cutting (m)*	*Mean Width (m)*	*Weighting*
1	4	40 + (4 × 4) = 56	$\frac{56+40}{2} = 48$	1
2	10	40 + (4 × 10) = 80	$\frac{80+40}{2} = 60$	4
3	16	40 + (4 × 16) = 104	$\frac{104+40}{2} = 72$	2
4	20	40 + (4 × 20) = 120	$\frac{120+40}{2} = 80$	4
5	18	40 + (4 × 18) = 112	$\frac{112+40}{2} = 76$	2
6	12	40 + (4 × 12) = 88	$\frac{88+40}{2} = 64$	4
7	6	40 + (4 × 6) = 64	$\frac{64+40}{2} = 52$	1

The dimensions can now be entered on dimension paper in the manner shown on the following sheet. The average width of each cross-section is squared with its depth and multiplied by the appropriate weighting factor to give a total weighted area of section of cutting. This area is converted to a volume by multiplying by the distance between the cross-sections modified to one-third to correct for the value of the weightings.

EXCAVATION FOR ROAD CUTTING

	48.00		Excavn. for cuttgs.;	To avoid a great deal of
	4.00		Commeg.Surf. 0.15 m (c.s.1	laborious and unnecessary
4/			below Original Surf.	labour in squaring, all
	60.00		cube $\times \frac{1}{3}$/50.00	dimensions have been entered
	10.00		(c.s.2	as superficial items, to be
2/			E220	subsequently cubed by
	72.00			multiplying the sum of the
	16.00		(c.s.3	areas by $\frac{1}{3}$ of the length
4/				between the cross-sections.
	80.00			
	20.00		(c.s.4	
2/				
	76.00			Total weighting is 18 and
	18.00		(c.s.5	the number of 50 m long
4/				sections of excavation is 6,
	64.00			so that $\frac{6}{18}$ or $\frac{1}{3}$ of the
	12.00		(c.s.6	distance of 50 m must be the
				timesing factor required.
	52.00			
	6.00		(c.s.7	

Material to be excavated is deemed to be naturally occurring soft natural material other than topsoil, rock or artificial hard material, unless otherwise stated in item descriptions (rule D1 of Class E).

Worked Examples (in Part 2 of this book)

As illustrations of Class E: Earthwork:

WE2 Excavation and Filling
WE5 Pumping Chamber
WE6 Sewage Holding Tank
WE7 Pumphouse
WE8 Stone Faced Sea Wall
WE14 Quay with Concrete and Timber Piles (only small amount of earthwork)
WE17 Estate Road

CHAPTER 6

CESMM3: Classes F–H

Concrete

Class F: ***In Situ*** **Concrete**
Class G: Concrete Ancillaries
Class H: Precast Concrete

Class F: *In Situ* Concrete

Class F in CESMM3 realistically prescribes separate bill items for the provision and placing of concrete. This separation is intended to assist the tenderer in relating prices more closely to costs and so simplifying estimating and assisting with the valuation of variations. A change of concrete mix or a variation in placing can be more readily accommodated by a change in the rate of one of the component items.

When measuring this class of work it is sensible to consider the placing element first in the order of taking off as this element leads to many more categories of items than does provision. Items for provision can be more readily computed from the placing items than vice versa. Placing is firstly categorised into the basic types; mass (non-reinforced), reinforced and prestressed (F5** to F7**) and measured by cubic metres. Blinding, bases, suspended slabs, walls and the like are further categorised by thickness; while (normally) detached columns, beams and casings to metal sections are categorised by cross-sectional area. These requirements reflect that placing on a per cubic metre basis is more expensive for thinner or smaller cross-sectioned structural members.

Rules M1 and M2 simplify the computation of concrete quantities by eliminating the need for deductions for reinforcement, prestressing components, and most cast in components, rebates, grooves, throats, chamfers, internal splays, pockets, holes, joints and the like, and the need for additions for small nibs or external splays. Internal splays arise from fillets placed inside formwork, thereby reducing the volume of concrete required, while external splays add to the volume of concrete. These rules result in a larger volume of concrete being measured than is actually required because significant voids are not adjusted while only small projections are ignored.

In costing this class of work the likely split of significant costs is as follows:

Provision: materials, labour in mixing, any small-scale mixing plant (in the case of ready mixed concrete all the foregoing would be replaced with the cost of concrete delivered to site).

Placing: cost of transporting within the locus of the work, labour and small plant in placing and curing.

Method-related charges: main batching plant and on large sites the means of transport from central batching plant to the locus of the work.

Provision of Concrete

The item descriptions for the provision of concrete use the terminology of BS 5328 *Methods for specifying concrete, including ready-mixed concrete*. Part 2 of this British Standard – *Methods of specifying concrete mixes* – is the most useful part to explain of the itemisation adopted for provision of concrete. The British Standard has been revised since the publication of CESMM3 but the changes can be incorporated fairly readily. The various types of concrete are as follows:

F1** is for 'Standard mixes' and these are described in Section 4 of BS 5328, Part 2, 1997; Table 5 giving mix proportions for 40 and 20 mm aggregates. Standard mixes state a performance strength (varying from grade 7.5 to 25) and the Contractor follows the tabular information to obtain the specified concrete.

F2** is for 'Designed mixes' with a compressive strength performance requirement and these are described in Section 1 of BS 5328, Part 2, 1997; Table 1. Compressive strengths are quoted from grade C7.5 to C60 but CESMM3 only lists up to grade C40. Higher strengths are not common but if they were necessary the '9' code can be used as follows: F293 – Provision of concrete, designed mix, grade C60, cement to BS 12 or BS 146, 20 mm aggregate.

F3** is for 'Designed mixes' with a flexural strength performance requirement and these are described in Section 1 of BS 5328, Part 2, 1997; Table 2. Grades are quoted as F3, F4 and F5 which ties in with F31* to F33* of CESMM3.

F400 is for 'Prescribed mixes' which are mixes where the proportions are specified by the Engineer and these are covered in Section 3 of BS 5328, Part 2, 1997.

F9** could be used for 'Designated mixes' which are not featured in CESMM3 but are described in Section 5 of BS 5328, Part 2, 1997. These designated mixes cover 'general' grades 0–4 (strength 7.5–20); FND all at grade 35; PAV at grades 35 and 40; and RC grades 30 to 50.

In all cases, concrete specifications are extremely comprehensive and complex documents, so that items should merely identify the relevant specification clauses rather than attempting to repeat descriptions at great length (see paragraph 5.11).

Placing of Concrete

This activity is covered in CESMM3 by F5** to F7** and the accompanying rules. The note at the foot of page 41 in the CESMM3 emphasises the effect of location on costs and the need to enlarge item descriptions in accordance with paragraph 5.10 where special characteristics affect the method and rate of placing concrete. Cost may be affected by height above or below ground, position and shape on plan, density of reinforcement, restrictions on access, unusual limitations on pouring, exceptional curing requirements and related aspects. The wording 'may be stated' in the footnote is intentionally non-compulsory as it would be almost impossible to be prescriptive for all possible situations. The onus is on individual bill compilers to apply this rule as and when they consider it appropriate.

The categories of thickness required in items for blinding, bases, suspended slabs and walls, although stated in fairly wide bandings, reasonably reflect the placing costs on a cubic metre basis. It should be noted that attached beams, columns, piers and other projections do not affect the category of thickness which is decided purely on the basic thickness of the member to which they are attached (rule D7). The volume of concrete of these integral features is however incorporated with the volume of the base, slab or wall (rules M3 and M4), unless in the rare circumstance that they are expressly required to be cast separately.

Detached columns, beams and casings are itemised separately and categorised by stages of cross-sectional area, again reflecting the cost implications of placing on a cubic metre basis. Narrow slabs and walls are categorised as beams and columns if they are less than 1 m wide or long (rule D8). Tapering members which cross the boundaries of thickness categories required in Class F may be dealt with in two ways: firstly, should the structural member concerned be of sufficient size then the work could be split into the appropriate thickness categories; secondly, the average thickness could be stated and a separate suitably described item created for the whole structural member.

Some components may cause problems in classification, for example a column cap which might be classified as a thickening of the slab, thickening of column or 'other concrete form' (for example, F680). With these alternative approaches available an additional item description should be inserted to show what has been done in accordance with paragraph 5.13. The classification of 'other concrete forms' might also be used to cover composite members, giving the principal dimensions or an identifying reference (rule A4). Box culverts could be classified in this way where it would be more helpful to the tenderer than the separate measurement of walls and slabs.

Complex beam shapes make the pouring of concrete more difficult. Hence rules D9 and A3 require beams which are rectangular or approximately rectangular over less than four-fifths of their length, or where they are of box or other composite section, to be separately shown in the bill as 'special beam sections', with details of their cross-sectional dimensions or a drawing reference.

Class G: Concrete Ancillaries

Formwork

The rules for the measurement of formwork are contained in G1** to G4** and the accompanying rules. Rules M1 and M2 provide guidelines to assist in deciding where formwork is measured. For instance formwork is to be measured to the surfaces of *in situ* concrete which require temporary support, except where otherwise stated in CESMM3.

The principal exceptions are:

(a) edges of blinding not exceeding 0.2 m wide

(b) joints and associated rebates and grooves

(c) temporary surfaces formed at the direction of the Contractor, such as surfaces of joints between pours

(d) surfaces of concrete which are expressly required to be cast against excavated surfaces

(e) surfaces of concrete which are cast against excavated surfaces inclined at an angle less than 45° to the horizontal.

Formwork to upper surfaces shall be measured to surfaces inclined at an angle exceeding 15° to the horizontal and to other upper surfaces for which formwork is expressly required (rule M3). The term 'expressly required' means that the Engineer instructs the formwork on the drawings, in the specification or otherwise. The likely reason for upper surface formwork (not exceeding 15° to the horizontal) being expressly required would be to prevent liquid concrete oozing out during placing owing to hydraulic pressure, for example to the upper surface of a horizontal projection where the pour will continue above that level. There is a certain knock-on effect to the Class F concrete placing costs if upper surface formwork occurs, because of the further difficulties in pouring through restricted access points and additional compaction problems. Thus such upper surface formwork should be so described unless it is close to vertical (rule A2).

Rule D1 lists the angles of inclination to the vertical applicable to horizontal (85°–90°), sloping (10°–85°), battered (0°–10°) and vertical (0°) plane formwork. It should be noted that 'plane' may be omitted from item descriptions (rule D2), as in practical terms the adjectives 'horizontal, sloping, battered and vertical' are completely understood on their own. While dealing with semantics, the 'plain' formwork found in the building standard method (SMM7) should not be confused with 'plane' in CESMM3!

Formwork is categorised by width in the Third Division – widths over 0.2 m being measured in square metres while not exceeding 0.2 m is measured in linear metres. The widest category has the rather unlikely value of exceeding 1.22 m being based on the width of a standard full sheet of plywood (2.44 × 1.22 m). The width of formwork is deemed to be 'exceeding 1.22 m' unless otherwise stated (rule D2). CESMM3 was formulated on the assumption that most formwork will be of timber and plywood construction but since then more use is being made of proprietary metal system formwork which has different width constraints; perhaps leading to a revision of the method in the future.

Formwork can be measured by length as a single item where concrete members or holes in them are of constant cross-section (note at bottom of page 43 of CESMM3). Typical examples are walls, columns and beams, where the formwork can normally be re-used several times without major dismantling. An additional description will identify the members by their principal dimensions, mark number or other reference as rule A5. This is a good approach, since it highlights situations where many re-uses of formwork may be possible and enables the Contractor to price accordingly. Components of constant cross-section are classified under 8 in the Second Division and by type of component in the Third Division.

Projections and intrusions are also measured as components of constant cross-section under G1-485 and G1-486 respectively. These features are defined in rules D4 and D5 respectively and as they represent details of relatively small sizes, they normally need not be further described (rule A5); thus projections and intrusions of different sizes or shapes may be grouped together within their respective items. It is also worth remembering that these features are neither added to nor deducted from the volume of concrete; see Class F, rules M2 and M1(d).

Where formwork is to be left in position for design purposes or through impossibility of removal, it becomes part of the Permanent Works and is to be measured in separately identifiable items (rule A1).

G1** to G4** separate formwork by the requirements for surface finish on the cast concrete. Significant cost differences can arise between the various finishes which Engineers may desire and the specification should additionally make quite clear what is acceptable as 'rough finish' (G1**) and what standard is actually required for 'fair finish' (G2**). 'Stated surface features' (G4**) are likely to have a higher surface relief than 'other stated finishes' (G3**) but as the specification will detail exactly what is required, bill compilers need not become too concerned whether they categorise any particular finish as G3** or G4** provided the relevant specification clause is quoted in the items.

With curved formwork separate items are to be inserted for each different radius and each different shape of multi-radius formwork (spherical, conical, parabolic, ellipsoidal), desirably stating the location in each case (rule A4).

The rules for the measurement of formwork to small and large voids are each given in four stages of depth in the third division and the maximum diameters of circular voids and areas of other voids are given in rule D3. The area occupied by small and large voids should not be deducted from the main formwork area (rule M6) which links through to Class F, where they also are not deducted from the volume of concrete – Class F: rule M1(e). On the other hand, bigger voids which exceed those defined as small and large (see table in rule D3) are deducted from formwork and their features measured in detail as normal formwork (rule M4).

The measurement of formwork is generally based on a broad brush approach as CESMM3 assumes that tenderers will obtain much of their costing information from the contract drawings. Such elements as support heights and systems, striking times and numbers of reuses should show up clearly on the drawings. Thus it is important that the bill gives appropriate locational information so that the drawings may be consulted as necessary. Some tendering contractors may opt to price some formwork as fixed and time-related method-related charges as certain cost elements are not directly related to individual measured items.

Reinforcement

The measurement of reinforcement is detailed in classification G5**. Separate items are required for different reinforcement materials and sizes of the preferred dimensions listed in BS 4449, with bars of a diameter of 32 mm or more grouped together.

Items for reinforcement are deemed to include supporting reinforcement (other than steel supports to top reinforcement) as rule C1. This general wording includes all support such as tying wire and means that no weight allowance is made for such support in the calculations of weights of the various items. On the other hand, the weight of support steel to top reinforcement is added into total weight of the relevant item (rule M8). Special joints in bar reinforcement, as defined in rule D7, are enumerated under G550 with the type of joint and bar stated (rule A8).

Bars exceeding 12 m in length before bending are to be given separately in multiples of 3 m to give the tenderer the opportunity of allowing in his rates for the supplier's 'extra' for long bars and additional handling and fixing costs (rule A7). Where no length is stated in the bill description this signifies 12 m or less, while the inclusion of 15 m would indicate bars with lengths exceeding 12 m and not exceeding 15 m.

Fabric reinforcement in contrast to bar reinforcement is measured in square metres giving the net area, the additional areas in overlaps being ignored (rule M9). The descriptions of fabric reinforcement either follow rules A9 or A10 dependent on the specified mesh, the work being measured under G56* or G57* as appropriate.

Joints

Movement joints and their associated features are measured under G6** Joints. The formation of the joint is measured by area, classified in categories of width and are only measured if expressly required (rule M10). 'Day' joints and any other joints formed at the Contractor's discretion are not measurable (rule M2c). The width used to categorise the joint is the full width, ignoring fillets etc. – in effect the distance between the outer faces of the concrete structure in which the joint is formed (rule M11). It is worth noting that formwork is not separately measured to joints (rule M2b) but the cost of formwork where required is deemed to be included with the items for 'formed surface joints': G63* and G64* (rules D8 and C3). Formed surface joints will normally include all vertical joints. Joints which do not require support whilst being formed are classed as 'open surface joints': G61* and G62*, and would normally include horizontal joints. The nature and specification of filler material is included in the descriptions of items as appropriate under G62* and G64*.

Further features and details of movement joints are separately measured; waterstops and sealed rebates or grooves are measured in metres while dowels are enumerated. All cutting and angles are deemed to be included in the items for waterstops (rule C4).

Post-tensioned Prestressing

The technology and execution of post-tensioned prestressing of concrete is highly specialised and consequently tendering contractors will gain almost all of the cost-significant information to build up their rates from the contract drawings and specification clauses. This fact is recognised by rule A12 which requires identification of each component and for the composition of tendons and anchorages to be stated. In consequence the bill items under CESMM3 (G7**) are very simple, normally only requiring two enumerated items for the tensioning element of each type of post-tensioned structural unit: one item for the tendon and associated components (rule C5) and one item for each jacking operation (rule M12). Tendons are classed as being incorporated within *in situ* or precast concrete and either horizontal which includes profiled (often elliptically shaped) tendons as rule D9 or inclined or vertical which are grouped together. Tendons are further itemised by length categories which are calculated in accordance with rule D10.

Concrete Accessories

Finishes to *in situ* concrete are of two types: finishing to top surfaces, in other words where no formwork has been used and the work is executed while the concrete is still green, measured under G81*; and finishing of formed surfaces where the work is executed after the concrete has set and the formwork has been stripped, measured under G82*. Items of top surface that are measurable include granolithic and similar finishes, stating the materials, thicknesses and surface finish of the applied layers (rule A13). The volume of these finishes shall not be included in the concrete measured in Class F.

Long inserts such as steel angles cast into concrete are measured in metres, while most other inserts, such as anchor bolts and pipe sleeves, are enumerated (G83 1–2). Items for inserts are deemed to include their supply unless otherwise stated (rule C7). The contractor is often left to decide whether inserts are cast or grouted into position and in these circumstances the normal rules apply (rule D11). However should grouting of inserts be expressly required then the items for inserts shall so state and specify the grouting materials and the sizes of openings (rule A16) and in addition formwork shall be separately measured (rule M16). The item description should contain sufficient information to identify the work and there should be sufficient separate items to accommodate significant cost differences. For example, pipes passing through walls or slabs should be enumerated in ranges of nominal bore. Rule A15 distinguishes between inserts which project from one surface of the concrete, those which project from two surfaces of the concrete, and those which are totally within the concrete.

Class H: Precast Concrete

The majority of precast concrete components are enumerated with the descriptions giving the position in the Works, specification of concrete and the mark or type number (rules A1 and A2). The tenderer will obtain the remainder of the information from the Drawings and Specification. The cost of the larger special components is influenced considerably by shape and size and the number required of each type; this information is given most effectively on drawings. Rule A2 prescribes that units (components) with different dimensions shall be given different mark or type numbers.

Hence rule A2 overrides the ranged classifications of length, area and mass listed in the second and third divisions of the classification table. Furthermore, paragraph 5.14 permits the use of specific dimensions in place of ranged dimensions in an item containing components with the same dimensions. The descriptions of the different precast concrete components (units) are built up in the following manner:

Precast Concrete Unit	*Mark Number*	*Principal Dimensions of Cross-section*	*Cross-sectional Area*	*Average Thickness*	*Area*	*Length*	*Mass*
Beams and columns	✓	✓				✓	✓
Slabs	✓			✓	✓		✓
Segmental units and units for subways, culverts and ducts	✓	✓					✓
Copings, sills and weir blocks	✓	✓	✓				✓

It should be noted that the above requirements of item descriptions for precast components often lead to the need for a fourth level of coding. For example, on a project there may be a number of precast concrete beams all the same length and section but with three variants of wall rest detail, requiring one item for each mark number coded thus: H113.1; H113.2 and H113.3.

Prestressed precast concrete may be pre-tensioned or post-tensioned and different approaches to the measurement of these two types of construction are required by CESMM3. Precast post-tensioned units may be in one piece or may comprise several precast components assembled and tensioned on site into longer structural units such as beams or bridge spans. Such work is measured under Class H for the precast concrete units (H3**) but the tensioning items are separately measured under Class G (G7**). These post-tensioned units should not be confused with pre-tensioned prestressed precast components which are normally ready to use factory produced units which are wholly measured under Class H (H2**) with the tendon and stressing detailed as per rule A3.

Rule D3 requires major concrete components cast adjacent to their final positions, such as railway bridge decks, to be measured as *in situ* concrete. However, large precast concrete bridge beams cast alongside the bridge and subsequently placed over each span are measured as precast units, since they involve the multiple use of formwork and the casting of the beams other than in their final position (rule D2).

Worked Examples (in Part 2 of this book)

As illustrations of Classes F: *In situ* Concrete and G: Concrete Ancillaries:

- WE3 Mass Concrete Retaining Wall
- WE4 Precast Prestressed Concrete Beams (post-tensioning measured under Class G)
- WE5 Pumping Chamber
- WE6 Sewage Holding Tank
- WE7 Pumphouse
- WE8 Stone Faced Sea Wall
- WE14 Quay with Concrete and Timber Piles (reinforced concrete decking)
- WE16 Navigation Lamp Platform (reinforced concrete platform in tidal estuary)

As illustrations of Class H: Precast Concrete:

- WE4 Precast Prestressed Concrete Beams (post-tensioning measured under Class G)
- WE7 Pumphouse (small precast units incorporated in brick walls)

CHAPTER 7

CESMM3: Classes I–L

Pipework

Class I: Pipework – Pipes
Class J: Pipework – Fittings and Valves
Class K: Pipework – Manholes and Pipework Ancillaries
Class L: Pipework – Supports and Protection, Ancillaries to Laying and Excavation

Introduction

The rules for the measurement of pipes and associated work occupy four classes of the CESMM3 Work Classification (I–L). These are all closely interrelated and should be considered as a composite class.

The rules in Class I cover pipework, Class J deals with pipe fittings and valves, Class K embraces manholes and work associated with pipework such as land drains, ditches, culverts, crossings and their reinstatement, while Class L is concerned with work related to the laying of pipes, such as extra cost items in trenching, bedding, haunching, surrounding, wrapping and pipe supports.

Class I: Pipework – Pipes

Pipework is measured under Class I in metres giving the nominal bore and trench depth ranges, although it is much more realistic to give the actual bore of the pipes as required by rule A2. Pipework items are comprehensive ones in that they include the following items in addition to the provision, laying and jointing of pipes:

(1) Jointing material (rule A2)
(2) Cutting of pipes (rule C1)
(3) Lengths occupied by fittings and valves and those built into chamber walls (rules M3 and M5)
(4) Excavation of trenches (rule C2)
(5) Backfilling of trenches with excavated material (rule C2)
(6) Upholding sides of excavation (rule C2)
(7) Preparation of surfaces (rule C2)
(8) Disposal of excavated material (rule C2)
(9) Removal of dead services (rule C2).

Although the classification table of Class I covers 512 different categories through classifications I 111 to I 888, nevertheless they cannot embrace every conceivable alternative. Hence rule A2 expands the First Division rules to include separate items for different nominal bores, pipe materials, joints and linings.

Pipework items additionally are to be located by referencing pipe runs to the drawings as per rule A1 so that tendering contractors may take any differences in location into account in their prices. This is an important concept in civil engineering contracts as the terrain can vary widely in different parts of large sites. Separation into different locations should be sufficient to allow contractors to assess variables such as unusual working conditions, restricted access, work in roads, soil conditions affecting trench support and similar cost-significant features.

To present the various categories and classifications of pipes and locations within bills as clearly as possible, it is good practice to give the type of pipe and location as descriptive headings followed by the various items in the depth ranges for the trenches.

Rule D3 defines that the depths used to classify trenches in the Third Division of Class I are the depths from the commencing surface to the pipe invert levels. This is a most convenient rule for the compilers of bills as the invert levels are normally readily gained directly from the drawings or drainage schedules. However estimators need to be aware that allowances in the rates require to be made for the inevitable additional depth of trench digging to accommodate the thickness of the pipe, the space for sockets and trimming to align and grade the pipeline.

The prescribed depth zones of trenches required in CESMM3 are the actual lengths of trench within each depth range rather than the average depth of trench for the whole of any particular pipe run (this is in contrast to the practice in building drainage measurement under SMM7). The approximate lengths of each depth category may be calculated by interpolation of the depths within each pipe run but in practice the most straightforward approach is to obtain the lengths graphically. This may be achieved by using a longitudinal drawing of the pipe run and superimposing a scale prepared with the CESMM3 depth ranges which is then slid along the drawing marking where the changes in depth range occur. With either approach it should be remembered that the Bill of Quantities is only required to contain 'estimated' quantities (paragraph 1.7) and in consequence reasonable accuracy is all that should be expected at the billing stage, detailed remeasurement being carried out on site of the actual work executed.

The measured lengths of pipes in trenches shall include the lengths occupied by fittings and valves (rule M3). This saves having to separately measure for the trench excavation occupied by these components which are themselves measured under Class J. However rule M3 also states that the lengths of pipes which are not in trenches shall exclude the lengths occupied by fittings and valves. Thus rule M3 creates fittings and valves effectively 'extra over' pipes in trenches but 'full value' when not in trenches; which ruling affects measurements under Class J.

The lengths of pipes entering manholes and the like are included in the measured lengths of pipe runs (rule M5). The exception is pipes and fittings which are part of a drop manhole construction where they are included with the item for the manhole measured under Class K. Thus typical lengths which would be measured for pipe runs are as follows:

Inside face of manhole to inside face of next manhole in plain runs.

Exterior face of drop manhole details to inside face of next ordinary manhole.

It is worth noting that the non-drop faces of drop manholes should be treated as ordinary manholes.

Should more than one pipe be expressly required to be laid in one trench then the items should so indicate and identify the pipe run (rule A5). Pipes which are not in trenches are defined in rule D1 and additionally described as rule A3.

Class J: Pipework – Fittings and Valves

All fittings and valves are enumerated with a full description in each item. Separate items are not required for excavation, preparation of surfaces, disposal of excavated material, upholding sides of excavation, backfilling and removal of dead services (rule C2).

The item descriptions for pipe fittings, such as bends, junctions and tapers are to include nominal bore, material, jointing and lining particulars, and reference made to applicable British Standards (rule A1). In general, lengths and angles of bends, junctions and branches need not be stated, except for cast iron or spun iron fittings exceeding 300 mm nominal bore and all steel fittings (rule A2). The latter fittings are expensive and the inclusion of principal dimensions such as the effective length, nominal bore and angle of a bend, will permit identification in the supplier's catalogue. Rule A6 also requires additional particulars in item descriptions of valves and penstocks.

The list of fittings and valves in the second division is not intended to be exhaustive and only gives the most commonly encountered components. Others can be added and coded as J*9*. Where pipe fittings, such as branches and tapers, cross the Third Division nominal bore ranges, they shall be classified in the larger size range (rule D1).

Straight specials are pipes either cut to length or made to order (non-standard lengths) (rule D2) and are measured only when expressly required (rule M2).

Rule A4 requires that fittings to pipework not in trenches shall be so described, which ties in with the pipe measurement rules in Class I which effectively cause the measurement of pipe fittings in trenches as extra over the cost of plain pipe while pipe fittings to pipes not in trenches are measured full value.

Class K: Pipework – Manholes and Pipework Ancillaries

Manholes, other chambers and gullies are not normally measured in detail but are enumerated in accordance with the principles listed in K1–3 and rules C3, C4, A1 and A2. They are identified by a type or mark number, which will be the reference for constructional details given in Drawings and Specification, and are deemed to include all items of metalwork and pipework, other than valves (rule C3). Differing manhole and other chamber arrangements will be evidenced by separate bill items containing different type or mark numbers. Excavation in rock or artificial hard material and backfill with other than excavated material is measured as an extra item in Class L.

Manholes with backdrops are separately classified in the Second Division of Class K, and in accordance with rule C4 the items are deemed to include the backdrop pipes and associated fittings. This requirement ties in with the measurement of pipes under Class I where the length occupied by the backdrop detail is excluded from the measured length of pipes.

Larger or more complex manholes and other chambers may be measured in detail in accordance with the relevant Work Classification rules of CESMM3 where it is considered that enumeration does not adequately cover the cost significance of the particular construction, as per the footnote to page 53 of CESMM3. Sewage holding tanks, pumping chambers and the like would benefit from detailed measurement which would allow for easier price adjustments should the final detailed design vary on site.

The filling materials for French and rubble drains are measured in cubic metres (K410 and K420) which seems a strange choice of unit considering that the trenches for these drains are measured quite logically in linear metres (K43*) further classified by cross-sectional area of excavation. The trench widths should be stated on the drawing in order to calculate the volumes of filling or to calculate the cross-sectional areas of these items. Rule M1 raises a further complication in that French drains with pipes incorporated shall have the pipe and trench measured under Class I but the filling with rubble or graded material measured under Class K. (See also Class I, rule A5.) Where this feature occurs it would be most helpful to an estimator if the relevant items were suitably cross-referenced between Classes I and K. Some bill compilers will be tempted to simplify the measurement of French drains by all inclusive linear items, firstly having noted the departure from the rules of CESMM3.

Ditches are measured in metres stating the cross-sectional area in the ranges listed in the third division. A lined ditch description shall include the nature and dimensions of the lining (rule A5).

The measurement of ducts and metal culverts is covered by K5** and is very similar to the measurement of pipes and trenches in Class I, except that fittings are deemed to be included.

Pipe crossings of streams are not measured where the width does not exceed 1 m (rule M5). Crossings of hedges, walls, fences, sewers or drains, and other stated underground services are separately enumerated, giving the appropriate pipe bore range in the description.

Reinstatement of surfaces after laying pipes, ducts and metal culverts is measured under K7** comprising breaking up and reinstatement of roads and footpaths (K71* to K74*), reinstatement of land (K75*) and strip topsoil from easement and reinstate (K760). All except the last item require classification by the pipe bore stated in bandings in order to convey the approximate width of trench reinstatement likely to be required. Lengths of reinstatement are measured along the centre line and include lengths occupied by manholes, rule M7. Where there are multiple pipes or ducts in one trench, the lengths measured and widths stated for reinstatement purposes are defined in rules D1 and D7. The requirements to specify the details of the various types of reinstatement work is covered by rules A8 to A10.

Timber and metal supports left in excavations (measured in m^2 of the supported surface) are only taken where it is a requirement of the Engineer (rule M11). Item descriptions of connections of new pipework to existing work shall identify the nature of the existing service and will include details of associated work such as sustaining flows and reconstructing benching in manholes (rule A12).

Class L: Pipework – Supports and Protection, Ancillaries to Laying and Excavation

This section covers work related to extra cost items in excavating and backfilling, specialised pipe laying methods, and the protection and support of pipes.

Where excavation and backfill of pipe trenches involve other than ordinary soft material, such as rock, mass concrete, reinforced concrete or other artificial hard material, then an item in m^3 is required to cover the 'extra cost' of dealing with these materials over and above the pipework items already measured in Class I. The quantity is computed by multiplying the average length, average depth and nominal width of trench excavation stated in the Contract, making allowance for battered trench sides (rule M4). Where no nominal width is stated it shall be taken as 500 mm greater than the maximum nominal distance between the internal faces of the outer pipe walls where this distance does not exceed 1 m, and as 750 mm greater than this distance where it exceeds 1 m (rule D1). An isolated volume of hard material shall not be measured separately unless its volume exceeds 0.25 m^3 (rule M8). Excavation which is expressly required to be carried out by hand shall form separate items (rule A1).

Backfilling above the Final Surface shall only be measured where the Engineer will not permit the use of excavated material, while excavation and backfilling below the Final Surface shall be measured only when required by the Engineer, for example 'soft spots' but not excess excavation (rule M7).

Similarly pipe laying in headings and by thrust boring and pipe jacking shall be measured only when expressly required (rule M9) and shall give the location so that it can be correlated with pipework items measured under Class I (rule A2). The plant and temporary works associated with thrust boring and pipe jacking will probably generate method-related charges. Pits for thrust boring and pipe jacking may either be 'specified requirements' in Class A or method-related charges where at the discretion of the Contractor.

The lengths measured for beds, haunches and surrounds to pipes (L3** to L5**) and wrapping and lagging of pipes (L60*) are taken along pipe centre lines and should include the lengths occupied by fittings and valves but should quite properly exclude lengths occupied by manholes and chambers, as per rules M11 and M12. Thus the lengths billed for these items will be marginally less than those billed under Class I for the pipes themselves as the Class L item lengths should exclude the thickness of each manhole wall entered by pipes (Class I, rule M5). The materials used shall be stated but not the cross-sectional dimensions, which are obtainable from the Drawings. Nominal bore ranges are given in the Third Division, although the actual nominal bore can be given where only one pipe size is involved (5.14 of CESMM3). The bed items include excavation and they can be combined with haunches or surrounds where they are of the same material (rules C1, D2 and A3).

Concrete stools and thrust blocks are enumerated and descriptions include the type of concrete and appropriate range of concrete volume, with no separate measurement of formwork or reinforcement (rule C2). Other isolated pipe supports are also enumerated but stating the principal dimensions, materials and the height measured in accordance with rule D5.

Worked Examples (in Part 2 of this book)

As illustrations of Classes I–L: Pipework:

WE6 Sewage Holding Tank
WE9 Sewer
WE10 Water Main
WE17 Estate Road (associated surface water drainage to road)

CHAPTER 8

CESMM3: Classes M–O

Metalwork and Timber

Class M: Structural Metalwork
Class N: Miscellaneous Metalwork
Class O: Timber

Introduction

This chapter covers two disparate structural materials in Classes M and O and non-structural metalwork in Class N. Compilers of Bills of Quantities should always note the exclusions printed under the main heading in any particular class of work and this is especially true of Classes M, N and O, for example timber piling and non-structural timbers are measured elsewhere.

Although not specifically mentioned in the rules of these classes, it is good practice under paragraph 5.10 to keep different pieces of construction billed separately with appropriate drawing references. This enables tendering contractors to decide if location, access or other circumstance affects their price for otherwise similar work. Additionally, such separation makes for much easier post contract cost control on site.

Class M: Structural Metalwork

The measurement of Structural Metalwork is split between off-site fabrication and on-site erection of the structural members and these processes are defined in rules C1 and C2. This separation recognises the completely different working practices and working environments between steel fabrication shops and open construction sites. In order to take off quantities of complex frames and the like, most bill compilers will prepare detailed abstracts of the structural members, listing the various components in order to build up the total quantities of each CESMM3 item. Although there is no requirement to issue such further information with Bills of Quantities it makes sense to give tenderers these breakdowns which will save them much time and effort. Martin Barnes in *CESMM3 Handbook* (Telford, 1992) gives several examples of abstract sheets and comments on their usefulness.

A considerable proportion of the cost of steelwork is in fabrication where activities such as welding on fillets and cutting holes are entailed. Hence detailed drawings of connections and fittings are necessary at the tendering stage and this is assumed in the rules for measurement.

Although steel is purchased by the tonne, the price will vary according to the section, size, length, quantity, quality, finish, and the requirements for testing and inspection. The rate per tonne for plates will also be influenced by their length, width and thickness.

Shop and site bolts are expensive and their number requires accurate assessment. Drawing office costs vary with the number of separate pieces of steel, their complexity and the number of drawings required. Fabrication costs are influenced by a whole range of production processes.

Erection costs are affected by many matters, including the number, size and weight or mass of pieces of steel and their location and the form of connections, in addition to site conditions and facilities.

The main items of structural metal are measured by mass in tonnes, while anchorages and bolts are enumerated. The weight of structural members for fabrication should include the aggregated weight of all the fittings attached to that member in the fabrication process. Fittings comprise such as caps, bases, gussets, end plates, stiffeners and the like.

Fabrication items are broadly categorised into main and subsidiary members for bridges, members for frames and other members. Rules A2 and A3 require tapered, castellated and cranked members to be identified.

Erection of members is categorised in a similar way as in fabrication and the weight will normally be the aggregated weight of all the fabrication items for that piece of construction.

The mass of members, other than plates or flats, is calculated from their overall lengths, with no deductions for splay cut or mitred ends (rule M2). No allowance is made for rolling margin, or the mass of weld fillets, bolts, nuts, washers and rivets (rule M4), or voids less than $0.1\,m^2$ (rule M5), and all fillets and connections are included in the metalwork rates.

Trestles, towers, built-up columns, trusses and built-up girders can be made from sections and/or plates and may be of compounded sections, lattice girders, plate girders or box type construction. Details of the members shall be given in accordance with rule A4. Light crane rails are generally included with the main beams or girders to which they are attached, while rails for heavier cranes (over 20 t capacity) are best kept separate together with their ancillary fittings, such as fixing clips and resilient pads. Anchorages and holding down bolt assemblies are suitably described and enumerated (rule M7).

Off-site surface treatment of metalwork is measured in m^2 under the classifications listed in the second division. Where blast cleaning is specified, the standard of finish should be stated, for example second quality to BS 4232. Painting systems shall also be clearly defined. Surface treatments carried out on site after the erection of structural metalwork are measured in accordance with the rules in Class V (Painting) (rule M8).

Testing will be covered under General Items and the supply, delivery, unloading, operation and dismantling of cranes and plant can be covered by erection rates or be included in method-related charges.

Class N: Miscellaneous Metalwork

This class covers metal components not specifically included elsewhere in CESMM3. Separate items are not given for erection and fixing or for the provision of fixings (rule C1). Item descriptions shall include the specification and thickness of metal, surface treatments and the principal dimensions of miscellaneous metalwork assemblies (rule A1). Alternatively, a more effective approach is often to identify the work by reference to material, construction and assembly details given in drawings and/or specification. This latter approach is particularly well suited to stairways and walkways, to avoid lengthy bill descriptions, using mark numbers for identification purposes as described in the footnote on page 63 of CESMM3.

There is a variety of units of measurement ranging from stairways and walkways in t; handrails, bridge parapets, ladders, walings and frames (measured on external perimeters) in m; cladding, flooring, panelling and duct covers in m^2; and tie rods, bridge bearings and tanks by nr. No deductions are made for openings or holes each not exceeding 0.5 m^2 in area in the calculations of masses or areas.

The classification table in Class N, although covering the most commonly occurring elements, is not comprehensive and non-standard items may be coded as N9**. Non-standard construction may be measured by the most appropriate unit and it would be good practice to provide suitable references to the drawings. Normally under rule C1 the fixing of metalwork is deemed included but should 'supply only' be required then this should be made clear in the relevant item descriptions in accordance with paragraph 3.3.

Class O: Timber

The rules for measurement of work in this class cover timber components, timber decking, and metal fittings and fastenings to the timberwork. The timber components are those used in permanent civil engineering work such as jetty timbers and fendering. Carpentry and joinery work to buildings is measured in accordance with Class Z.

The approach to the measurement of timberwork is straightforward with decking measured in m^2 (void allowance of 0.5 m^2) and components by length (m). The nominal gross cross-sectional dimensions or thicknesses (unplaned), grade or species, impregnation requirements or special surface finishes shall be stated in item descriptions (rule A1). In addition, the structural use and location of timber components exceeding 3 m in length are to be stated in item descriptions (rule A2).

Metal fittings and fastenings are enumerated under the categories listed in the Second Division, and the materials, types and sizes of fittings and fastenings shall be stated in item descriptions (rule A4). Separate items are not required for fixing timber components and decking, or for boring, cutting and jointing (rule C1).

Worked Examples (in Part 2 of this book)

As illustrations of Class M: Structural Metalwork:

WE11 Steel-Framed Gantry
WE12 Timber Jetty (structural steel framing incorporated with timber piling)

As illustrations of Class N: Miscellaneous Metalwork:

WE7 Pumphouse (single item for access cover)
WE11 Steel-Framed Gantry (chequer plate flooring)
WE16 Navigation Lamp Platform (handrails and access ladder)

As illustrations of Class O: Timber:

WE12 Timber Jetty (structural timber members, decking and handrails)
WE14 Quay with Concrete and Timber Piles (associated structural timbers)

CHAPTER 9

CESMM3: Classes P and Q

Piling

Class P: Piles
Class Q: Piling Ancillaries

Introduction

The measurement of piling works in CESMM3 separates the main items for the piles in Class P from the ancillaries in Class Q which comprise extra labours, preboring, pile extensions, tests and the like. The measured items reflect as far as possible the practical cost implications for each type of pile construction as the cost significance of the piling plant and the costs involved in moving and setting it up around the site are reflected in the itemisation. However, some contractors will find merit in recovering these costs as fixed and time-related charges under the CESMM3 provisions for method-related charges. In this respect, piles can be an important part of marine works and therefore subject to the provisions of paragraph 5.20 'Work affected by bodies of water'. Such work may have to be executed from barge-based piling rigs with the resultant additional costs possibly best recovered on a method-related charge basis.

Class P: Piles

The rules in Class P aim to obtain a set of prices for each piling operation, which will lead to equitable payment in the event of variations. The bill items relate to groups of piles which are piles of the same type, material and cross-section in a single location. On a small contract all the piles might be regarded as in a single group.

Two or three separate billed items are generated for each group of piles by the classifications in the third division, depending on the type of pile. They embrace the following elements:

(1) number of piles in a group to cover the plant and labour costs involved in moving the rig from one pile position to the next, setting up at each position and preparing to drive or bore

(2) length of piles in the group, covering the material cost of the piles; the concreted lengths of cast in place piles shall be measured from the cut-off levels to the toe levels expressly required (rule M3)

(3) total depth bored or driven; raked piles shall be identified in the item descriptions and their inclination ratios stated (rule A2). Items for piles are deemed to include disposal of excavated material (rule C1).

The pile materials and section characteristics shall be given in item descriptions; section characteristics being the diameter for cast in place concrete piles, the cross-sectional area for preformed concrete or timber piles, and the mass per metre and cross-sectional dimensions for isolated steel piles.

Rule A5 requires contiguous bored piles to be identified because of the added costs in care and accuracy necessary with this type of work which is usually the basis for constructing pre-formed retaining walls.

Sometimes piles may be of hybrid construction, for example partly bored then driven piles. In such cases a suitable descriptive heading should be given referring to the appropriate drawings and specification followed by measured items reflecting the particular operations. See Worked Example 13 in Part 2 of this book which comprises hybrid piling.

Interlocking steel sheet piles (P8**), being quite different in nature from the individual piles in the remainder of Class P, are not enumerated but are measured in an entirely different way. Both the driving and materials items are measured by area, found by multiplying the mean undeveloped horizontal lengths of pile walls by the depths (rule M7). Corner, junction, closure and taper piles are classed as 'Length of special piles' (P8*1) and measured in linear metres stating their type in the item descriptions (rules D7 and A12). As these special piles are included in the areas of sheet piling under rule M7, they are in effect being measured as extra over the main area item of sheet piling. Closure and taper piles are only measured when expressly required by the Engineer (rule M8).

Rule M1 establishes the 'Commencing Surface' from which piles are driven or bored, as the surface adopted in the Bill of Quantities at which boring or driving is expected to begin. The measurement of cutting off surplus lengths of adding extensions is covered in Class Q.

Class Q: Piling Ancillaries

Work incidental to piling operations, other than backfilling empty bores for cast in place concrete piles, is only measurable when expressly required (rule M1). Hence work undertaken by the Contractor at his own choosing will not be reimbursed unless it is covered in rates for items outside Class Q. Items for piling ancillaries are also deemed to include disposal of surplus materials unless otherwise stated (rule C1).

Work ancillary to piling is classified by pile type and size in a similar manner to Class P, for identification purposes, but ranges are used instead of actual cross-sectional dimensions. Cast in place piles may be concreted through a tremie pipe where water stands in the shaft, but this does not require specific mention.

Where the base of a cast in place pile is to be enlarged, the diameter shall be stated (rule A1), although the price will only cover the cost of the extra material around the shaft previously measured under Class P.

Pile extensions are measured in two items:

(1) number of pile extensions, to cover the cost of preparing piles to receive extensions and of making joints

(2) length of pile extensions to cover the cost of material in them, subdivided between those which do not exceed 3 m and those exceeding 3 m, and including the material to be used in the item description (rule A6).

The driving of extended piles is covered by Class P. Preparing heads of piles to receive permanent work is enumerated, while cutting off surplus lengths is taken as a linear item.

Removing obstructions (Q7) is priced on an hourly basis for breaking out rock or artificial hard material above the founding stratum of bored piles (rule M11). It is measured only when expressly required to bored piles, when the Engineer can maintain control and keep records. Extraction of piles is classed as non-standard work, since it is not listed in Class Q, and suitable codes will be Q 3–6, 9*.

The pile testing items in Q8 differentiate between loading tests to normal piles and raking or preliminary piles.

Worked Examples (in Part 2 of this book)

As illustrations of Classes P: Piles and Q Piling Ancillaries:

WE8 Stone Faced Sea Wall (steel sheet piling)
WE12 Timber Jetty (timber Piles)
WE13 Hybrid piles (part bored, part driven *in situ* concrete piles)
WE14 Quay with Concrete and Timber Piles
WE15 Steel Sheet Piling
WE16 Navigation Lamp Platform (preformed concrete piles driven in tidal estuary)

CHAPTER 10

CESMM3: Classes R–T

Roads, Rails and Tunnels

Class R: Roads and Pavings
Class S: Rail Track
Class T: Tunnels

Introduction

These classes are principally concerned with transportation infrastructure, although in the case of Class T the tunnels may be for any purpose. It is worth noting the exclusions from these classes, as for example the excavation and earthworks to provide the formation level, are measured under Class E: Earthworks; while the roads, pavings and rail track items only cover the specialised make up of these constructions above that formation level.

Class S: Rail track includes items for removal and repair of existing track but strangely Class R: Roads and Pavings does not have any mention of the very common tasks of repair and resurfacing of existing roads nor of jointing new roads to old.

Airport runway construction should also be measured in accordance with Class R as would any other paved areas for other purposes.

Class R: Roads and Pavings

Class R in CESMM3 prescribes rules for the measurement of sub-bases, bases and surfacings of roads, airport runways, light-duty pavements, footways, cycle tracks and other paved areas, together with the necessary kerbs, channels and edgings, traffic signs and surface markings. Landscaping, drainage, fences and gates, and gantries and similar structures supporting traffic signs are measured in accordance with the appropriate classes.

The various courses of road materials in sub-bases, bases and surfacings are each measured separately in m^2, describing the material and giving the depth of each course or slab and the spread rate of applied surface finishes. The third division thickness ranges are overridden by rule A1 requiring the actual depth to be stated. This provision recognises that the Third Division thickness ranges are really only convenient for item coding purposes but the accurate thicknesses are essentially quoted in the item descriptions because of the expensive nature of many road building materials.

Work to surfaces inclined at an angle exceeding 10° to the horizontal is so described and measured separately (rule A2). No deductions shall be made for manhole covers and the like less than 1 m^2 in area (rule M1).

The details of the construction work draw heavily on 'Specification for Highway Works' (Department of Transport). Thus sub-bases of granular material may be either DTp Specified type 1 or type 2. Type 1 can consist of crushed rock, crushed slag, crushed concrete or well-burnt non-plastic shale within a specified grading range, whereas type 2 also includes natural sands and gravels and there are variations in the grading range. In like manner concrete carriageway slabs may be of DTp specified paving quality jointed reinforced concrete (JBC). This is concrete of grade C40 complying with BS 5328, with a minimum cement content of 320 kg/m^3 of ordinary Portland cement (OPC) and with the average value of any four consecutive test results at 7 days having a strength of not less than 31 $N/mm.^2$

Tolerances in surface levels and finishes have considerable impact on plant and labour costs and bill descriptions need to be extended to cover differing or special tolerance requirements, in accordance with paragraph 5.10 of CESMM3.

With concrete pavements, item descriptions for steel fabric reinforcement to BS 4483 shall include the fabric reference, while descriptions of other fabric reinforcement shall state the material, sizes and nominal mass/m^2 (rule A4). The area of additional fabric in laps is not measured (rule M3).

Separate items are not required for formwork to slabs or joints in concrete pavements (rule C1). Construction joints are measured only when they are expressly required (rule M7) and the dimensions, spacing and nature of components to joints shall be given in item descriptions (rule A6).

Kerbs, channels and edgings are measured as linear items including concrete beds and backings, with the details given in item descriptions (rule A7). The different cross-sections of precast concrete kerbs with bullnosed, 45° splayed and half battered faces relate to the prescribed details in BS 7263. Kerbs, channels and edgings laid straight or to curves with a radius exceeding 12 m are grouped together.

Although excavations for kerbs, channels and edgings should be strictly measured under Class E: Earthworks, the note at the foot of page 77 in CESMM3 allows this work to be conveniently included with the relevant items in Class R provided that the appropriate preamble statements are given in accordance with paragraph 5.4.

Traffic signs are enumerated giving the details listed in rule A8. Road studs are also enumerated while line surface markings are measured as linear items and in the case of intermittent markings shall exclude the gaps (rule M9).

Class S: Rail Track

As the title of this class of work suggests, the coverage is limited to that work directly concerned with the track and its immediate foundations. In the case of new railway construction the cuttings, embankments, drainage, structures and the like would all be measured in detail under the other appropriate work classes of CESMM3. The gauge of the track does not rate any specific mention in the rules of CESMM3 which may seem strange to a lay person. In practice the method of measurement renders the actual gauge to have little cost significance but in reality the gauge will show clearly on the drawings and in the specification. It is considered good practice to mention the gauge in the bill descriptive headings, particularly in the fairly unlikely event of having more than one track gauge in one project. The majority of track work in the United Kingdom is laid to 'standard gauge' which measures 1435 mm between the rails.

Traditionally rails and accessories such as sleepers and chairs were bulk purchased by the railway companies directly from manufacturers at favourable cost and thus tenders were invited for laying the track only. Although this system is not as universally adopted as in the past, CESMM3 continues to cater for the separation of supply and laying of track and accessories in the measured items. Track foundations alone are covered by items that include both supplying and laying. 'Supply' includes delivery of components to the site (rule C3), while 'laying' comprises all work subsequent to delivery of components to the site (rule C8). Where track is not to be supplied by the Contractor, the location is to be stated in accordance with rule A13 of Class S.

Separate items are required for bottom ballast, placed before the track is laid, and top ballast, which is placed after the track is laid. The volume of top ballast includes the volume occupied by the sleepers (rule M1). The ballast rates must allow for the cost of boxing up, trimming to line and level and tamping after the track has been laid.

Enumerated items for the supply of sleepers shall state the type, size and identify fittings attached by the supplier (rule A8). Item descriptions for the supply of rails shall give the section reference or cross-sectional dimensions and the mass/metre of the rail (rule A9). Item descriptions for turnouts and crossings shall state the type and shall be deemed to include timbers, fittings and check rails (rules A10 and C6), while the enumerated items for chairs, base plates, fishplates (in pairs) and related items are deemed to include fixings, keys, clips, bolts, nuts, screws, spikes, ferrules, track circuit insulators, pads and conductor rail insulator packings (rule C5).

There are two basic types of track in use in the UK; firstly the traditional British 'bull head' rail which is like an 'I' in cross-section and sits in a chair wedged tight by a key; secondly the modern version of 'flat-bottomed' rail which has a girder style base and a hardened steel upper running rail which may sit on a flat plate on timber sleepers or sit directly on concrete sleepers and is normally held in place by proprietary clips. Bull head rails now mainly occur on secondary lines, in sidings or other low-speed locations whereas all high-speed main-line track tends to be in flat-bottom track on concrete sleepers with the rail welded into continuous lengths of about 4800 metres.

It is unnecessary to give lengthy descriptions of materials for linear track laying items, the type and mass/metre of rail and type of joint and sleeper only being required by rule A15. Laying plain track is measured along the centre line of the track (two rail) and includes sleepers and fittings (rule C9), and shall include the lengths occupied by turnouts and diamond crossings (rule M8). Forming curves in plain track are separated according to the radius (not exceeding and exceeding 300 m), and constitute 'extra over' straight track items to pick up the additional costs. The term 'plain track' denotes track consisting of ordinary lengths of running rails. Item descriptions for laying turnouts and diamond crossings shall state their type and length (rule A16).

The important elements of measuring track laying under rules S6** may be summarised as follows:

S6*1 Laying plain track measured in metres along the centre line of the two running rails. Length includes curved track and lengths occupied by turnouts and diamond crossings.

S6*2 & S6*3 Forming curves in plain track measured in metres (in effect extra over the plain track).

S6*4 & S6*5 Laying turnouts and diamond crossings enumerated (again in effect extra over the plain track as their lengths are not deducted from plain track).

Work to existing track work is included in CESMM3 and incorporates all the tasks which are required for track maintenance and upgrading projects. The classification of S2** covers taking up existing track, with the track measured in metres and other items enumerated. Item descriptions shall state the amount of dismantling, details of disposal of track, and the type of rail, sleeper and joint (rule A3). Another classification (S3 1–5 0) provides for the measurement of lifting, packing and slewing existing track, measured by number, but stating the length of track (rule D3), maximum distance of slew and the maximum lift (rule A5). This entails separate items for dealing with different lengths.

Class T: Tunnels

Tunnelling may be undertaken for transportation schemes such as roads or railways but often may be for more mundane reasons such as sewers and water supply installations. Class T is limited to driven tunnels as under rule M1 cut and cover construction is excluded, such work being measured under other appropriate classes of CESMM3.

The cost of tunnelling is influenced greatly by the nature of the material to be excavated and supported, and because of its relative inaccessibility before work is under way, it cannot be assessed accurately at tender stage. The work is highly mechanised and therefore extremely expensive, but is also subject to severe constraints owing to limitations of access and area of working face, and the uncertainty of ground conditions.

The cost uncertainty is generally greater than with other types of civil engineering work and the rules of measurement take this into account by limiting the risk borne by the Contractor, principally through the measurement of compressed air working, temporary support and stabilisation.

Thus rule A1 prescribes that work expressly required to be executed under compressed air shall be measured separately stating the gauge pressure in stages. Items are also to be included as specified requirements under Class A for the provision and operation of plant and services for this work. Hence the responsibility for deciding the extent of compressed air work and the operative air pressure rests with the Engineer when formulating the Bill. Any deficiencies will be subsequently rectified through variation orders.

Rule M8 prescribes that 'both temporary and permanent support and stabilisation shall be measured', and these are not restricted to the normal 'expressly required' provision. Thus the Contractor will be reimbursed for the amount of support and stabilisation he provides at the billed rates, regardless of the quantity inserted in the Bill. This work includes installing rock bolts or steel arches, erecting timber supports, lagging between arches or timbers, applying sprayed concrete or mesh or link support, pressure grouting and forward probing. Hence most of the risk to the Contractor arising from the extent of support and stabilisation is removed.

Some engineers fear that contractors will be tempted to undertake more support work than is really justified, having inserted favourable rates in the Bill. There are however safeguards built into the contractual arrangements: the Engineer is empowered by the ICE Conditions of Contract to supervise the construction of the works and also the Contractor when pricing the Bill is in competition with other tenderers. Furthermore there is little incentive for the Contractor to slow down the driving operation to carry out unnecessary support work.

Much of the foregoing discussion has involved the possible additional costs occasioned by difficulties and variations in the strata through which the tunnel is being driven. Should the site investigations reveal (or should there be reasonable grounds to suppose) that distinctive variations in the ground conditions will pertain in different sections of the same tunnel then it would be competent to invoke paragraph 5.8 which allows for separation of such parts of the work to reflect those variations in strata and possible methods of construction. Likewise should certain locations or access points to parts of the work appear to be cost significant then separation under paragraph 5.8 would again be prudent.

Excavation of tunnels and shafts are separately measured in cubic metres with the diameter stated as rule D2 and the volume calculated in accordance with rule M2. Item descriptions shall state whether the excavations are straight, curved or tapered while tunnels are assumed to be horizontal up to an inclination of less than 1 in 25 and shafts are generally assumed to be vertical unless otherwise stated (rule A3). Excavation items for tunnels and shafts are separated into work in rock or in other stated material (T11* to T14*). Excavation in other cavities (T15* and T16*) are defined in rule D1 as transitions, breakaways and intersections between tunnels and shafts which are outside the normal profiles of the tunnels or shafts. Excavation rates are deemed to include disposal of spoil and dead services off the site unless otherwise stated (rule C1). It is sometimes the case that materials from tunnel excavations are quite suitable for use as filling materials measured under the Earthworks section and rule M19 of Class E accommodates this occurrence.

In addition to the volume measurement of excavations, the excavated surfaces are measured in square metres separating areas in rock from other stated material (T170 and T180). These surface items cover the excavation, trimming and disposal of overbreak and the subsequent back grouting to fill voids.

As most tunnels and shafts are circular in cross-section CESMM3 assumes this to be the case but rule A6 defines the dimensions to be stated should another shape of cross-section be designed. In the case of more complex cross-sectional requirements reference to drawn information is the best way to define the coverage of an item.

The volume of excavation, and areas of excavated surfaces and *in situ* linings are based on payment lines shown on the drawings, while any cavity formed outside these payment lines is deemed to be overbreak. Where no payment lines are shown on the drawings, the overbreak starts either at the limit of the permanent work to be constructed in the tunnel or shaft or at the minimum specified size of the void required to accommodate the permanent work (rules M2, M4 and M5). Separate items for excavation and linings are needed for curved or tapered tunnels and shafts, tunnels sloping at 1 in 25 or steeper, and inclined shafts (rule A3).

Linings to tunnels, shafts and other cavities may be of *in situ* concrete (T2** to T4**) or of preformed segmental sections (T5** to T7**). Sprayed *in situ* concrete linings are measured by area while cast concrete linings are measured by volume with formwork in square metres. The thickness of *in situ* linings should be measured in accordance with rule M5. Preformed segmental linings are measured by the number of rings, since both the cost of lining materials and of labour is proportional to them, and this eliminates the need to make an accurate prior assessment of creep. Item descriptions for preformed segmental linings are to state the nominal ring width and list the components of one ring of segments, often including the number of bolts, grummets and washers, and the maximum weight of a piece of segmental lining (rule A9).

Pressure grouting is measured in detail under T83* and refers to the support and stabilisation of the ground surrounding a tunnel and would normally be expressly required by the engineer. It is important to note that pressure grouting is a separate element and quite distinct from any required back grouting which fills voids caused by overbreak. Back grouting is not separately measured in CESMM3, being included as part of the rates for the excavated surfaces items measured under T17* and T18* and specified under rule A5.

Worked Examples (in Part 2 of this book)

As illustrations of Class R: Roads and Pavings:

WE8 Stone Faced Sea Wall (concrete slab pavement in promenade)
WE17 Estate Road (concrete carriageway and bitumen macadam footpaths)

As illustration of Class S: Rail Track:

WE18 Rail Track (new passing loop formed from siding)

As illustration of Class T: Tunnels:

WE19 Tunnel (tunnel for sewer scheme)

CHAPTER 11

CESMM3: Classes U–W Walling, Painting and Waterproofing

Class U: Brickwork, Blockwork and Masonry
Class V: Painting
Class W: Waterproofing

Introduction

These work classes represent trades which are also common in the building industry but although some similarities are evident to the rules of SMM7, overall the CESMM3 coverage is generally simpler and more straightforward.

It is worth noting that 'masonry' in CESMM3 is strictly restricted to mean stone walling, whereas in SMM7 the word is used more generically to encompass walling built of bricks or blocks of any material. To avoid any confusion it is best to use the word masonry only in the CESMM3 sense in the context of civil engineering Bills of Quantities.

Class U: Brickwork, Blockwork and Masonry

The rules for the measurement of brickwork, blockwork and masonry within civil engineering have to cover widely differing situations, ranging from half brick thick leaves of cavity construction through to the less common very thick structural walling. Walls which do not exceed 1 metre thick are categorised in four bands of thickness and measured by square metres but if over 1 metre thick are given in cubic metres (U*1* to U*5*). However for pricing accuracy, the actual nominal thickness of each type of wall must be stated in item descriptions (rule A5), the thickness bandings being purely for coding purposes. No deductions from volumes and areas in Class U shall be made for voids each not exceeding 0.25 m^2 in cross-sectional area

Isolated walls having a length on plan not exceeding four times their thickness shall be classed as piers and measured in linear metres in the same way as columns as U*60 (rule D2). However attached columns and piers of the same material as the wall or facing to which they are attached are measured as pilasters as U*76.

The item descriptions must state the nominal sizes of the bricks, blocks or stones and specify the types of materials, bonding, mortar and pointing (rules A1 and A3), this being best achieved by appropriate descriptive headings.

The Third Division classifies the work according to its general form such as vertical straight walls, vertical curved walls, battered straight walls, battered curved walls, vertical facing to concrete, battered facing to concrete and casing to metal sections.

Where walls are built of cavity or composite construction, each of the two skins shall be measured separately and suitably identified (rules M1 and A4). Wall ties across cavities and tying brickwork or blockwork to concrete, and concrete infills to cavities are each measured separately in m^2 (U18 5–6). The composite wall rules will also apply to brick walls built mainly of common bricks with facing bricks on the external face, and each will need to be measured separately with the average thickness stated.

Surface features such as rebates and band courses are measured as linear items with no additions to or deductions made from the main brickwork quantities (rules M2 and D3). The cross-sectional dimensions of surface features are stated in the item descriptions only where they exceed 0.05 m^2 (rule A7). Item descriptions for surface features shall include sufficient particulars to identify special masonry and special or cut bricks and blocks, and to enable the estimator to calculate a realistic price for the work (rule A6). These features are consequently partly extra over the plain wall as no deductions are made but are also partly full value should they incorporate a projection. Conversely sills and copings are dealt with in a quite different way; they are excluded (deducted) from the areas and volumes of walling (rule M2), and the items cover both labour and materials as the material is required to be stated in the items measured under U*71.

Fair facing which is measured in m^2 under U*78 covers all fair facing except for masonry where it is deemed to be included (rule C1). This provision seems strange as masonry facing is usually much more expensive than any facing requirement on brick or blockwork. As a consequence rule A2 requires item descriptions for masonry walls to state the surface finish so that an all inclusive price may be calculated. However rule A2 also requires the surface finish to be stated for facing to concrete, casing to metal sections, columns and piers which might infer that the rates for these elements should also include 'surface finishing' – but is this the same thing as 'fair facing'? Any confusion should be eliminated otherwise claims might ensue, the onus being on the compiler of the bill to make the item descriptions clear and unambiguous.

Supposing a project has simple facing brick outer leaves to cavity wall construction; CESMM3 seems to infer that an item for the brickwork should be measured under U211 then a further item (for the same quantity) taken for fair facing should be measured under U278. If the design required a natural stone rubble wall outer leaf then only one all inclusive item would be measured under U811. This is contrary to the ethos of having simple rules of measurement which exists in the majority of the other work classes of CESMM3. Many Engineers and Quantity Surveyors will be tempted to make an exception to CESMM3 for fair facing and incorporate a similar deemed to include provision to apply to brick and block in the same way that rule C1 applies to masonry.

Item descriptions of damp-proof courses and joint reinforcement must include the materials and dimensions (rule A8). Building in of pipes and ducts are enumerated in two size ranges: the smallest covering pipes and ducts with a cross-sectional area not exceeding 0.05 m^2 and the largest exceeding 0.05 m^2, stating the lengths in the descriptions where they exceed 1 m (rule A10).

Class V: Painting

Painting work under Class V is limited to on-site treatments as any painting carried out prior to delivery to site is either deemed to be included with the component or in the case of structural metalwork is measured separately under Class M.

Each type of painting material is separately categorised in the First Division and the number of coats or film thickness stated in the items (rule A1). The separation of different kinds of paint means that separate items are required for each layer of different material rather than a single item for a complete treatment comprising primer, undercoats and topcoat as would be the case for work measured under SMM7.

Preparation for the work is deemed included under rule C1 but requires to be detailed in the item if there is more than one type of preparation on the same surface (rule A2). These requirements only really affect the item descriptions as all types of preparation will require to be fully defined in the contract specification and included in the price.

The First Division classifies the type of paint, the Second Division the type of surface and the Third Division different inclinations, restricted widths and isolated areas. Widths, not exceeding 1 m, are measured in two linear categories without distinguishing between different inclinations (rule M2). The enumerated isolated group provision can be applied only where the total surface area of each group does not exceed 6 m^2, and shall identify the work and state its location (rules D1 and A3). A typical example would be a coat of arms on wrought iron entrance gates.

No deductions are made for holes and openings in painted surfaces each not exceeding 0.5 m^2 in area (rule M1). In computing the painted area of metal sections, no allowance is made for connecting plates, brackets, rivets, bolts, nuts and the like (rule M4). The area of painted pipework surfaces is obtained by multiplying the pipe length by the barrel girth without deduction of flanges, valves and fittings; but equally no additional allowance is made in the measurement for painting such features (rule C3).

It will be noted that lower surfaces inclined at an angle not exceeding 60° to the horizontal are combined with soffit surfaces and that upper surfaces are subdivided into two categories. When considering types of surface, rough concrete is distinguished from smooth concrete because of the differences in labour and material requirements and resultant costs.

Class W: Waterproofing

The rules for the measurement of waterproofing are fairly similar to those for painting with comparable surface inclinations (excluding soffits but additionally including curved and domed surfaces), restricted widths and isolated areas. Dampproofing, tanking and roofing are each kept separate and item descriptions must include the material (classified in accordance with the Second Division) and the number and thickness of coatings or layers (rule A1 to Class W). Separate items are not required for preparation of surfaces, joints, overlaps, mitres, angles, fillets and built-up edges or for laying to falls and cambers (rule C1).

Waterproofing is measured as the size of the surface covered and no deduction shall be made for holes or openings not exceeding $0.5\,m^2$ in area (rule M1). Isolated groups of surfaces as dealt with under W**8 have similar requirements as in the Painting rules and are covered by rules M4, D2 and A2. The classification of curved or domed surfaces applies only where the radius of curvature is less than 10 m (rule D1).

Worked Examples (in Part 2 of this book)

As illustrations of Class U: Brickwork, Blockwork and Masonry:

WE7 Pumphouse (brickwork basement and superstructure)
WE8 Stone Faced Sea Wall (granite facing to sea wall and parapet wall to promenade)

As illustrations of Class V: Painting;

WE7 Pumphouse (painting doors and windows)
WE11 Steel-Framed Gantry (painting structural steelwork)
WE12 Timber Jetty (painting steel sections)

As illustration of Class W: Waterproofing:

WE7 Pumphouse (asphalt tanking and roofing)

CHAPTER 12

CESMM3: Classes X–Z

Miscellaneous, Renovation and Incidental Works

Class X: Miscellaneous Work
Class Y: Sewer and Water Main Renovation and Ancillary Works
Class Z: Simple Building Works Incidental to Civil Engineering Works

Introduction

The titles of these three work classes accurately describe their contents, which by their nature encompass a very diverse range of work tasks and treatments. Class X was originally the last section in the first edition of CESMM, Class Y was added to CESMM2 introducing sewer renovation only while water main renovation was added to CESMM3 along with the new Class Z.

Class X: Miscellaneous Work

This class is concerned with the measurement of fences, gates and stiles, drainage to structures above ground, such as gutters and downpipes, and rock filled gabions.

Item descriptions for fences, gates and stiles shall give their type, and principal dimensions, and also details of foundations where appropriate (rules A2 and A3). Fences are measured as linear items and gates and stiles are enumerated. The height and width classification ranges are for coding purposes only, and actual heights and widths will be given in item descriptions. Fences erected to a curve of a radius not exceeding 100 m or on a surface inclined at an angle exceeding 10° require specific mention because of the additional cost (rule A1). Items for fences are deemed to include excavation, preparation of surfaces, disposal of excavated material, upholding sides of excavation, backfilling, removal of existing services, concrete, formwork and reinforcement (rule C1) and also end posts, angle posts, straining posts and gate posts (rule C2).

Gutters and downpipes are measured as linear items, including holderbats and brackets, but fittings such as bends, angles, stopends, outlets, swan necks and shoes are enumerated (rule D3). Item descriptions shall include the type, materials and principal dimensions of components (rule A5).

Gabions are wire or plastic mesh cages filled with loose rock or crushed stone and common sizes are 2 × 1 × 1 m and 2 × 1 × 0.5 m. They are used extensively for revetment and linings in sea and river defences.

Item descriptions for rock filled gabions shall include the particulars listed in rule A6. Rock filled gabions exceeding 300 mm thick are classed as boxed gabions and those not exceeding 300 mm thick as mattress gabions.

Class Y: Sewer and Water Main Renovation and Ancillary Works

Introduction

This type of work has become very commonplace since the 1980s because of the largely Victorian era sewers and water mains installed in the major British cities reaching the end of their useful lives with leakage and collapse becoming quite frequent symptoms. The very costly and disruptive remedy of physical removal and replacement of these services can, in many cases, be postponed for many years by extending their life with pipeline linings and other remedial work as covered within Class Y.

This is the only section of CESMM3 which is entirely concerned with work of a repairing and alteration nature but it also incorporates the rules from the Pipework section for new manholes. It is possible that such renovation work might be part of a larger civils project but more often it will be issued as a specialist contract in its own right with the bill comprising Class A: General Items followed by the renovations under Class Y. In this respect the temporary works associated with this class of work frequently represent a high proportion of the cost of the permanent works necessitating careful consideration of the specified requirements in the General Items. It is most likely that this class of work will be undertaken by firms with specialist skills and equipment rather than general civil engineering contractors.

Measurement of Sewer Renovation

Section Y of CESMM3 covers the preparation, stabilisation and renovation of existing sewers and the work connected with new or existing manholes.

Cleaning and closed circuit television surveys are commonly used to assess the condition and remedial requirements of existing sewers. These elements are covered under 'preparation', Y110 and Y130 respectively. Should the employing authority wish to be clear on the extent and nature of any remedial work before becoming contractually committed then it would be prudent to have these exploratory tasks carried out as a separate preliminary contract. The contract documentation for the main contract should then more closely reflect the extent and method of executing the works. However some contracts are let on the basis of optional methods of remedial work which involve the Engineer issuing further instructions after the true nature of the problems have been established. As with most work of a largely concealed nature, the clear allocation of risk between the contracting parties is an important element of any agreement if disputes are to be avoided.

The principal characteristics of the main sewer are to be stated (rules A2 and A5), while rules A3 and A4 distinguish between 'man entry' and 'no man entry' sewers where the Engineer dictates the choice of method.

The preparation of existing sewers under classification Y1** includes preparatory work such as removal of silt, grease, encrustation and tree roots, which is carried out prior to sewer renovation. Most items of preparation work to existing sewers are enumerated (removing intrusions, plugging laterals and local internal repairs), while cleaning and closed-circuit television surveys are measured as linear items, and filling laterals and other pipes in m^3, with locations clearly defined as in rule A1. Stabilisation of existing sewers can be carried out by pointing (in m^2), pipe joint sealing (by number), or external grouting (grout holes by number and grout injected in m^3).

The measurement of cleaning to existing sewers is classified very simply in Y1 1 0, although it will be necessary to identify differing cleaning requirements and standards for varying locations billed in accordance with rule A1. The cleaning items are deemed to include making good damage resulting from the cleaning work but not otherwise (rule C2). For example, the Contractor cannot be held responsible for sewer damage exposed by the cleaning but not caused by it.

Removing intrusions in existing sewers are classified into three groupings in Y1 2 1–3. An intrusion is a projection into the bore of the sewer. Artificial intrusions may encompass isolated projecting bricks, projecting rubber O rings and dead services. While laterals comprise any drains or sewers which are connected to the sewer being renovated, which are prepared by cleaning (Y1 1 0) or by sealing (Y1 4–5*), with sealing/filling of laterals and other pipes measured in m^3. Local internal repairs covered by Y1 6 1–3 are repairs to the structural fabric of the sewer which are to be carried out from inside the sewer. Typical examples are isolated patch repairs, repairs to bellmouths and Y junctions and repairs around laterals.

Stabilisation of existing sewers is carried out by pointing, joint sealing and grouting as Y2 1–3*. As already remarked, the location of all work in Class Y should be stated by reference to the drawings (rule A1) and this is especially important in the case of stabilisation items as the location of a particular operation can be very cost significant. Other generators of separate items which should not be overlooked are differences in specification within treatments such as for example in remedial pointing where it may be hand pointing or pressure pointing in different parts of the same project. External grouting is only measured where it is expressly required to be carried out as a separate operation from annulus grouting in Y3 6 0 (rule M4), and consists of the grouting of voids outside the existing sewer from inside it other than voids grouted in the course of annulus grouting (rule D3).

Renovation of existing sewers encompasses a variety of techniques and materials for improving the performance of sewers, each with their distinct advantages and disadvantages, and including sliplining (lengths of pipe lining jointed before being moved into permanent positions), *in situ* jointed pipe lining (lengths of pipe linings jointed at the permanent positions), segmental lining (circular or non-circular sewer linings normally made up from pairs of upper and lower segments jointed near their springings), stated proprietary lining, and gunite coating of stated thickness – all measured as linear items.

Certain of these pipe lining systems are completed by annulus grouting between the new lining and the old sewer wall as defined in rule D4, measured by cubic metres under Y360. Rule M5 requires that the volume measured for annulus grouting does not include the volume measured for external grouting under Y232. However, annulus grouting can include other voids incidental to that operation such as filling in cracks and holes in the existing sewer wall. The test as to whether it is annulus or external grouting is decided by the necessity for holes for the grout. Should the work require holes to be drilled in the existing sewer wall, or cracks in the sewer wall to be prepared for the purpose of grouting, then it falls to measured as external grouting. Holes are not measurable with annulus grouting as the work should be accomplished by applying the grout from the open ends of the lining as the work proceeds.

Where the Contractor is permitted to choose the appropriate renovation technique to be used, the procedure will be described in the preamble as 5.4 of CESMM3. Curved work is defined as *in situ* jointed pipe lining and segmental lining curved to an offset which exceeds 35 mm per metre (rule A9).

Laterals may also need realigning or jointing and are inserted as enumerated items, with the item descriptions including the type of lining to which laterals are to be connected and identification of laterals which are to be regraded (rule A10). Lateral items are deemed to include the work involved in connecting to the lining within 1 m from the inside face of the lined sewer (rule C6). Where the grading work involves a longer length of lateral, a separate item is required to cover the work.

The installation of new manholes and the abandonment, removal and replacement of existing manholes are enumerated. Full details of work to existing manholes shall be included in item descriptions (rule A15). Class Y6** prescribes the rules for the measurement of new manholes and these are identical to those contained in Class K1** (pipework – manholes) and the associated measurement, definition, coverage and additional description rules. Items for new manholes which replace existing manholes shall be deemed to include breaking out and disposal of existing manholes (rule C11 of Class Y).

Interruptions to work through excessive flows are measured under Clause Y8** only where a minimum pumping capacity is expressly required and for periods of time during normal working hours, when the flow in the sewer exceeds the installed capacity requested by the Engineer, and the work is interrupted (rule M7). The unit of measurement is the hour, and the Engineer shall prescribe the minimum pumping capacity which he considers adequate. Rules A1 and A2 subdivide the interruption item by location and sewer type and size. Because of the large variations in costs within this class of work, interruptions are further categorised in the Second Division into preparation, stabilisation and renovation of sewers and work on laterals and manholes. Renovation is further broken down in the Third Division to reflect the different methods employed.

Interruptions are more likely to be included in contracts where the engineer has access to reliable data on the normal flow rates and considers that more competitive tenders will be submitted if the risk of delays caused by flash flooding are assumed by the employer, rather than the possibility of over compensation for those risks by the contractor. It should also be noted that remedying any consequential damage to the work caused by such excessive flows would not be included either in the time claim for interruptions or in the cost of repairs as these costs would normally be at the contractor's risk under the contract.

Measurement of Water Mains Renovation

This was a new section inserted in CESMM3 in parallel with renovation of sewers. Cleaning of water mains to be renovated is measured in metres taken along the centre lines, and shall include the space occupied by fittings and valves and state the nominal bore (Class Y5 1* and rule M6). Removing intrusions and pipe sample inspections are enumerated, while closed circuit television surveys, cement mortar lining and epoxy lining of existing mains are taken as linear items.

Pipe sample inspections and closed circuit television surveys shall include work carried out either before or after cleaning and lining (rule D5), while items for sample survey inspections shall be deemed to include replacing the length removed by new pipework (rule C7). Item descriptions for linings include the materials, nominal bores and lining thicknesses (rule A11).

Class Z: Simple Building Works Incidental to Civil Engineering Works

Introduction

Class Z of CESMM3 encompasses carpentry and joinery, insulation, windows, doors and glazing, surface finishes, linings and partitions, piped building services, ducted building services, and cabled building services. This was an entirely new section introduced in CESMM3 and is intended to deal with simple building works which are incidental to civil engineering works, such as the pumphouse illustrated in Worked Example 7 in Part 2 of this book. Work covered by classes contained elsewhere in CESMM3, such as drainage, metalwork, brickwork, blockwork and masonry, painting, asphalt work, and roof cladding and coverings, will be measured in accordance with the procedures prescribed in those classes. More sophisticated building work is better measured in accordance with the Standard Method of Measurement of Building Works (SMM7).

Carpentry and Joinery

Structural and carcassing timber is classified according to its location in the building, such as floors, walls and partitions, flat roofs, pitched roofs, plates and bearers and the like (Z11*), and measured in metres. Strip and sheet boarding are measured in m^2, stairs and walkways, and units and fittings enumerated and miscellaneous joinery, such as skirtings, architraves, trims and shelves separately measured as linear items.

When measuring lengths and areas for carpentry and joinery items, no allowance is made for joints or laps (rule M1), and no deduction for holes and openings each not exceeding 0.5 m^2 in area (rule M2). Sizes in item descriptions shall be nominal sizes unless otherwise stated (rule D1), while item descriptions shall state the materials used and identify whether sawn or wrought and any treatment, selection or protection for subsequent treatment (rule A1).

The item descriptions of most structural and carcassing timbers shall state the gross cross-sectional dimensions (rule A4), while those for stairs and walkways, and units and fittings, shall identify the shape, size and limits (rule A6).

Insulation

Insulation is classified according to type and location and measured in m^2 under Z2**, stating the materials and the overall nominal thickness (rule A7).

Windows, Doors and Glazing

Windows and doors are enumerated and classified according to the material and type of component as Z3 1–3*, which distinguishes between windows and window sub-frames and doors and frames or lining sets. Item descriptions for windows, doors and glazing shall indentify the shape, size and limits of the work (rule A8), and are deemed to include fixing, supply of fixing components and drilling or cutting of associated work (rule C2). Items of ironmongery are separately enumerated and described. Glazing is measured in m^2 with the item descriptions identifying the materials, nominal thicknesses, method of glazing and securing the glass (rule A10), while hermetically sealed units are separately itemised (rule A11). Patent glazing is measured in m^2 and classified as to roofs, opening lights or vertical surfaces.

Surface Finishes, Linings and Partitions

The principal finishes are classified as *in situ* finishes, beds and backing; tiles; flexible sheet coverings; and dry partitions and linings as Z4 1–4* with separate items for floors, sloping upper surfaces, walls and soffits, all measured in m^2, except surfaces with a width not exceeding 1 m, which are measured in metres in two separate width classifications (not exceeding 300 mm and 300 mm–1 m). Suspended ceilings are measured in m^2 in three depth of suspension ranges, as amplified by rule A21, while bulkheads are taken in metres and access panels and fittings enumerated. Proprietary system partitions are taken as linear items and classified as solid, fully glazed and partially glazed, with door units enumerated (Z4 7 1–4).

Items for surface finishes, linings and partitions are deemed to include fixing, supply of fixing components and drilling or cutting of associated work (rule C3), and also preparing surfaces, forming joints, mitres, angles, fillets, built-up edges and laying to cambers or falls (rule C4), while suspended ceilings include associated primary support systems and edge trims (rule C6). The materials, surface finish and finished thickness shall be included in item descriptions (rule A17).

Piped Building Services

Pipework and insulation are each measured separately in metres, while pipework fittings, equipment and sanitary appliances and fittings are each enumerated (Z5**). Lengths of pipes are measured along their centre lines and include the lengths occupied by fittings (rule M6). Items for piped services are deemed to include fixing, supply of fixing components and commissioning (rules C7 and C8). Item descriptions shall include details of location or type (rule A22), and pipework descriptions shall give materials, joint types and nominal bores (rule A23).

Ducted Building Services

The linear items of ductwork distinguish between circular and rectangular ductwork and between straight and curved ducts, with the lengths measured along their centre lines (rule M7). Fittings and equipment are enumerated and classified under Z63*. Item descriptions shall include locational and other details as rules A26, A27 and A28.

Cabled Building Services

Cables, conduits, trunking, trays, earthing and bonding are measured in metres, with their associated fittings enumerated, with the cables classified according to their positioning as Z7 1*. Guidance on measuring the lengths of the various components is provided in rules M8, M9 and M10. Final circuits and equipment and fittings (box fittings in the case of conduits) are enumerated and classified as Z7 7–8*.

Items for cabled building services are deemed to include determining circuits, terminations and connections, providing draw wires and draw cables, cleaning trunking, ducts and trays and threading cables through sleeves; fixing and supply of fixing components; and commissioning; while items for conduits are deemed to include fittings other than box fittings (rules C11, C12, C13 and C14). Item descriptions shall include locational and other details as rules A29, A30 and A31.

Worked Examples (in Part 2 of this book)

As illustration of Class X: Miscellaneous Work:

WE7 Pumphouse (drainage above ground)

As illustrations of Class Y: Sewer and Water Main Renovation and Ancillary Works:

WE20 Sewer Renovation
WE21 Water Main Renovation

As illustration of Class Z: Simple Building Works Incidental to Civil Engineering Works:

WE7 Pumphouse (door, windows and associated items)

PART 2

Worked Examples

Refer to the Preface to this book for advice on referencing the Worked Examples.

List of Worked Examples:

WORKED EXAMPLE 1

Demolition and Site Clearance

Cross-references

Explanatory Chapter

This worked example includes material which is explained within part of Chapter 4 CESMM3 – Class D: Demolitions and Site Clearance. This section of CESMM3 covers demolition and site clearance of natural and artificial items above the original surface of the site, and tree roots or stumps below the surface. It is worth noting that all other removals below the original surface are not part of Class D, being taken in other Work Classes of CESMM3.

Related Worked Examples

Explanatory example within the text of Chapter 4 covering Class B: Ground Investigation.

WE2 Excavation and Filling (straightforward excavations, as follow on from this work)

WE6 Sewage Holding Tank (straightforward excavations, as follow on from this work)

Introduction

Worked Example 1 covers the measurement of typical site clearance and demolition items.

Paragraph 14 of CESMM3 allows the actual dimension to be stated rather than a range as given in a Work Classification, and adoption of this option has much to commend it in the case of demolition and site clearance items in order to give the Contractor relevant information for costing purposes. This is demonstrated in Worked Example 1 in items D414 and D511.

Where there is more than one example of the same item in this Classification then each should be suitably identified should there be significant differences in cost.

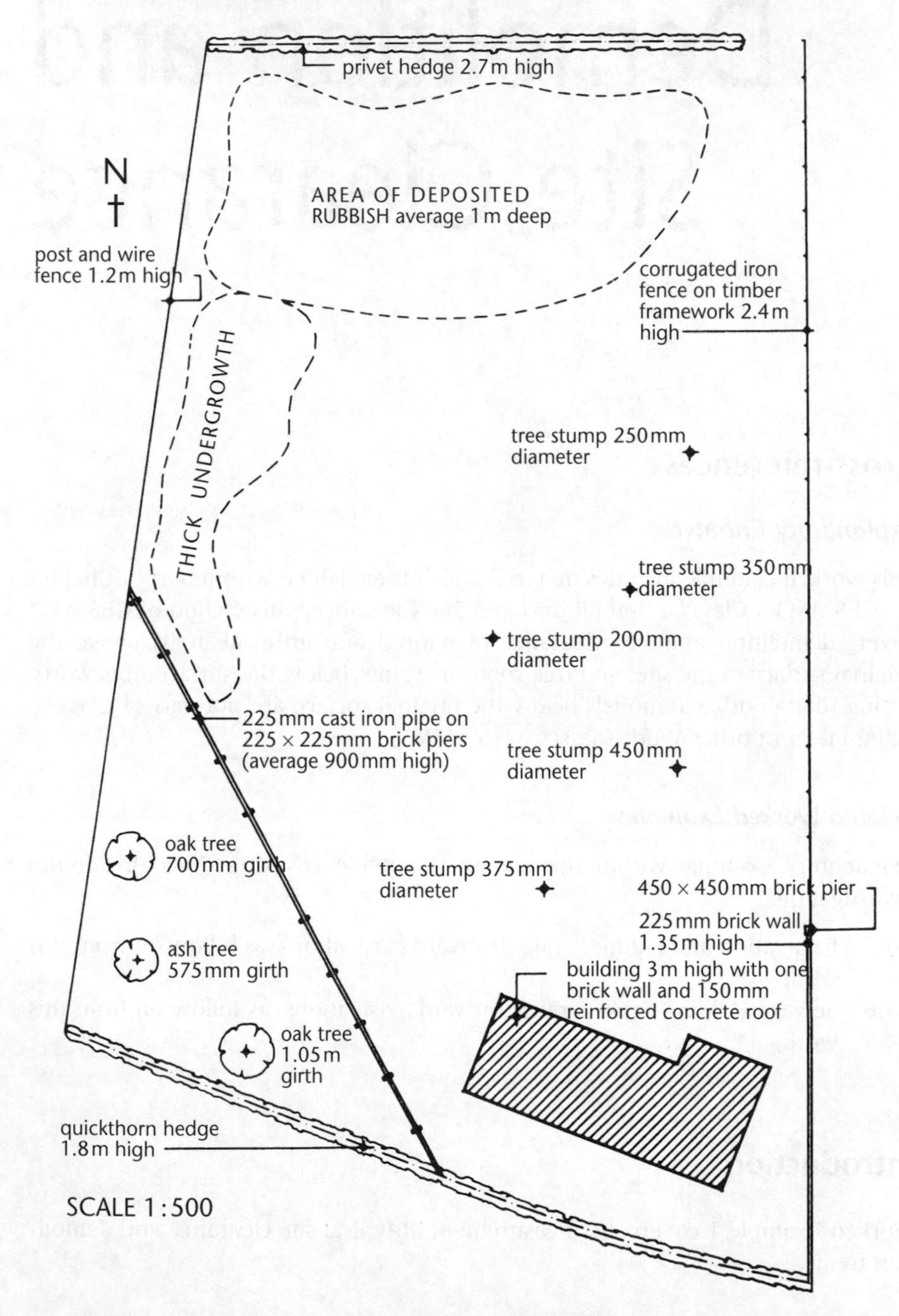

DEM. & SITE CLEARANCE

Dim	Qty	Description	Notes
			Code numbers from CESMM3 inserted after item descriptions for identification purposes.
78.00 45.00		Gen. clearance as Dwg. WE1 inc. fences and hedges. D100	General clearance includes the demolition and clearance of all articles, objects and obstructions except buildings and other structures, and larger trees, stumps and pipelines. Area is reduced to hectares prior to billing.
2		Trees girth 500 mm–1 m; holes back filld. w. excvtd. mat. D210	Felling of trees enumerated with girth classification as D2 1-5, and deemed to include removal of the stumps where they are also required to be removed (rule C3 of Class D). The nature of any backfilling material is to be stated (rule A3 of Class D).
1		Tree girth 1–2 m; ditto. D220	
5		Stumps diameter 150–500 mm. D310	All existing stumps of the same diameter classification as D310.

1.1

DEM. & SITE CLEARANCE (Contd)

		Description	Waste	Notes
			bldg. – main area 18.500 7.000 129.500 projn. 6.000 2.000 12.000 total area 141.500 3.000 total vol. 424.500 m³	Cubic contents calculated in 'waste' with each step suitably annotated.
Sum		Bldg. bwk. & r.c. roof vol. 250–500 m³ (425 m³). D414		Buildings to be demolished are entered as a sum with volume above ground level given in the description, in accordance with the ranges in D411–8. It is more helpful to the Contractor to be given the actual volume, as in this example.
			wall 23.75 0.23 1.35 7.36 pier 0.45 0.45 1.50 0.30 7.66	
Sum		Bdy. wall, bwk. vol. 8 m³. D511		Dimensions are entered in the order of length, thickness and height. Distinction is made between a wall of which the volume can be given under D51, and linear fences included under general clearance. The actual volume is given as it is so far below 50 m³.
45.00		Pipeline nom. bore 225 mm. D610		Pipe supports are included in the price without the need for specific mention (rule C4 of Class D).

WORKED EXAMPLE 2

Excavation and Filling

Cross-references

Explanatory Chapter

This worked example includes material which is explained in Chapter 5 CESMM3 – Class E: Earthworks. This class covers excavation, filling and landscaping works.

Related Worked Examples

WE1 Demolition and Site Clearance (prior considerations before commencing excavation work)
WE5 Pumping Chamber (basement excavations)
WE6 Sewage Holding Tank (straightforward excavations)
WE7 Pumphouse (basement excavations)
WE17 Estate Road (road cutting excavations)

Introduction

Worked Example 2 covers the measurement of excavation and filling to create a level playing field 72 × 36 m within an area of sloping ground. The work involves creating sloping side banks to the excavations and the filling to suit the contours, with the banks specified to be set to a slope of 1 in 2.5. Side bankings compounded with naturally sloping ground create a problem in assessing the horizontal component of the banks. To make the task more straightforward the existing ground is assumed to slope evenly throughout. These calculations may be solved mathematically or by computer software packages which generate solutions to earthwork problems, but for the purposes of explaining this example it is considered best to assess the dimensions graphically. In any case, it should be remembered that all quantities in civils contracts are subject to remeasurement and that the bill quantities are 'estimated', thus reasonable accuracy is required rather than adopting pedantic and over-laborious approaches to such work.

The excavation is reduced to formation datum 150.000 with the whole of the level area and the banks being topsoiled 150 mm deep, thus the level playing surface will finish at datum 150.150.

There is just sufficient fill material resulting from the excavations to complete the filling work but there is an overall shortfall of topsoil requiring some importation. Excavation of topsoil is in cubic metres while filling to stated levels is in square metres, making the reconciliation of the existing available volumes with the required importation volume slightly more awkward. This problem is solved by calculating the area of existing 150 mm thick topsoil excavated over the plan area of the new banks and deducting this from the item for the area of topsoiling the new sloping banks.

Cut and Fill Calculations

The 150.000 contour line is first plotted on the plan since this represents the demarcation line between the excavation and filling. Intermediate points on the contour line are found by interpolating between known spot or ground levels. For instance, taking the two levels in the bottom left-hand corner (SW), the difference between the two adjacent spot levels is 150.860 – 149.285 = 1.575 m, and the distance of the 150.000 level point from the edge of the area is

$$\frac{0.715}{1.575} \times 12.000 = 5.450\,\text{m}$$

The method of working adopted for this example is to calculate the volumes of excavation and fill in the main area (that is, 72 m × 36 m) from calculated average depths and to follow with the volumes of the banks. This is the simplest and quickest method although there are many alternative techniques. The average depths of excavation and fill are most conveniently found by suitably weighting the depth at each point on the grid of levels, according to the area that it affects. Generally this involves taking the depths at the extreme corners of the area once, intermediate points on the boundary twice and all other intermediate points four times. The sum of the weighted depths is divided by the total number of weightings (number of squares × 4) to give the average weighted depth for the whole area.

An alternative is to calculate the cross-sectional area on each grid line, including the section of adjacent bank, and to weight the areas in accordance with Simpson's rule. The banks at the end of each area would have to be added to the volumes of excavation and fill respectively.

Schedules of depths and the dimensions of excavation and fill now follow.

DRAWING WE2: EXCAVATION AND FILLING
is overleaf

EXCAVATION AND FILLING

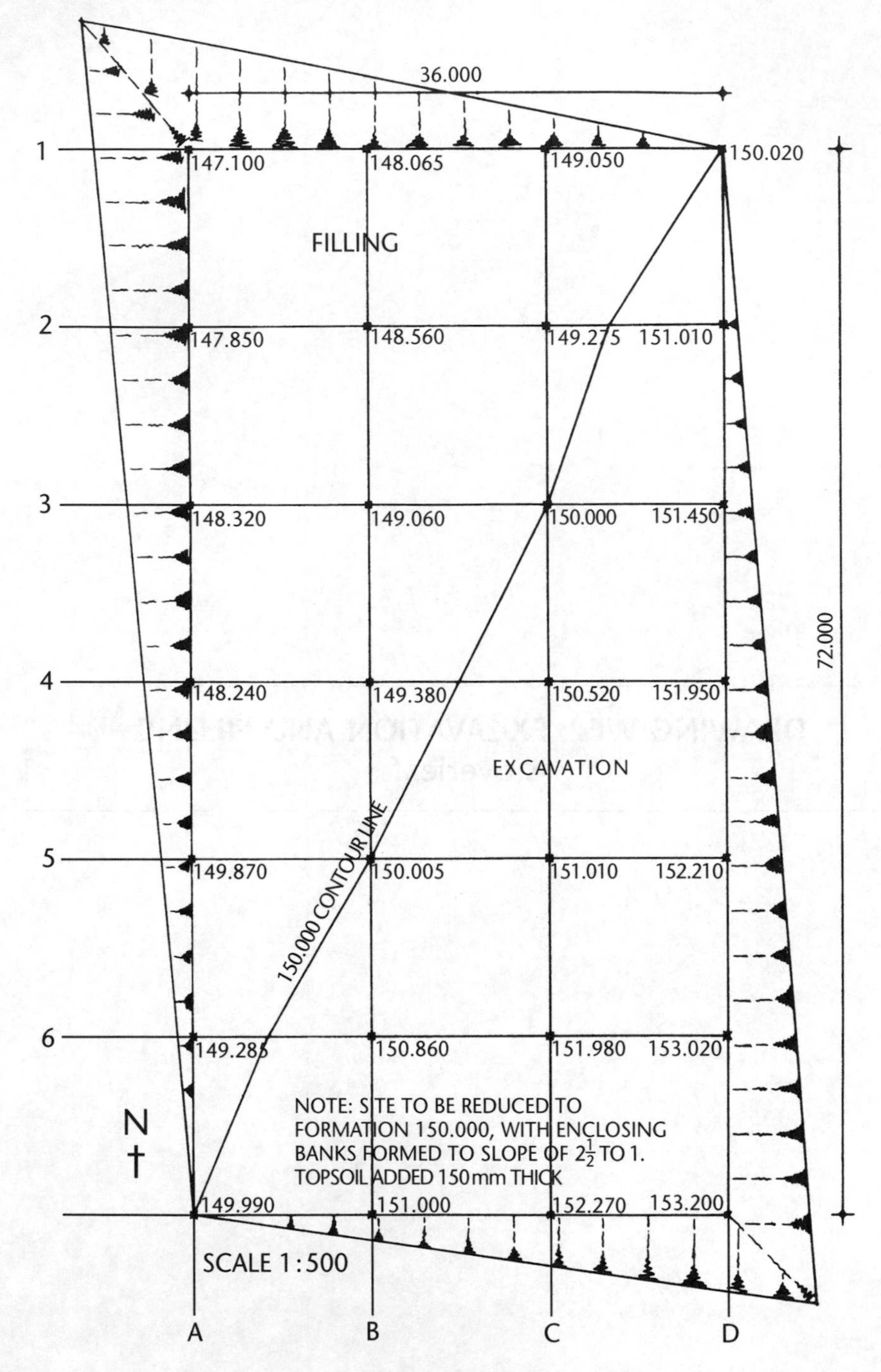

EXCAVATION AND FILLING

AVERAGE DEPTH OF EXCAVATION TO MAIN AREA (EXCLUDING BANKS)

POINT	GROUND LEVEL	DEPTH OF EXCAVATN.	WEIGHTING	WEIGHTED DEPTH OF EXCAVATN.	COMMENTS
D1	150.020	0.150	1	0.150	150mm topsoil.
D2	151.010	1.010	1	1.010	(To weight this twice would give excessively high excavation
C3	150.000	0.150	3	0.450	quantities. 150mm topsoil; affects 3 squares.)
D3	151.450	1.450	2	2.900	
C4	150.520	0.520	3	1.560	
D4	151.950	1.950	2	3.900	
B5	150.005	0.150	3	0.450	150mm topsoil.
C5	151.010	1.010	4	4.040	
D5	152.210	2.210	2	4.420	
B6	150.860	0.860	3	2.580	
C6	151.980	1.980	4	7.920	
D6	153.020	3.020	2	6.040	
A7	149.990	0.150	1	0.150	150mm topsoil.
B7	151.000	1.000	2	2.000	
C7	152.270	2.270	2	4.540	
D7	153.200	3.200	1	3.200	
			36	45.310	
	Average depth of excavation (including topsoil)			1.258	

NOTE: The contour line is virtually coincident with the corners of intermediate squares.
The total weighting of 36 is equivalent to 9 complete squares with 4 effective levels to each.

EXCAVATION AND FILLING (Contd)

AVERAGE DEPTH OF FILL TO MAIN AREA
(EXCLUDING BANKS)

POINT	GROUND LEVEL	DEPTH OF FILL	WEIGHTING	WEIGHTED DEPTH OF FILL	COMMENTS
A1	147.100	2.900	1	2.900	
B1	148.065	1.935	2	3.870	
C1	149.050	0.950	2	1.900	
D1	150.020	–	1	–	negligible quantity.
A2	147.850	2.150	2	4.300	
B2	148.560	1.440	4	5.760	
C2	149.275	0.725	3	2.175	
A3	148.320	1.680	2	3.360	
B3	149.060	0.940	4	3.760	
C3	150.000	–	3	–	
A4	148.240	1.760	2	3.520	
B4	149.380	0.620	3	1.860	
A5	148.870	1.130	2	2.260	
B5	150.005	–	3	–	negligible quantity.
A6	149.285	0.715	1	0.715	
A7	149.990	0.010	1	0.010	
			36	36.390	
		Average depth of fill		1.011	
		Add replacement of topsoil		0.150	Much more convenient to add the additional 150 mm at the end rather than adding it to each individual depth.
		Average total depth of fill		1.161	

2.2

EXCAVATION AND FILLING

Sloping banks at corner A1

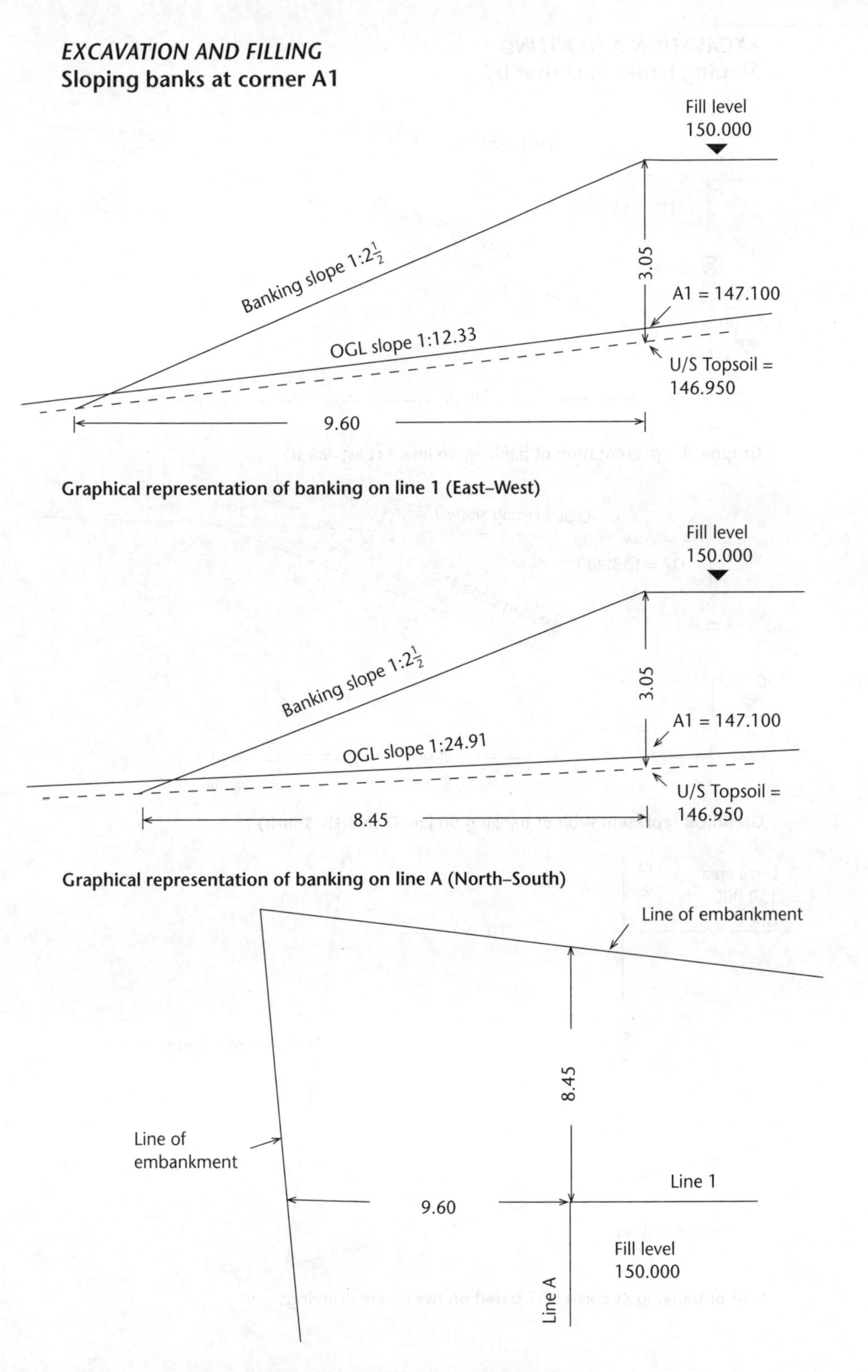

Plan of banking at corner A1 based on the above drawings

2.3

EXCAVATION AND FILLING
Sloping banks at corner D7

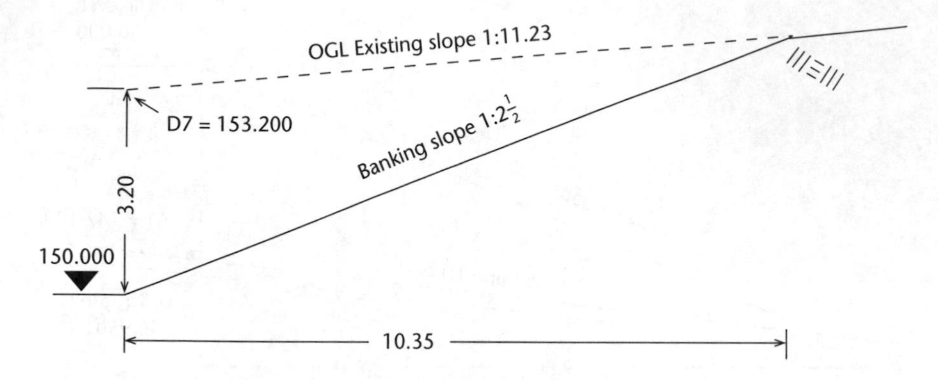

Graphical representation of banking on line 7 (East–West)

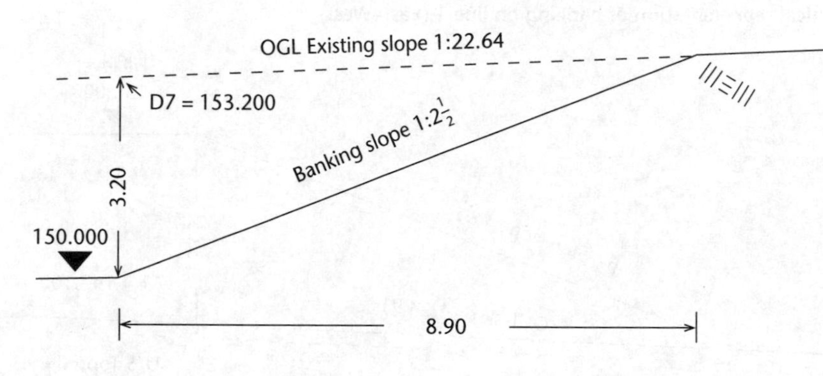

Graphical representation of banking on line D (North–South)

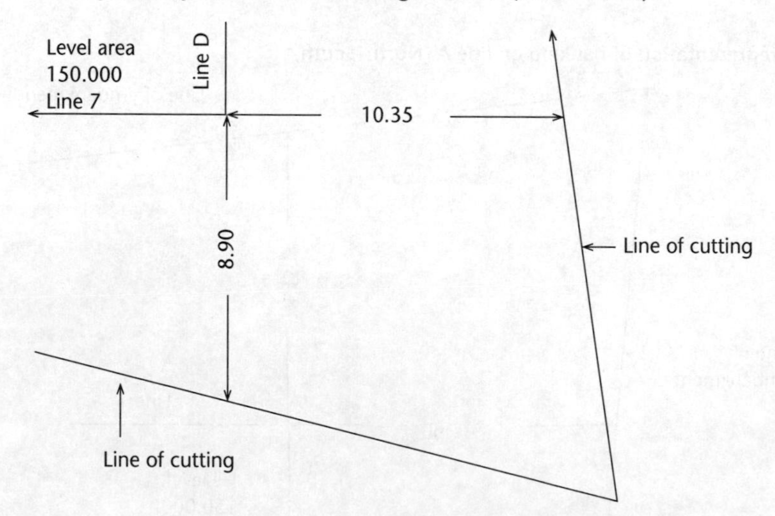

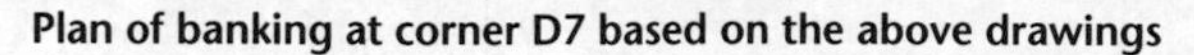

Plan of banking at corner D7 based on the above drawings

EXXCAVATION AND FILLING (Contd)

Class E: Earthwork

Timesing	Dimensions	Description	Notes
		Gen. excavn. topsoil, max.	Area of dig where filling
½/	72.00	depth n.e. 0.25 m.	required therefore excav.
	36.00	E411.1	complete & rule A4 does not
	0.15	(level area	require further description.
½/	72.00		
	11.10		
	0.15	(west slope	
½/	36.00		
	11.20		
	0.25	(north slope	
		Gen. excavn. topsoil, max.	Area of dig with further
½/	72.00	depth n.e. 0.25 m, excvtd.	excavation below therefore
	36.00	surf. u/s of topsoil.	rule A4 applies. Not all bill
	0.15	E411.2	compilers would split these
½/	72.00		items taking all in E411.2.
	12.10		
	0.15	(east slope	
½/	36.00		
	11.90		
	0.15	(south slope	
		Gen. excavn., max. depth	
		2–5 m comncg. surf. u/s of	(Rule A4)
		topsoil	Paragraph 5.21.
		E425	All taken for disposal but
		&	next item will use most of
			volume for filling.
		Excavn. ancillaries, disposal	(Rules D4, D5)
		of excavtd. mat.	Av. depth of excavn. = 1.258
½/	72.00	E532	Deduct topsoil = 0.150
	36.00		Net depth of dig = 1.108
	1.11	(level area	
⅓/ ½/	72.00		Pyramid shape: vol. =
	10.35	(east slope	one-third base area × altitude.
	3.20	(pyramid shaped excavn.	Base is a triangle: area = half
⅓/ ½/	36.00		base × ht. Thus a third times
	8.90	(south slope	a half times multiplier.
	3.20	(pyramid shaped excavn.	
⅓/	11.00		Pyramid with four-sided base,
	10.30		with approximately a
	3.20	(corner area of slope	rectangular base.

2.5

EXCAVATION AND FILLING (Contd)

Timesing	Dimensions	Description	Notes
		Fillg. to embankments E623	(Rules D6, C3) Deemed to be non-selected excavn.
		&	
		Ddt. Disposal excavtd. mat. E532	Volume balanced against last item by deducting disposal.
½/	72.00 36.00 1.16	(level area	(Only 16 m³ approx. left for disposal). Average depth of fill includes removed topsoil depth (see table).
⅓/ ½/	72.00 9.60 3.05	(west slope (pyramid shaped filling	Pyramid shape: vol. = one-third base area × altitude. Base is a triangle: area = half base × ht. Thus a third times a half times multiplier.
⅓/ ½/	36.00 8.45 3.05	(north slope (pyramid shaped filling	
⅓/	10.30 9.70 3.05	(corner area of filling	Pyramid with four-sided base, with approximately a rectangular base. Depth at point A = 2.90 + 150 mm for topsoil excav. = 3.05.
		Filling thickness 150 mm, excvtd. topsoil E641.1	(Rules A14, D8, M19) In effect replacing topsoil to main area now levelled.
	72.00 36.00	&	
		Landscapg. grass seedg. E830.1	(Rules C4, A18) Note that no measurement is made for prep. or trimming as deemed included.
		Filling thickness 150 mm, imported topsoil, inclined at angle of 10°–45° to horiz. E642	(Rule A14) Not sufficient excvtd. topsoil to complete work so imported taken here and balanced by next item.
		&	
		Landscapg. grass seedg. inclined at angle exc. 10° to horiz. E830.2	(Rule A18) Measured directly as triangles on slope.
½/	72.00 12.94		
½/	36.00 12.73	(excvtd. banks	
½/	72.00 11.88		
½/	36.00 11.99	(filled banks 2.6	

EXCAVATION AND FILLING (Contd)

		Description	Notes
		Filling thickness 150 mm, excvtd. topsoil, inclined at angle of 10°–45° to horiz. E641.2	
1251.00		&	$1251 m^2$ is qty of strip orig. topsoil caused by slopes but $1338.48 m^2$ now required for topsoiling new banks. Balanced here by converting excavn. meas. in cubic m (E411).
1.00		Ddt. Filling imported topsoil a.b. E642	

2.7

WORKED EXAMPLE 3

Mass Concrete Retaining Wall

Cross-references

Explanatory Chapter

This worked example includes material which is explained in part of Chapter 6 CESMM3 – Classes F: *In Situ* Concrete and G: Concrete Ancillaries. These sections of CESMM3 cover provision and placement of *in situ* concrete, formwork and accessories.

Related Worked Examples

WE5 Pumping Chamber (reinforced *in situ* concrete)
WE6 Sewage Holding Tank (more complex shaped example of reinforced *in situ* concrete)
WE7 Pumphouse (simple concrete foundation and reinforced suspended slabs)
WE8 Stone faced sea wall (*in situ* mass concrete wall part stone faced)
WE14 Quay with Concrete and Timber Piles (concrete pile caps and suspended quay slab)
WE16 Navigation Lamp Platform (simple reinforced concrete pile cap)

Introduction

Worked Example 3 covers the measurement of a simple mass concrete retaining wall. The basic requirements of CESMM3, Classes F and G are demonstrated on a straightforward piece of construction.

Placing of concrete in walls (F54*) is classified by the thickness of the wall and in this example the wall is tapered in thickness leading to two items; see items

F543 and F544 in the worked example. Some bill compilers would prefer to measure the placing in one item and this could be done under 'Other concrete forms' (F580) with a suitable description and/or drawing reference (rule A4). This aspect is further discussed in Chapter 6.

The top of the wall has no specific finish required and no item is therefore given (rules M13, M14). However should a finish such as steel trowelling be specified this would be measured under G812 in square metres.

Although earthwork dimensions have been omitted, the granular fill to provide drainage behind the wall has been included in the take off (E618). In practice this quantity may also have to be taken as a deduction from 'filling to structures' (E613) depending on how that filling item had been measured.

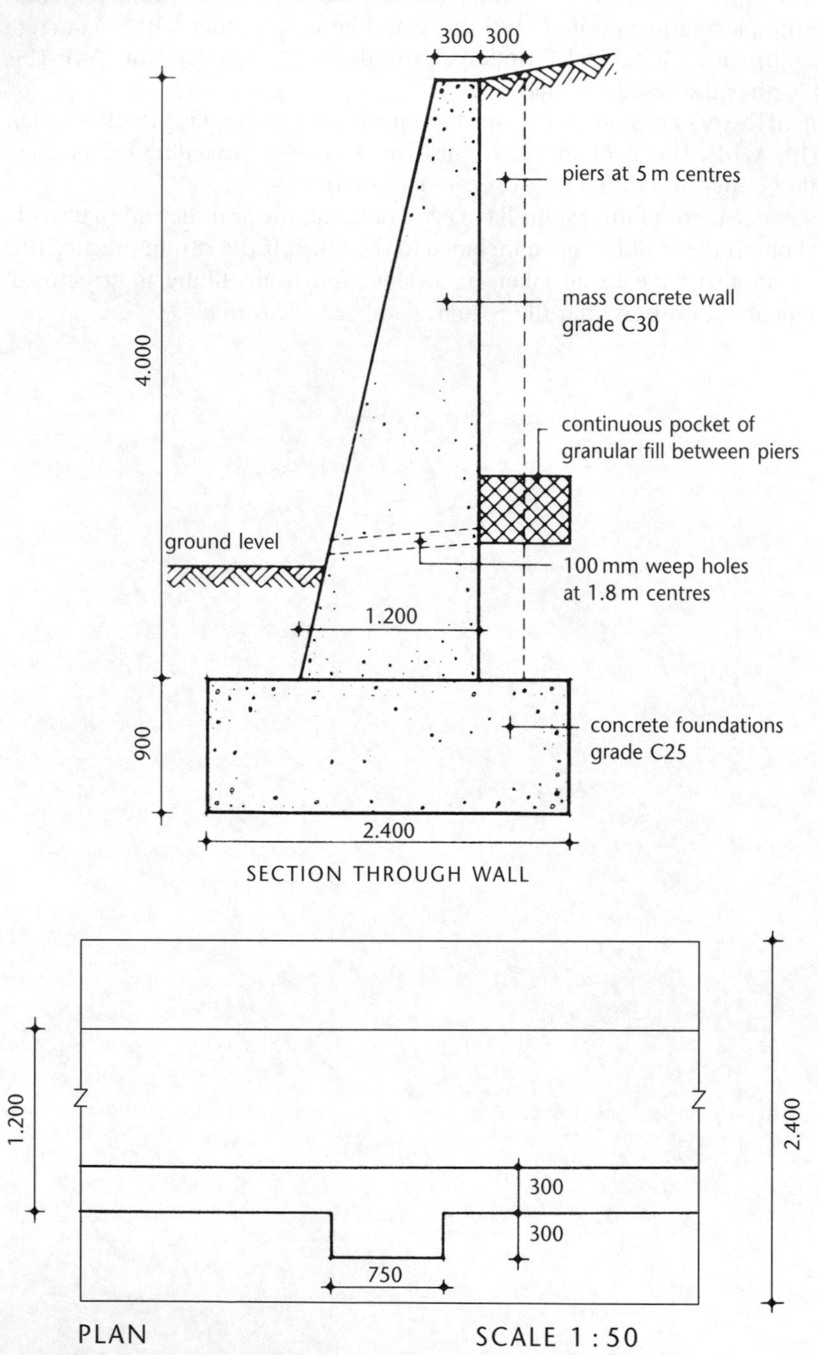
MASS CONCRETE RETAINING WALL
300 300
piers at 5 m centres
mass concrete wall
grade C30
4.000
continuous pocket of
granular fill between piers
ground level
100 mm weep holes
at 1.8 m centres
1.200
900
concrete foundations
grade C25
2.400
SECTION THROUGH WALL
1.200
2.400
300
300
750
PLAN
SCALE 1 : 50

MASS CONCRETE RETAINING WALL

For the purpose of this example a 30 m length of wall has been taken and the earthwork dimensions have been omitted.

Note: the principles adopted in this example would apply equally well to the measurement of reservoirs, settling tanks, bridge abutments, etc. built in concrete.

Timesing	Dimensions	Description	Notes
			The code numbers in CESMM3 have been inserted after each item for identification purposes. They can also form the bill item references.
		In situ concrete Provisn. of conc.	
	30.00 2.40 0.90	Designed mix grade C25, cement to BS 12, 20 mm agg. To BS 882, min. ct. content 120 kg/m³. F253	The measurement of concrete is subdivided into provision and placing. The concrete mix may be 'standard', 'designed' or 'prescribed'. The use of the grades in section 2 of BS 5328 simplifies the approach.
		plers: 5⌊30, 6 + 1 av. thickness of wall: 1.200, 300, 2⌊1.500, 750	
	30.00 0.75 4.00	Designed mix grade C30, ct. to BS 12, 20 mm agg. to BS 882, min. ct. content 180 kg/m³ F263	Note the extensive use of abbreviations and the standard order of dimensions, i.e. length, breadth and height. Reference can be made in the item description to sampling requirements as a specification clause.
7/	0.75 0.30 4.00	(piers	Piers are taken at both ends of retaining wall.
		Placg. of conc.	
	30.00 2.40 0.90	Mass bases, thickness: ex. 500 mm. F524	It is good practice to adopt the appropriate standard terminology (F52*).

MASS CONCRETE RETAINING WALL (Contd)

			ht. of 300–500th. wall.	
				1.200
				300
				900
				$4.000 \times \frac{2}{9} = 0.89$
			av. thicknesses	
			500	300
			1.200	500
			2|1.700	2|800
			850	400
			ht. of wall ex. 500th.	
			4.000	
			890	
			3.110	
	30.00		Mass wall, thickness:	
	0.40		300–500 mm.	
	0.89			F543
7/	0.75			
	0.30			
	0.89			(piers
	30.00		Mass wall, thickness:	
	0.85		ex. 500 mm.	
	3.11			F544
7/	0.75			
	0.30			
	3.11			(piers
			Concrete Ancillaries	
			Fwk. fair finish	
	30.00		Slopg.	G225
	4.10			

Note build up of dimensions in 'waste'.
The thickness of wall determines the amount of tamping or vibrating that has to be carried out for a given volume of concrete – this affects the price and the thickness is therefore classified in accordance with the ranges in the third division of Class F. The wall has to be subdivided into the part not exceeding 500 mm thick and that exceeding it.
Attached piers are included with the wall in accordance with rule M3 of Class F.
Assumed that concrete in wall foundation will be cast against excavated surfaces.
Wrot formwork has been taken for the full height of the wall as it would probably be difficult to use sawn formwork for the bottom section below ground only and it will avoid any snags arising from variations in the finished ground level.
Formwork shall be deemed to be to plane areas and to exceed 1.22 m wide unless otherwise stated (rule D2 of Class G).
Note longer length of sloping face (scaled from drawing).
Described as sloping and not battering as exceeds 10° from vertical.

MASS CONCRETE RETAINING WALL (Contd)

Timesing	Dimensions	Squaring	Description	Notes
			less piers 30.000	
			7/750 5.250	
			24.750	
			Fwk ro. finish.	
	24.75		Vert. G145	
	4.00			
7/	0.75		Vert. width 0.4–1.22 m.	The formwork to the faces and returns of the piers is kept separate from that to the wall face, as the narrow widths generate separate bill items. Both are superficial items as they exceed 200 mm wide.
	4.00		(pier faces	
			G144	
7/2/	0.30		Vert. width 0.2–0.4 m.	
	4.00		(pier retns.	
			G143	
			1.800 | 30.000	
			17	
			Inserts	Measured as inserts in accordance with G832. Separate items are not required for adapting formwork, as the inserts are not required to be grouted into preformed openings (rule M16 of Class G).
17/	1		100 mm clayware land drain, 1 m lg., cast in on rake, totally within conc. vol. G832	
			ClASS E: Earthwork	Note: If expansion jointing was required between the various sections of wall, the non-extruding expansion jointing for the full cross-sectional area would be measured in square metres, with the strip of sealing compound on the outer face of the wall taken as a linear item.
	24.75		Granular fill in continuous pocket behind wall.	
	0.60			
	0.45		E618	

WORKED EXAMPLE 4

Precast Pre-stressed Concrete Beams

Cross-references

Explanatory Chapter

This worked example includes material which is explained in part of Chapter 6 CESMM3 – Classes H: Precast Concrete and G: Concrete Ancillaries. These sections of CESMM3 cover precast concrete units and post-tensioned prestressing in precast concrete respectively.

Related Worked Example

WE7 Pumphouse (precast concrete lintels incorporated in brick walls)

Introduction

This example comprises 40 identical beams of a complex constructional form, namely precast post-tensioned pre-stressed concrete. Post-tensioned pre-stressing is an exclusion from Class H: Precast Concrete, being measured under Class G: Concrete Ancillaries. This approach is quite different from that for precast pre-tensioned pre-stressed concrete units which are covered entirely within Class H as enumerated items. The reason for adopting that distinct approach for post-tensioned units is to adequately reflect the complex and skilled on-site executed tensioning processes. The pre-tensioned precast units on the other hand are normally factory-produced units delivered to site ready for incorporation in the works. Refer to Chapter 6 for further discussion of this matter.

Most precast concrete components are easy to identify as such (rule D2) but rule D3 deals with the situation where site precasting may be adopted in certain circumstances for work which in nature and characteristic is really *in situ* concrete. The 40 beams in this example are cast on site but should be treated as precast as they would make multiple use of the formwork during their manufacture and as such are an exception to rule D3.

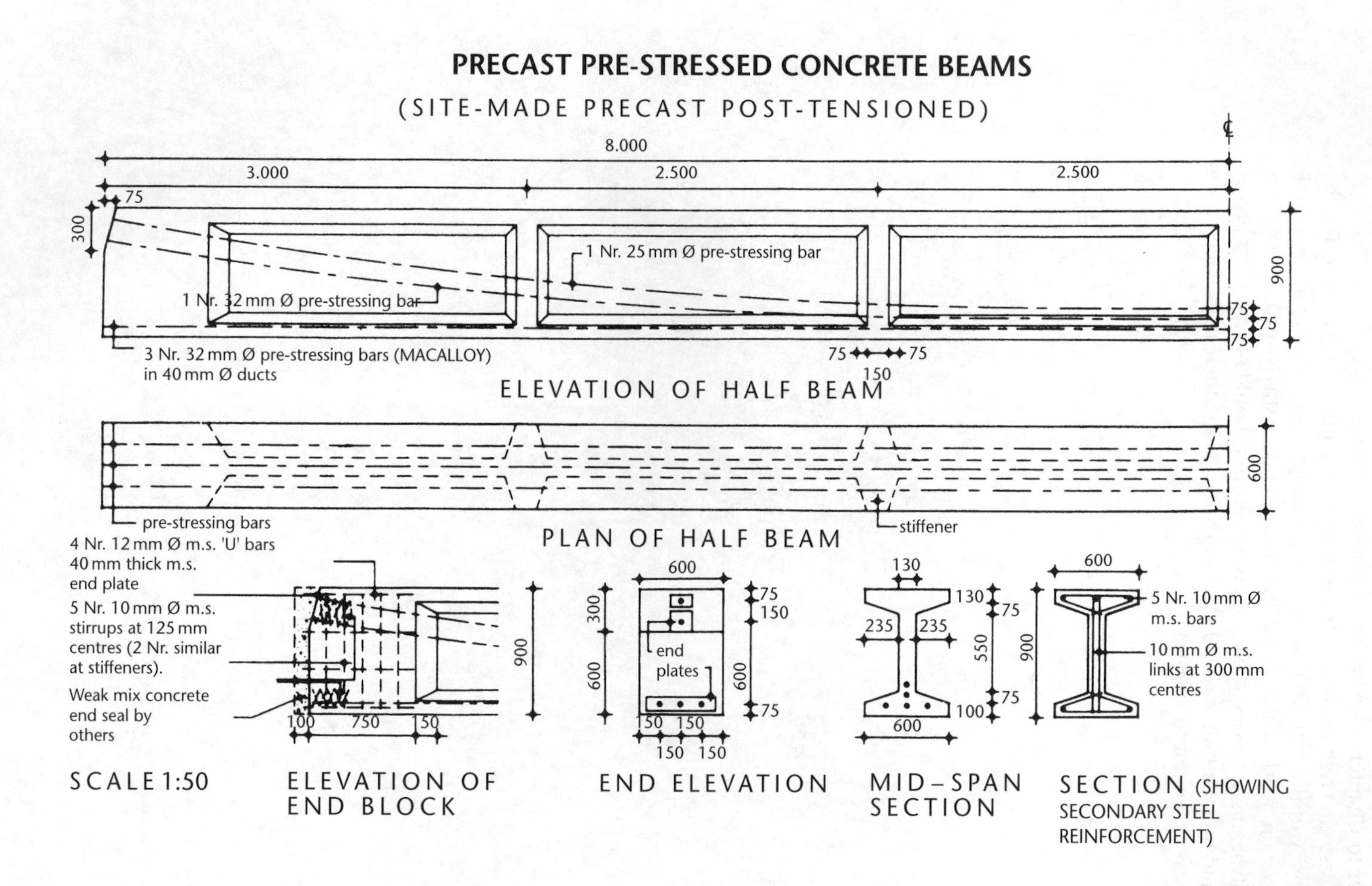
PRECAST PRE-STRESSED CONCRETE BEAMS
(SITE-MADE PRECAST POST-TENSIONED)
8.000
3.000
2.500
2.500
1 Nr. 25 mm Ø pre-stressing bar
1 Nr. 32 mm Ø pre-stressing bar
3 Nr. 32 mm Ø pre-stressing bars (MACALLOY)
in 40 mm Ø ducts
ELEVATION OF HALF BEAM
pre-stressing bars
stiffener
PLAN OF HALF BEAM
4 Nr. 12 mm Ø m.s. 'U' bars
40 mm thick m.s. end plate
5 Nr. 10 mm Ø m.s. stirrups at 125 mm centres (2 Nr. similar at stiffeners).
Weak mix concrete end seal by others
end plates
5 Nr. 10 mm Ø m.s. bars
10 mm Ø m.s. links at 300 mm centres
SCALE 1:50
ELEVATION OF END BLOCK
END ELEVATION
MID–SPAN SECTION
SECTION (SHOWING SECONDARY STEEL REINFORCEMENT)

PRECAST PRE-STRESSED CONCRETE BEAMS

(40 Nr Site-made precast post-tensioned beams forming road bridge deck)

Class H: Precast Concrete

Timesing	Dimension	Squaring	Description	Notes
			Precast conc. grade C40 as spec. clauses H 5–9, in bridge deck spans ref. Dwg. WE 4, prepared for post-tensioning in final position.	(Rule A1) Position in the works and spec. of conc. to be stated.
	40		Prestressed post-tensioned beams mark nr. WE 4, 600 × 900 mm 'I' section, length 16 m, mass 12 t. H357	(Rules A1, C1, D1, D2) Note: Rule A3 does not apply to post-tensioned work. Actual lengths and mass stated as all 40 are identical.

Class G: Concrete Ancillaries

Timesing	Dimension	Squaring	Description	Notes
			Post-tensioned prestressing as spec. clause G73 'Macalloy System' with anchorages all as Dwg. WE4 to precast bridge deck beams.	(Rules A12, C5, D9, M12) Ducts, grout, components etc. deemed included.
	40		25 mm Horiz. intl. tendons in precast conc. len. 15–20 m. G735.1	(Rules M12, D9)
4/	40		32 mm Horiz. intl. tendons in precast conc. len. 15–20 m G735.2	4 × 32 mm in each beam.
5/	40		External jacking operations G750	(Rule M12) Assume jacking required from 1 end only.

WORKED EXAMPLE 5

Pumping Chamber

Cross-References

Explanatory Chapters

This worked example includes material which is explained in Chapter 5 CESMM3 – Class E: Earthworks; and part of Chapter 6 CESMM3 – Classes F: *In situ* Concrete and G: Concrete Ancillaries. These sections of CESMM3 cover excavations and excavation ancillaries; provision and placement of *in situ* concrete, formwork, reinforcement and concrete accessories.

Related Worked Examples

WE2 Excavation and Filling (playing field levelling)
WE3 Mass Concrete Retaining Wall (non-reinforced *in situ* concrete)
WE6 Sewage Holding Tank (excavations and a more complex shaped example of reinforced *in situ* concrete)
WE7 Pumphouse (excavations and simple concrete foundation and reinforced suspended slabs)
WE8 Stone Faced Sea Wall (excavations affected by tidal water and *in situ* mass concrete wall part stone faced)
WE14 Quay with Concrete and Timber Piles (concrete pile caps and suspended quay slab)
WE16 Navigation Lamp Platform (simple reinforced concrete pile cap)

Introduction

Worked Example 5 covers the measurement of a chamber which could have been considered for measurement under Class K: Pipework – Manholes and Pipework Ancillaries (K237). However the pumping chamber is somewhat more complex than usual and consequently the optional approach of giving a detailed measurement of the work offered by the note at the foot of page 53 of CESMM3 has been adopted. This choice is necessarily subjective and each case should be considered on its merits and the size and context of the particular job. (See Worked Examples 9 and 10 for examples of manholes and chambers enumerated under Class K.)

Having chosen the detailed measurement approach, Worked Example 5 covers the measurement of a pumping chamber involving simple basement excavation and reinforced concrete construction. The basic requirements of CESMM3, Classes E, F and G are demonstrated on a fairly simple piece of construction.

The access covers in the roof slab are omitted from the drawing and not measured here, but as they are likely to be in metal they would be best measured under Class N: Miscellaneous Metalwork (see Worked Example 7 Pumphouse). Such metal covers are mostly incorporated with manholes or other similar chambers and simply included in the appropriate item under Class K (rule A2) but, should they be required independently, CESMM3 does not appear to cover them specifically.

PUMPING CHAMBER

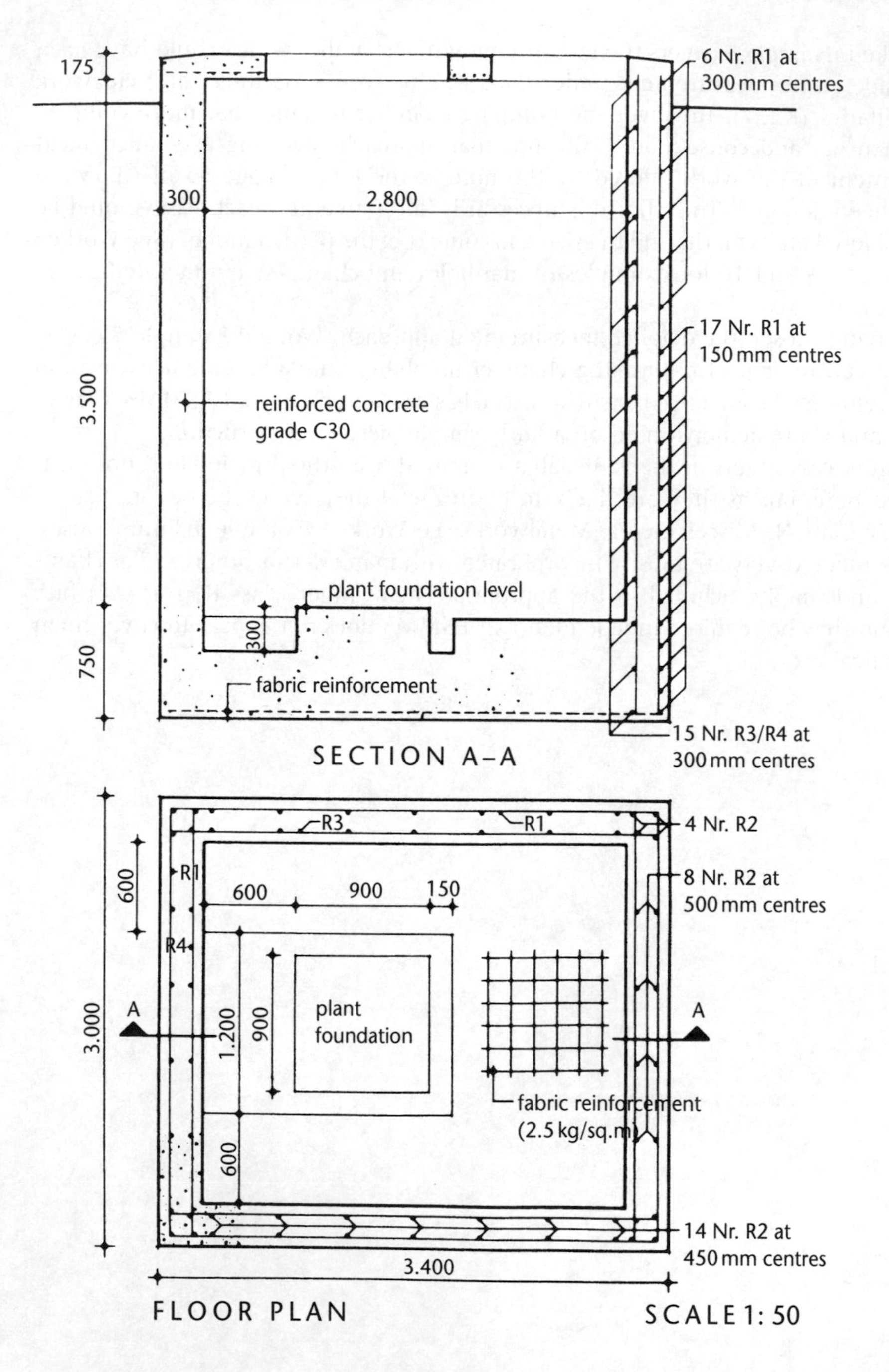

BAR SCHEDULE

Note: All bars are 12 mm diameter

BAR REFERENCE	SHAPE OF BAR	LENGTH	TOTAL NUMBER
R1	L SHAPED 1.650 / 1.800	3.450	92
R2	STRAIGHT (in two lengths)	2.500	120
R3	STRAIGHT	3.300	34
R4	STRAIGHT	2.900	37
R5	STRAIGHT	1.400	4
R6	STRAIGHT	1.100	8
R7	STRAIGHT	800	10
R8	STRAIGHT	600	5

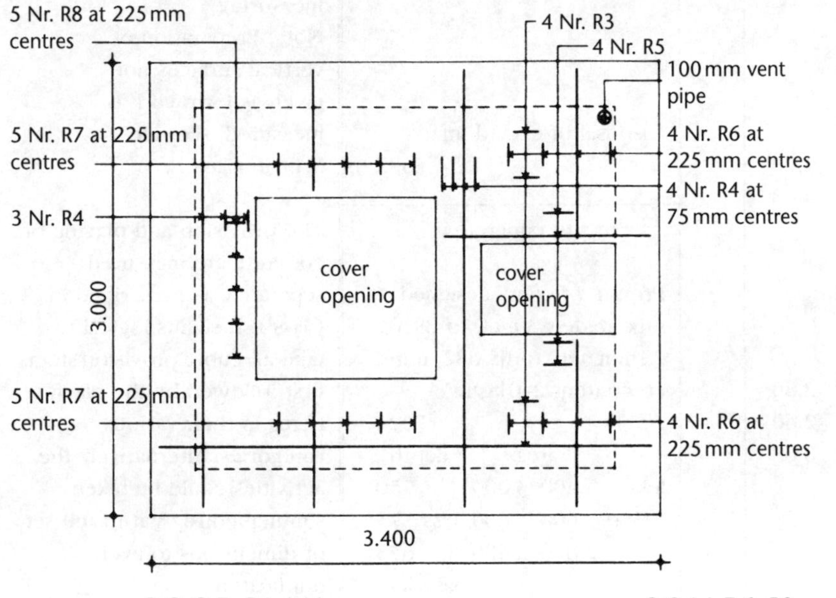

ROOF PLAN SCALE 1:50

PUMPING CHAMBER

Dimensions	Description	Notes
	total depth 175 3.500 750 4.425 less ht. above grd. 350 4.075	Excavation for pits and similar structures is measured as total depth, but taken in the stages listed in the Third Division of Class E. It is not considered necessary to separate the topsoil for subsequent reuse, because of the small quantity involved.
3.40 3.00 4.08	Earthwks. Gen. excavtn., max. depth: 2–5 m. E425	
3.40 3.00	Excavn. ancillaries Prepn. of excvtd. surfs. E522	Separate items are not required for upholding sides of excavation or additional excavation to provide working space (rule Cl of Class E), but disposal of excavated material requires measuring. Note: Preparation of vertical surfaces not given as formwork is measured, see rule M11 in Class E.
3.40 3.00 4.08	Disposal of excvtd. mat. E532	
2.80 2.40 0.68	In situ concrete Provsn. of conc. designed mix grade C30, ct. to BS 12, 20 mm agg. to BS 882, min. ct. content 240 kg/m^3. F223	The provision and placing of concrete are measured separately as prescribed in Class F. It seems logical to take all cubic provision items first followed by the placing items in their various categories. Alternatively the activities could be taken simultaneously with each set of dimensions to avoid duplication.
	area / depth less 3.400 3.000 / 750 2/300 600 600 / less 75 2.800 2.400 / 675 base len. 600 900 150 1.650	
1.65 1.20 0.23	Ddt. ditto. area ard. plant. fdn.	

PUMPING CHAMBER (Contd)

Dimensions		Description	Notes
		Provsn. of conc. a.b. F223	
0.90		Add ditto. (plant fdn.	Note method of building up
0.90		ht.	the girth of the chamber
0.30		3.500	wall, measured on its centre
		750	line, by taking the internal
		4.250	perimeter and adding the
11.60		len.	thickness of the wall for each
0.30		2.800	corner.
4.25		(walls 2/ 2.400	
		5.200	
		10.400	The order of measurement
3.40		add corners 4/300 1.200	follows a logical sequence –
3.00		11.600	the order of construction on
0.18		(cover slab	the site – base, walls and
			cover slab.
1.20		Ddt. ditto.	
1.20			Deduction of concrete is
0.18			made for the openings as
			they exceed the area of 'large
0.90			voids' as defined in rule D3
0.60			of Class G.
0.18		(cover opgs.	
		Placg. of conc.	
		Reinforced	
2.80		Bases and ground slabs,	Bases are measured in cubic
2.40		thickness: ex. 500 mm.	metres, distinguishing
0.68		F624	between different classes of
			concrete (mass, reinforced
			and prestressed) and
1.65		Ddt. ditto (area ard.	separating into the thickness
1.20		plant fdn.	ranges listed in the Third
0.23			Division.
			It is deemed desirable to
0.90		Small plant base,	keep the concrete in the
0.90		thickness: 150–300 mm.	plant base separate from the
0.30		F622	remainder because of its
			small volume.
11.60		Walls, thickness:	The walls are 300 mm thick
0.30		150–300 mm.	and so fall within the
4.25		F642	thickness range of 150–300 mm.
3.40		Susp. slab thickness:	All suspended slabs are
3.00		150–300 mm.	measured in cubic metres.
0.18		F632	

5.2

PUMPING CHAMBER (Contd)

Timesing	Dimensions	Squaring	Description	Side notes
			Placg. of conc. Reinforced	
	1.20		Ddt. ditto. F632	Same deductions for openings as before, as does not fall within the inclusion provisions in rule M1 of Class F.
	1.20			
	0.18		(cover opgs.	
	0.90			
	0.60			
	0.18			
			Conc. ancillaries	Formwork providing rough and fair finishes must be distinguished and the plane classified in accordance with the second division of Class G (horizontal, sloping, battered, vertical and curved).
			Fwk. fair fin: 2/1.650 3.300	
			1.200	
			4.500	
	4.50		Vert. width:	
	0.23		0.2–0.4 m. (sump	
4/	0.90		(plant fdn.	Widths not exceeding 200 mm are measured as linear items and greater widths in square metres.
	0.30		G243	
			Conc. Accessories	
	2.80		Finishg. of top surfs., steel	To obtain smooth finish to concrete base.
	2.40		trowel. G812	
	4.50		Finishg. of formed surfs.,	To vertical surfaces to sump and plant base.
	0.23		steel trowel.	
			G823	
	3.60			
	0.30			
			Conc. ancillaries	Note build up of external girth of pumping station.
			Fwk. ro. fin.	
			11.600	Alternatively, the external dimensions of the chamber could be taken: 3.400
			add 4/300 1.200	3.000
			12.800	2/ 6.400
			less pt. 4.250	12.800
			above g.l. 225	
			4.025	
	12.80		Vertical (ext. face	
	4.03		of walls	Unnecessary to state width as it exceeds 1.22 m (rule D2 of Class G).
			G145	

PUMPING CHAMBER (Contd)

Timesing	Dimensions	Squaring	Description	Side notes
			Fwk. fair fin.	
	12.80 0.23		Vertical width 0.2–0.4 m. (ext. face of walls G243 3.500 75 3.575 11.600 less corners 1.200 10.400	Taking smooth face of concrete to 75 mm below ground level to allow for any irregularities in the finished ground surface. The formwork to the edges of the cover slab are taken later.
	10.40 3.58		Vertical (int. face of walls G245	Wrought formwork to internal faces of walls.
			Conc. accessories	
	11.60 0.30		Finishg. of top slopg. surfs., steel trowel G812	Sloping top surfaces to edges of cover slab. CESMM3 (Class G) does not require the inclusion of the word 'sloping', but additional information may be given in accordance with 5.13 where advisable.
			Conc. Ancillaries Fwk. fair fin.	
	2.80 2.40		Horizontal G215	Formwork to underside of cover slab.
	1.20 1.20 0.90 0.60		Ddt ditto. G215 (cover opgs. 1.200 900 1.200 600 2/ 2.400 2/ 1.500 4.800 3.000	Formwork to underside of openings deducted as they exceed the large void areas prescribed in rule D3 of Class G.
	4.80 3.00		Vert. width: 0.1–0.2 m. (sides of opgs. G242	Linear items of formwork as not exceeding 200 mm wide.
	12.80		Ditto. (edges of cover slab G242	The cover slab would be constructed later than the walls, after the plant has been installed – hence the need for a separate 150 mm strip of formwork to the edge of the cover slab.

PUMPING CHAMBER (Contd)

Timesing	Dimensions	Squaring	Description	Notes
			Conc. accessories Inserts	
	1		100 mm dia. c.i. pipe proj. from one surf. G832	Items for inserts shall be deemed to include their supply unless otherwise stated (rule C7 of Class G).
			Conc. ancillaries Reinforcement	
			3.400 3.000 less 2/40 80 80 3.320 2.920	40 mm cover has been allowed to the fabric reinforcement to all edges in base slab.
	3.32 2.92		High yield steel fabric to BS 4483, nominal mass 2–3 kg/m², ref. A142. G562	Laps are not measured (rule M9 of Class G). Item descriptions for high yield steel fabric to BS 4483 shall state the appropriate reference (rule A9 of Class G)
			M. S. bars to BS 4449 R3 R4 34 37 less bars in 4 7 cover slab 30 30	
92/	3.45		Diam. 12 mm (R1	Check the bar bending schedule against the Drawings before extracting the quantities from it. If no schedule is supplied, it will usually be necessary to prepare one.
120/	2.50		(R2	
30/	3.30		(R3	
30/	2.90		G514 (R4) (walls	40 mm cover is provided to the reinforcement unless otherwise specified and the normal allowance for hooked ends is an addition of 12 times the diameter of the bar for each hooked end. The total length of bar will be weighted up and billed in tonnes. Separate items are not required for supporting reinforcement (rule C1 of Class G).
4/	3.30		Diam. 12 mm (R3	
7/	2.90		(R4	
4/	1.40		(R5	
8/	1.10		(R6	Bars exceeding 12 m in length are given separately in stages of 3 m (rule A7 of Class G).
10/	0.80		(R7	
5/	0.60		(R8 G514 (cover slab	

5.5

WORKED EXAMPLE 6

Sewage Holding Tank

Cross-references

Explanatory Chapters

This worked example includes material which is explained in Chapter 5 CESMM3 – Class E: Earthwork; part of Chapter 6 CESMM3 – Classes F – *In situ* Concrete and G: Concrete Ancillaries; and a small sample of incidental work from Chapter 7 CESMM3 – Classes J and K: Pipework. These sections of CESMM3 cover excavations and excavation ancillaries; provision and placement of *in situ* concrete, formwork and concrete accessories; ventilation pipework and access manholes.

Related Worked Examples

- WE2 Excavation and Filling (playing field levelling)
- WE3 Mass Concrete Retaining Wall (non-reinforced *in situ* concrete)
- WE5 Pumping Chamber (excavations and a straightforward example of reinforced *in situ* concrete)
- WE7 Pumphouse (excavations and simple concrete foundation and reinforced suspended slabs)
- WE8 Stone Faced Sea Wall (Excavations affected by tidal water and *in situ* mass concrete wall part stone faced)
- WE9 Sewer (comprehensive coverage of pipework items from Classes I, J, K and L)
- WE14 Quay with Concrete and Timber Piles (concrete pile caps and suspended quay slab)
- WE16 Navigation Lamp Platform (simple reinforced concrete pile cap)

Introduction

Worked Example 6 covers the measurement of a chamber which could have been considered for measurement under Class K: Pipework – Manholes and Pipework Ancillaries (K234). However the holding tank is more complex and larger than usual and consequently the optional approach of giving a detailed measurement of the work offered by the note at the foot of page 53 of CESMM3 has been adopted. This choice is necessarily subjective and each case should be considered on its merits and the size and context of the particular job. (See Worked Examples 9 and 10 for examples of manholes and chambers enumerated under Class K.)

Having made the choice to adopt detailed measurement, the work involves general excavation and reinforced concrete construction with some items of pipework. The basic requirements of CESMM3, Classes E, F and G are demonstrated on a more complex piece of construction.

**DRAWING WE6: SEWAGE HOLDING TANK
is overleaf**

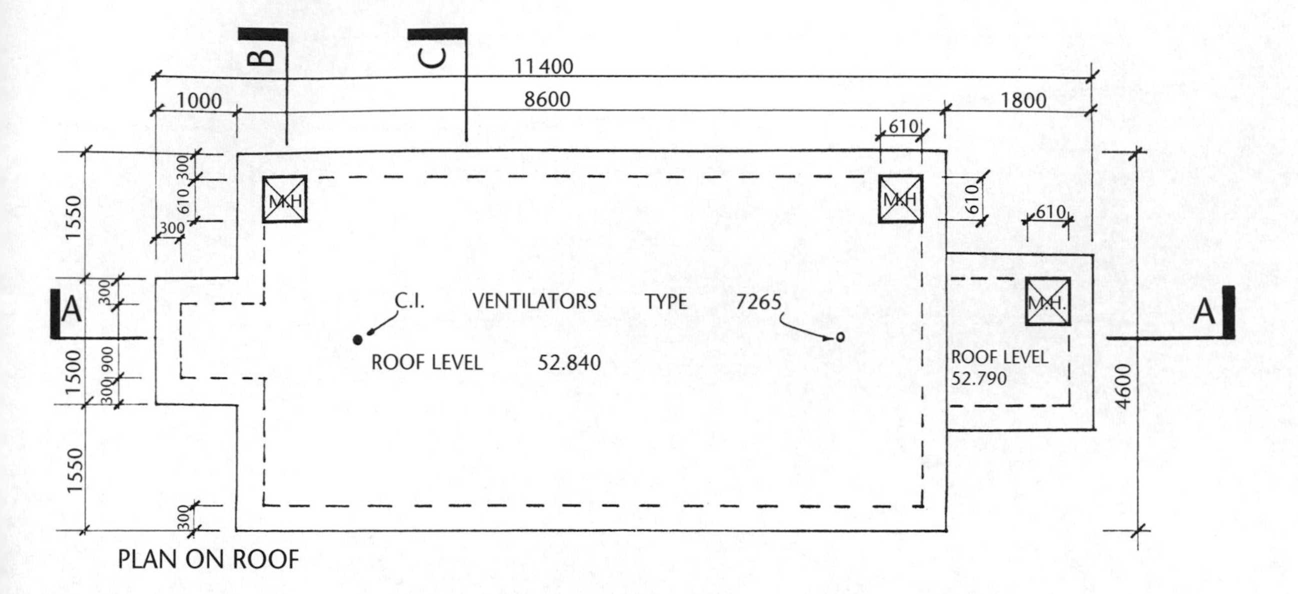

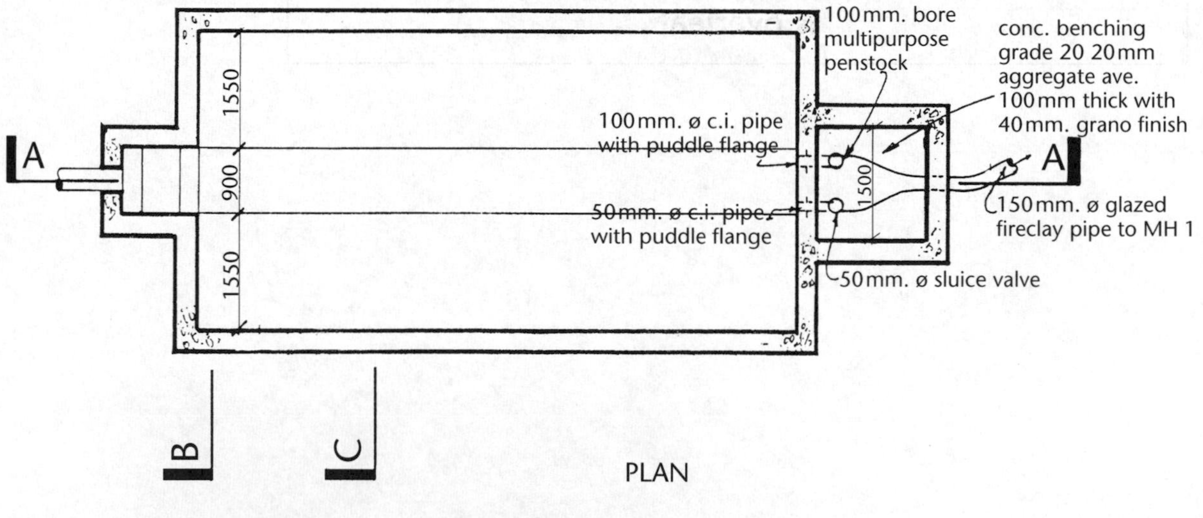

SEWAGE HOLDING TANK

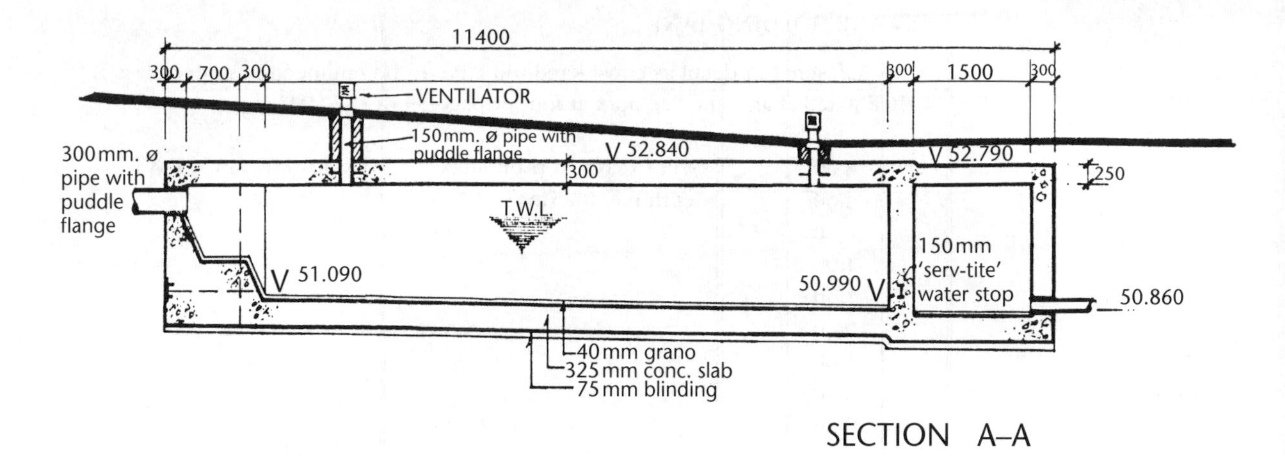

SECTION A–A

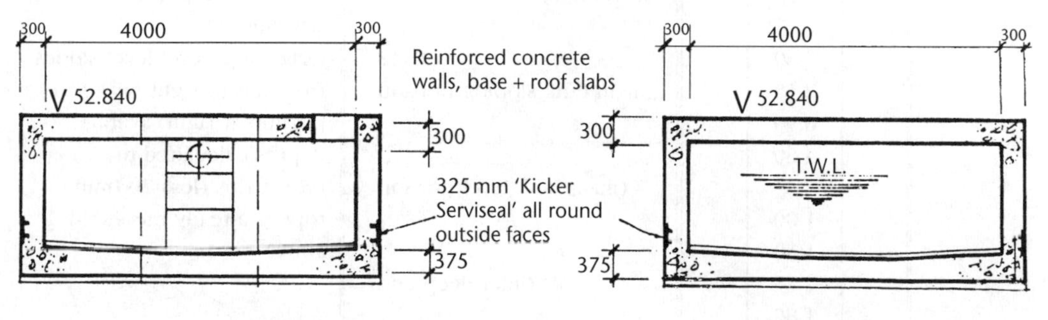

SECTION B–B

SECTION C–C

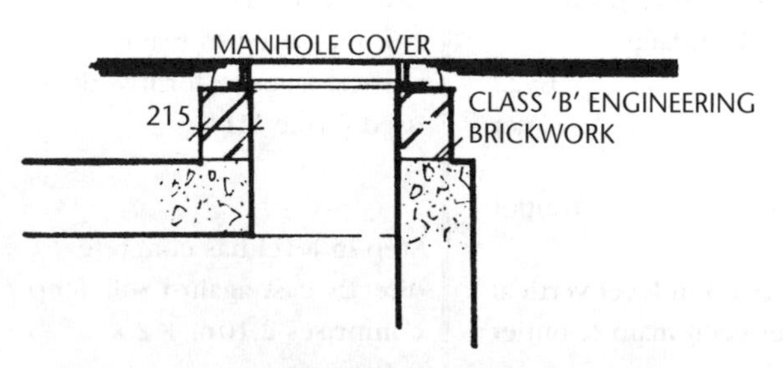

TYPICAL MANHOLE COVER DETAIL

SEWAGE HOLDING TANK

Note: Measured in detail as considered too large to be enumerated under Class K: Other stated chambers. See note at foot of page 53 of CESMM3.

Class E: Earthworks

Dimensions	Description	Notes
8.60	Gen. excavn. topsoil, max.	(Rules M1, M6, C1, A4)
4.60	depth n.e. 0.25 m.	
0.20	E411	
1.00		
1.50		
0.20	(inlet	
1.80		
2.10		
0.20	(outlet	
	Gen. excvn. max. depth 2–5 m, comncg. surf. u/s of topsoil. E425	(Rules D1, A4, M6)
	&	
	Excvn ancillaries, disposal of	(Rules M1, D4, D5) Rule D5
7.70	excvtd. mat.	saves long repetitious wording.
4.60	E532	Original ground level slopes
2.55	(main tank sloping portion	from left to right with level
0.90		portion at right, average
4.60		depths calculated to
2.35	(main tank level portion	reflect this (less 200 mm
1.00		topsoil already measured
1.50		above).
2.75	(inlet deep end	
1.80		
2.10		Outlet floor 130 mm
2.48	(outlet level end	deeper than main tank.
2.10		
0.30	(additional depth at	
0.13	junction of two slab levels, main to outlet	
8.60	Excvn. ancillaries prep.	(Rules M11, D5)
4.60	of excavd. surfaces.	Not measured to main
1.00	E522	vertical faces as formwork is
1.50	(inlet	used – rule M11.
1.80		
2.10	(outlet	
2.70		Step in level has concrete
0.13	(step in level vertical (between main & outlet	directly cast against soil. Step comprises 2.10 m + 2 × 0.30 m.

SEWAGE HOLDING TANK (Contd)

Dimensions	Description	Notes
	Filling to structures	(Rules M16, D6, C3)
7.70	E613	Following average depth
4.60	&	principles as in gen. excvn.
0.45	Ddt Disposal of excavtd. mat.	and allowing for return of
0.90	E532	topsoil.
4.60		
0.10	(main tank level portion	
1.00		
1.50		
0.60	(inlet	
1.80		
2.10		
0.15	(outlet	
8.60	Filling depth 200 mm excvtd.	(Rules M16, D8, C3)
4.60	topsoil.	Stated depths filling items are
1.00	E641	measured in m^2.
1.50		
1.80		
2.10		
8.60	Landscaping, hydraulic	(Rule C4) i.e. rules M22 &
4.60	mulch seeding.	M23 deemed included.
1.00	E820	(Rule A18 – in this case slope
1.50		less than 10 degrees.)
1.80		
2.10		

Class F: In situ Concrete

Dimensions	Description	Notes
	Provsn. of conc. designed	(Rules M1 & M2)
	mix grade C7.5, ct. to BS	Provision and placing of
	12, 20 mm agg.	concrete are measured
		separately as per
8.60	F213	Class F. In this example the
4.60	&	provision and placing are
0.08		billed at the same time to
1.00	Placg. of conc. mass,	avoid repeating dimensions.
1.50	blinding, thickness n.e.	This is the opposite approach
0.08	150 mm. F511	to that used in Worked
		Example 5.
1.80		(Rule D6)
2.10		
0.08		
2.10	(step in levels	
0.08		
0.08		

SEWAGE HOLDING TANK (Contd)

Timesing	Dimensions	Squaring	Description	Side notes
			Provsn. of conc. designed mix grade C25, ct to BS 12, 20 mm agg.	(Rules M1 & M2)
	8.60		F253	Average thickness of base
	4.60		&	calculated as 6(2 × 375 + 4
	0.34			× 325) = 341.
	1.00		Placg. of conc. reinforced,	
	1.50		bases, thickness	
	0.33		300–500 mm.	
	1.80		F623	
	2.10			
	0.33		(thicknessing at inlet	
	0.90			
	0.85			
	0.50			Thicknessing treated in similar manner to integral beams rule M4.
			Provsn. of conc. designed mix grade C25, ct to BS 12, 20 mm agg.	(Rules M1 & M2) Girth of main tank walls: 2 × 8.60 = 17.20
	27.20		F253	2 × 4.00 = 8.00
	1.51		&	2 × 1.00 = 2.00
	0.30			Total 27.20
	5.10		Placg. of conc. reinforced,	Girth of outlet tank walls:
	1.68		walls, thickness 150–300 mm.	2 × 1.80 = 3.60
	0.30		F642	1.50
	2.10			5.10
	0.13		(extra ht. at step at outlet	
	0.30			
½/	0.90		(thicknessing at inlet	Thicknessing treated in
	0.60			similar manner to integral
	0.15			piers rule M3.
			Provsn. of conc. designed mix grade C25, ct to BS 12, 20 mm agg.	(Rules M1 & M2)
	8.60		F253	Rule M1 manholes not
	4.60		&	deducted as large voids per
	0.30			rule D3 of Class G.
	1.00		Placg. of conc. reinforced,	
	1.50		susp. slab, thickness	
	0.30		150–300 mm.	
	1.80		F632	
	2.10			
	0.25			

6.3

SEWAGE HOLDING TANK (Contd)

Class G: Concrete Ancillaries

Timesing	Dimensions	Description	Notes
		Fwk. fair fin.	
		Sloping, width 0.4–1.22 m.	(Rules M1, M2, D1, D2)
	0.90	G224	
	0.70	(inlet sloping detail	
	0.90		
	0.50		
		Vert. width n.e. 0.1 m.	Note this width is measured
		G241	in linear metres.
	2.10	(step between 300 and 250 roof slab	
		Vert. width 0.4–1.22 m.	(Rule M6 – no ded. for insert
	0.90	G243	pipe.)
	0.40	(inlet back	
		Vert. width 0.4–1.22 m.	
2/	1.00	G244	
	1.00	(inlet internal sides average	
2/	1.00		
	2.10	(inlet external sides	
		Vertical	(Rule D2) Width deemed to
	4.60	G245	exceed 1.22 m.
	2.10	(external faces) (inlet end	
2/	8.60		
	2.15	(sides average depth	
2/	1.25		
	2.20	(main tank outlet end	
2/	1.80		
	2.28	(outlet tank sides	Ht. net 80 mm deeper due to
	2.10		step in levels of base and roof.
	2.28	(outlet tank end	
2/	1.55	(internal faces)	
	1.48	(main tank inlet end	
2/	8.00		
	1.48	(main tank sides av. depth	
	4.00		
	1.53	(main tank outlet end	
4/	1.50		
	1.71	(outlet tank	Ht. net 80 mm deeper as above.
		For large voids, depth	(Rule D3) Depth is in effect
	3	n.e. 0.5 m. G275	the slab thickness.
		(manholes	Area = $0.61 \times 0.61 = 0.372\,m^2$.

SEWAGE HOLDING TANK (Contd)

Timesing	Dimensions	Squaring	Description	Notes
			Fwk. fair fin., removed via manholes	(Rule A1) Formwork left in; in this case just difficult to strike and remove; paragraph 5.10.
			Horizontal, width 0.4–1.22 m.	(Rules M1, D1, D2)
	0.90		G214	
	1.00		(inlet soffit	
			Horizontal.	(Rules M1, M2, D1, D2, M6)
	8.00		G215	Manholes not deductible.
	4.00		(main tank soffit	
	1.50			
	1.50		(outlet soffit	
			Reinforcement	
			Measurement of bar and fabric reinforcement would be inserted here. Details omitted from plans for clarity but work would follow the same principles demonstrated in Worked Example 5.	
			Joints	
			Joints, plastic waterstop 150 mm 'Servtite'.	(Rules A11, C4, M11)
			G651	
	2.10		(main/outlet	
			Joints, plastic waterstop 325 mm 'Kicker Serviseal'.	Actual dimensions given – rule A11.
			G654	
2/	11.40		(all outer faces	
2/	4.60			
			Concrete Accessories	
			Finishg. of top surfs., wood float.	Smooth finish on top to obtain similar finish to fair finish formwork.
	8.60		G811	
	4.60			
	1.00			(Rules M13, M15)
	1.50			
	1.50			
	2.10			
			Finishg. of top surfs., granolithic finish 40 mm thick.	(Rules C6, A13)
	8.00			
	4.00			
	1.50		G814	
	1.50		(outlet tank	
	0.90			
	0.50		(level part of inlet	

6.5

SEWAGE HOLDING TANK (Contd)

Timesing	Dimension	Squaring	Description	Side notes
			Conc. Acc. cont.	
			Finishg. of formed surfs., granolithic finish 40 mm thick to slopes.	Unusual situation where fwk. and subsequent grano finish required. '9' code represents a non-standard item. Quantities from fwk. item G224.
	0.90			
	0.70		G829	
	0.90			
	0.50		(inlet slopes	
			Inserts, other inserts, projecting from one surf. of conc.	(Rules D11, C7, A14, A15)
	1		50 mm bore cast iron pipe with puddle flange, 400 mm long. G832.1 (main/outlet	Decimal point in coding to allow further items within same category.
	1		100 mm bore cast iron pipe with puddle flange, 400 mm long. G832.2 (main/outlet	
	2		150 mm bore cast iron pipe with puddle flange, 400 mm long. G832.3 (ventilators	
	1		300 mm bore cast iron pipe with puddle flange, 400 mm long. G832.4 (inlet	
	1		150 mm bore plain cast iron pipe, 450 mm long. G832.5 (outlet	

6.6

SEWAGE HOLDING TANK (Contd)

Class J: Pipework – Fittings and Valves

Quantity	Description	Notes
	Cast iron fittings and valves as specified	
1	100 mm penstock. G881 (outlet	
1	50 mm sluice valve. G891.1	Sluice valves not listed in CESMM thus code '9' used.
2	150 mm ventilators type 7265, complete with 150 mm plain cast pipe connections av. 400 mm long, and half bk. thick class B eng. bwk. protection eyes to ground level. G891.2	Non-standard fitting with which it is sensible to include the short lengths of connecting pipe rather than introducing Class I for small quantity.

Class K: Pipework – Manholes

Quantity	Description	Notes
3	Manholes, brick – class B eng. bwk. between conc. tank slabs and grd. level, av. 400 mm deep, with c.i. cover, as detail drawing. K111	

6.7

WORKED EXAMPLE 7

Pumphouse

Cross-references

Explanatory Chapters

This worked example includes material which is explained in Chapter 5 CESMM3 – Class E: Earthwork; Chapter 6 CESMM3 – Classes F: *In Situ* Concrete, G: Concrete Ancillaries and H: Precast Concrete; Chapter 11 CESMM3 – Classes U: Brickwork, Blockwork and Masonry, V: Painting and W: Waterproofing; part of Chapter 12 CESMM3 – Class Z: Simple Building Works incidental to Civil Engineering Works; and a single item from Chapter 8 CESMM3 – Class N: Miscellaneous Metalwork.

These sections of CESMM3 cover excavations and excavation ancillaries; provision and placement of *in situ* concrete, formwork, reinforcement and concrete accessories, simple precast concrete; and the many basic building items comprising the traditional construction of the basement and superstructure of the pumphouse.

Related Worked Examples

WE3 Mass Concrete Retaining Wall (non-reinforced *in situ* concrete)
WE5 Pumping Chamber (excavations and a straightforward example of reinforced *in situ* concrete)
WE6 Sewage Holding Tank (excavations and a more complex shaped example of reinforced *in situ* concrete)
WE8 Stone Faced Sea Wall (excavations affected by tidal water and *in situ* mass concrete wall part stone faced)
WE14 Quay with Concrete and Timber Piles (concrete pile caps and suspended quay slab)
WE16 Navigation Lamp Platform (simple reinforced concrete pile cap)

Introduction

Worked Example 7 covers the measurement of a pumphouse comprising a basement and superstructure constructed traditionally of concrete foundation slab, ground floor slab and roof with structural brick walls. There are many ancillary items covering joinery, roof waterproofing, painting and the like, resulting in numerous items from many classes of CESMM3.

Within Class E: Earthworks, the pumphouse construction provides an example of vertical preparation of excavated surfaces being required because of the brick walling being built directly against the vertical face of the excavation. Vertical preparation is a fairly rare occurrence – see Chapter 5 for a full discussion on where trimming and preparation of excavated surfaces should be measured.

DRAWING WE7: PUMPHOUSE
is overleaf

PUMPHOUSE

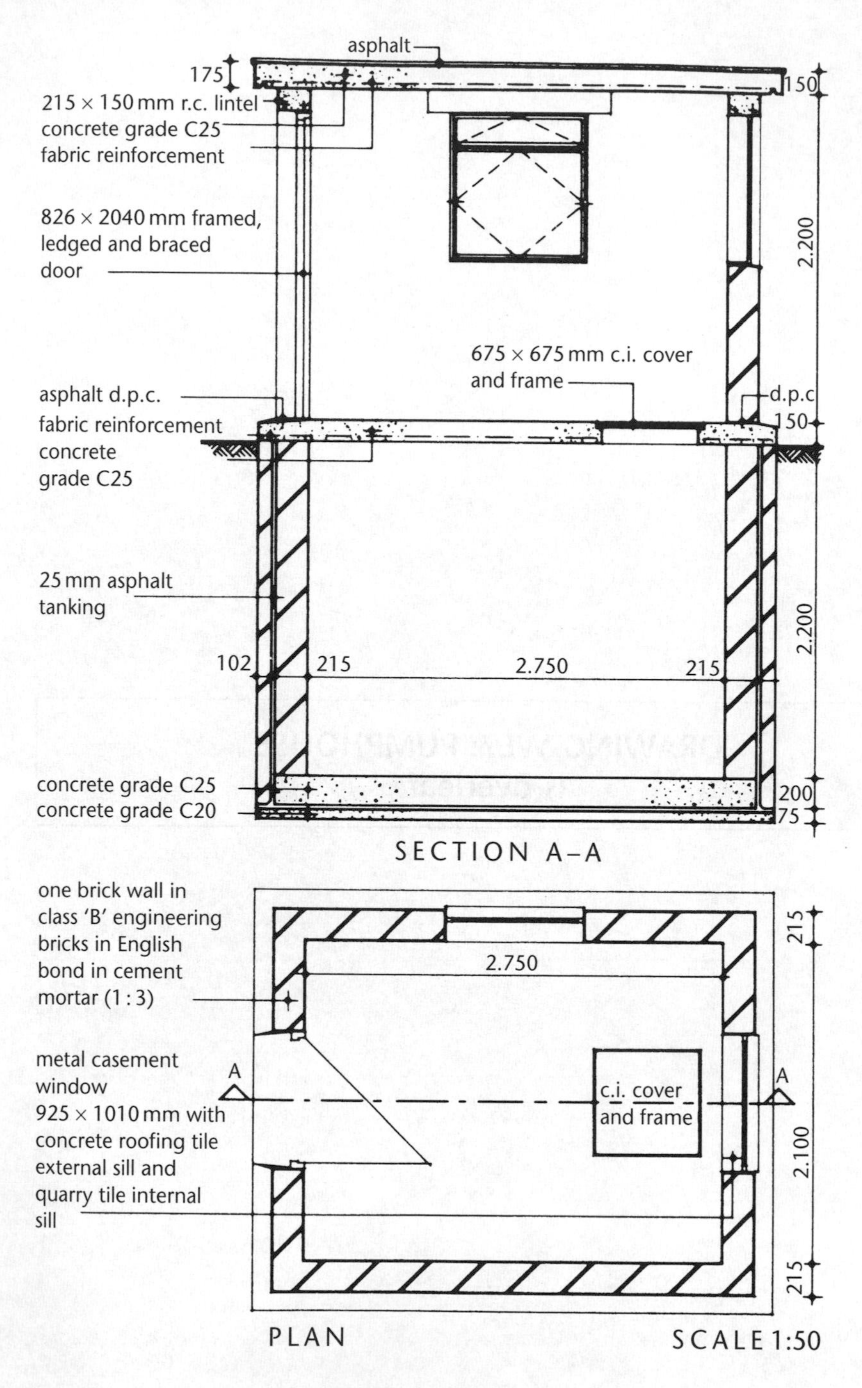

asphalt
175
215 × 150 mm r.c. lintel
concrete grade C25
fabric reinforcement
826 × 2040 mm framed, ledged and braced door
675 × 675 mm c.i. cover and frame
asphalt d.p.c.
fabric reinforcement
concrete grade C25
d.p.c
150
2.200
150
25 mm asphalt tanking
102
215
2.750
215
2.200
concrete grade C25
concrete grade C20
200
75
SECTION A–A
one brick wall in class 'B' engineering bricks in English bond in cement mortar (1 : 3)
metal casement window 925 × 1010 mm with concrete roofing tile external sill and quarry tile internal sill
A
A
2.750
c.i. cover and frame
215
2.100
215
PLAN
SCALE 1:50

PUMPHOUSE

Timesing	Dimensions	Description	Notes
		Pumpwell	
		Earthworks	Buildings of this type are often encountered on civil engineering contracts, where the bulk of the work is civil engineering.
		len. width	
		add 2.750 2.100	
		inner walls 2/215 430 430	
		asp. 2/25 50 50	
		outer walls 2/102 204 204	Under CESMM3 the work is measured in accordance with Class Z, which sets out the rules for the measurement of carpentry, joinery, finishes and services, while the other components are measured in accordance with the rules prescribed in the appropriate sections, such as earthworks, concrete, brickwork, pipework, painting and waterproofing work.
		3.434 2.784	
		depth	
		2.200	
		conc.slab 200	
		asp. 25	
		blindg.conc. 75	
		2.500	
	3.43 2.78 2.50	Gen.excavn., max. depth: 2–5 m E425 & Disposal of excavtd. mat. E532	
	3.43 2.78	Prepn. of excvtd. surfs. E522.1	Preparation of excavated surface to receive concrete blinding.
2/ 2/	3.43 2.50 2.78 2.50	Prepn. of excvtd. surfs. vertical. E522.2	(Rules D5, M11, A8) Preparation also required to vertical faces owing to brickwork being built directly against excavated surface.
		In situ concrete	The provision of in situ concrete is separated from the placing and measured in m^3 with the particulars normally extracted from BS 5328.
	3.43 2.78 0.08	Provsn. of conc., designed mix grade C20, ct to BS 12, 20 mm agg. to BS 882; min. ct. content 210 kg/m^3. (blindg. F213 & Placing of conc., mass blindg. thickness: n.e. 150 mm. F511	Placing of blinding concrete is measured in m^3; giving the appropriate thickness range. Formwork is not measured to the edges of the blinding concrete as they do not exceed 0.2 m in width (rule M2a of Class G).

7.1

PUMPHOUSE (Contd)

Dimensions	Description	Notes
	waterproofg.	
3.43 2.78	Tankg. of asp. to upper surfs. inclined at an L n.e. 30° to hor; mastic asp. to BS 6577 in 2 coatgs: thickness: 25 mm. W211	The item description shall state the materials used and the number and thickness of coatings or layers (rule A1 of Class W). Separate items are not required for angle fillets and the like (rule C1).
	In situ concrete len. width 2.750 2.100 add walls 2/215 430 430 3.180 2.530	
3.18 2.53 0.20	Provsn. of conc., designed mix grade C25, ct. to BS 12, 20 mm agg. to BS 882; min. ct. content 280 kg/m³. (base F233 & Placg. of conc. mass bases & grd. slabs; thickness: 150–300 mm. F522	Follow with the in situ concrete base slab, comprising separate provision and placing items. Select the appropriate work classification from the Second Division and the thickness range from the Third Division.
	Conc. accessories	
3.18 2.53	Finshg. of top surf., steel trowel. G812	Finishing to top surface of the base slab to a smooth finish is measured in m² stating the method to be used. It is considered unnecessary to deduct the area of finishing under the walls.
	Brickwork girth 2.750 2.100 2/4.850 9.700 add corners 4/215 860 10.560	Note the method of obtaining the length of wall measured on its centre line.
	Eng. bwk. Class B to BS 3921 in Eng. bond in c.m. (1:3).	
10.56 2.20	Vert. st. wall, nom. thickness: 215 mm, in basement wall to pumpg. chbr. U321.1	Some additional descriptive information has been given as provided for in CESMM3 5.13.
9.70 2.20	Fair facg. U378	Internal fair face is measured to the surface in m².

7.2

PUMPHOUSE (Contd)

Timesing	Dimensions	Squaring	Description	Notes
			Waterproofg. ht. 2.200 200 2.400 len. 10.560 add walls 4/215 860 asp. 4/25 100 11.520	Note build up of dimensions of asphalt in waste, starting with the girth previously calculated for the 215 mm brick wall on its centre line.
	11.52 2.40		Tankg; of asp. to surfs. inclined at an L ex. 60° to hor; mastic asp. to BS 6577 in 3 coatgs. thickness: 25 mm. W213	It is necessary to give both the thickness and the number of coatings of asphalt tanking, which can vary between horizontal and vertical coatings (see rule A1 of Class W). The ranges of angles of inclination of the waterproofed surfaces are listed in the Third Division of Class W.
			Brickwork 12.436 less 4/102 408 12.028	
			Eng. bwk. class B. to BS 3921 in stretcher bond in c.m. (1:3)	
	12.03 2.40		Vert. st. wall, nom. thickness: 102.5 mm, in protective wall to asphalt tanking. U311	Brickwork items shall include the types and nominal dimensions of bricks or refer to the appropriate British Standards (rule A1 of Class U).
			Superstructure Floor In situ conc.	
	3.43 2.78 0.15		Provsn. of conc. designed mix grade C25, ct. to BS 12, 20 mm agg. to BS 882; min. ct. content 240 kg/m³. F233 & Placg. of conc. reinfd. susp. slab; thickness n.e. 150 mm. F631	The leading dimensions are the same as for the blinding concrete at the base of the pumping chamber. The placing item description must include 'reinforced'. No deduction is made for the area (0.46 m²) occupied by the cast iron cover as it does not exceed the upper limit of a large void as prescribed in rule D3 of Class G and provided for in rule M1e of Class F.

7.3

PUMPHOUSE (Contd)

Times	Dim.	Qty	Description	Side notes
			Conc. ancillaries Fwk. fair fin.	
	2.75 2.10		Hor. (u/s of flr. slab G215 3.434 2.784 ^{2}/6.218 12.436	Formwork is deemed to be to plane areas and to exceed 1.22 m wide, unless otherwise stated (rule D2 of Class G). The wall surfaces are excluded.
 4/	12.44 0.68		Vert. width 0.1–0.2 m. (edges of slab (edges to cover opg. G242	Linear items as not exceeding 0.2 m wide.
			Conc. accessories	It is not considered necessary to distinguish between the main horizontal surface and the sloping surfaces and the periphery. No deduction is made for the opening as the area does not exceed 0.5 m² (rule M15 of Class G).
	3.43 2.78		Finishg. of top surfs, steel trowel. G812	
			Reinft. less 3.434 2.784 cover ^{2}/20 40 40 3.394 2.744	20 mm cover has been allowed to the fabric reinforcement at the edges of the slab, but excluding the opening for which no deduction of reinforcement is made.
	3.39 2.74		Fabric high yield stl., to BS 4483, nom. mass 2–3 kg/m², ref. A142 G562	Item descriptions for high yield steel fabric to BS 4483 shall state the fabric reference (rule A9 of Class G).
			C.i. cover & fr.	No directions for measurement given in Class N of CESMM3, so enumerated with a suitable description, including reference to the appropriate British Standard and coded as CESMM paragraph 4.5.
	1		Cover & fr., c.i. to BS 497, ref. MCIR 60/60, set in. conc. flr. slab. N999	

PUMPHOUSE (Contd)

Timesing	Dimensions	Squaring	Description
			Bwk.
			Eng. bwk. class B to BS 3921 in Eng. bond in c.m. (1:3)
	10.56 2.20		Vert. st. wall, nom. thickness: 215 mm to superstructure of pumphse U321.2
2/	10.56 2.20		Fair fcg. U378
	10.56		Dpc, hor., width: 215 mm of asp. to BS 6577, 25 mm th. in 2 layers. U382

Girth of wall on its centre line calculated previously for 215mm wall to pump well.

The location of the work is included in the description to indicate that it is above ground in accordance with 5.13. Adjustment of brickwork for the door and windows will be made when measuring these components.

Fair facing is measured to both faces of the wall, with the centre line girth forming the mean of the inside and outside measurements. It appears to be the intention of CESMM3 to measure fair facing to brickwork, which consists of the pointing and careful handling of the bricks, as rule C1 of Class U states that items for masonry shall be deemed to include fair facing, inferring that brickwork items do not. It would however seem more logical to describe the brick wall as built fair and pointed both sides.

Damp-proof courses are measured as linear items irrespective of their width and the description is to include the material and the dimensions. The plane has been added under rule 5.13.

PUMPHOUSE (Contd)

Dimensions	Description	Notes
	Roof	
	In situ conc.	
	2.750 2.100	The sub headings act as sign-posts and help others to find their way through the dimensions.
	add	
	walls 2/215 430 430	
	o'hg. 2/150 300 300	
	3.480 2.830	
3.48 2.83 0.16	Provsn. of conc. designed mix grade C25, ct. to BS 12, 20 mm agg. to BS 882; min. ct. content 240 kg/m³. F233	The concrete is separated into the two items of provision and placing. In determining the thickness range for placing the concrete, the varying thickness of 150 to 175 mm has to be taken into account.
	&	
	Placg. of conc., reinfd. susp. slab; thickness: 150–300 mm. F632	
	Conc. ancillaries Fwk. fair fin.	Unbroken area between walls of pumphouse finished to a smooth surface to give a satisfactory appearance.
2.75 2.10	Hor. (u/s of rf. slab G215	
	3.480 2.830 2/6.310 12.620	
12.62	Vert. width 0.1–0.2 m. (edges of slab G242	Linear item as not exceeding 0.2 m wide, but distinguishing between those in horizontal and vertical planes. Forming the grooves on the soffit is not measured (rule M2b of Class G).
	&	
	Hor., width 0.1–0.2 m. (eaves soff. G212	
	Conc. accessories	
3.48 2.83	Finishg. of top surf., stl. trowel. G812	Measured in m² stating the method to be used. It is not necessary to state that the surface is sloping.
	Conc. ancillaries Reinft.	Note insertion of basic calculations in waste as these form an important part of the taking off procedure. The letters 'abd' (as before described) eliminate the need for the repetition of full descriptions.
	less 3.480 2.830	
	cover 2/20 40 40	
	3.440 2.790	
3.44 2.79	Fabric high yield stl. a.b.d. G562	

PUMPHOUSE (Contd)

Dim.	Description	Notes
3.48 2.83	Roofg. asp. upper surfs. inclined at an ∠ n.e. 30° to the hor.; mastic asp. to BS 6577 in 2 coatgs., thickness: 25 mm. W311	The item description shall state the materials used and the number and thickness of coatings or layers (rule A1 of Class W). This item is deemed to include preparing surfaces, forming joints, overlaps, mitres, angles, fillets, built-up edges and laying to falls or cambers (rule C1 of Class W). Where protective base layers are required, these are measured separately as W4**.
	Door	
1	Dr., wrot. swd., frd., ledged & braced, 826 × 2040 × 50 mm th., as specfn. clause -. Z313	The description shall include the size of the door (rule A8 of Class Z).
2	Hinges, pressed stl. tee, 300 mm lg. Z341	Doors and ironmongery items are deemed to include fixing (rule C2 of Class Z), and materials shall be stated in item descriptions for ironmongery (rule A9 of Class Z). Alternatively, doors and their associated frames and ironmongery can be combined in single comprehensive items (footnote on page 103 of CESMM3).
1	Latch, cylinder rim night, Yale 77. Z343	
	add 826 fr. less reb. 2/62 124 950 add 2.040 fr. less reb. 62 2.102	Build up of overall dimensions of door frame in waste.
1	Dr. fr., wrot. swd., 112 × 75 mm, reb. × 2102 × 950 mm ov'll. Z314	The door frame is enumerated giving the sizes (rule A8 of Class Z). Alternatively, the item description could refer to a drawing.

PUMPHOUSE (Contd)

Timesing	Dimensions	Description	Notes
		Paintg.	Painting is measured in accordance with Class V. Painting to door surfaces with three coats of oil paint and including preparation work of knotting, priming and stopping (rules A1 and A2 of Class V). No distinction is made in CESMM3 between painting internal and external surfaces. The timesing factor of $1\frac{1}{9}$ makes allowance for the painting of edges to frames, ledges and braces of the door.
$2/1\frac{1}{9}/$	0.83 2.04	Kps & ③ oil paint on tbr. surfs. inclined at an ∠ ex. 60° to the hor. (dr. surfs. V323	
		826 2/2.040 4.080 add angles 2/75 150 5.056	Build up of length on centre line of door frame to be painted in waste.
	5.06	Kps & ③ oil paint on tbr. surfs., width n.e. 300 mm. (dr. fr. V326	
		Wdws.	Metal windows are enumerated giving the size. The items are deemed to include fixing, supply of fixing components and drilling and cutting of associated work (rule C2 of Class Z).
2/	1	Wdw., st., hot dip galvsd., size 925 × 1010 mm to BS 6510, as specfn. clause –. Z321	
2/	0.90 0.20	Glazg., stand. plain glass, clear float, nom. thickness: 3 mm, to BS 952, to stl. wdws. fxd. w. met. putty & stl. clips. Z351	Glazing item descriptions shall state the materials, their nominal thickness and method of glazing and securing the glass (rule A10 of Class Z).
2/	0.90 0.75		
		Paintg.	The painting to the metal windows is taken as metal sections in m², although it is not clear from CESMM3 as to whether this is the intended approach. Additional information is given in accordance with 5.13. No distinction is made between internal and external painting.
2/2/	0.93 1.01	Prime & ③ oil paint to met. sectns. of wdws. (mesd. pane area on b.s.). V370	

7.8

PUMPHOUSE (Contd)

Timesing	Dimension	Description	Side notes
		Adjustment of dr. & wdw. opgs.	The brickwork and fair facing is deducted for the areas occupied by the door, windows and lintels, as they each exceed 0.25 m² in area (rule M2 of Class U). The abbreviated 'ddt.' is used frequently for deduct, along with many other standard abbreviations listed in Appendix 1. The location of each item is shown clearly in waste.
		dr. wdws.	
		add lintel 950 925	
		beargs. 2/100 200 200	
		1.150 1.125	
	0.95 2.10	Ddt. vert. st. wall, nom. thickness: 215 mm in (dr. & fr. eng. bwk.a.b. U321.2	
2/	0.93 1.01	(wdws.	
	1.15 0.15	(lintel to dr.	
2/	1.13 0.15	(lintels to wdws.	
2/	0.95 2.10	Ddt. fair facg. (dr. & fr. U378	The same areas, twice timesed, are deducted for fair facing, to cover both internal and external faces.
2/2/	0.93 1.01	(wdws.	
2/	1.15 0.15	(lintel to dr.	
2/2/	1.13 0.15	(lintels to wdws.	
		Precast r.c. lintels to mix grade C25/20 mm agg. reinfd. w. 2 nr. 12 mm m.s. bars.	The lintels have been measured in accordance with the rules in Class H for precast concrete beams, as being the most appropriate item, and giving the specification of the concrete as rule A1 and the principal dimensions as rule A4 of Class H. Precast items are deemed to include reinforcement, formwork, joints and finishes (rule C1 of Class H).
	1	Lintel, 150 × 215 × 1150 mm lg. mass: n.e. 250 kg. H111.1	
	1	Lintel, 150 × 215 × 1125 mm lg.; mass; n.e. 250 kg. H111.2	

PUMPHOUSE (Contd)

Timesing	Dimensions	Squaring	Description	Side notes
2/	2.10 0.10		Fair facg. (dr. reveals	Fair face is measured to door and window reveals in m². The windows have reveals finished fair face both internally and externally, and hence the additional timesing factor of two.
2/2/2/	1.01 0.10		(wdw. reveals U378	
			Surf. finishes	
2/	0.93		Wdw. sill, ext.; 2 cos. of conc. rfg. tiles, 25 mm total thickness; width: 110 mm. Z425.1 & Ditto., int., clay quarry tiles, 18 mm th.; width: 150 mm. Z425.2	The tile sills are measured by length as they do not exceed 300 mm wide, and the item descriptions shall include the material, surface finish where appropriate, and finished thickness (rule A17 of Class Z).
			Drainage to structures above grd. PVCu as spec. clause X34	
	2.83		Gutters 125 mm diam. X331	Assume that gutters and downpipes are required (not shown on dwg.). (Rules D3, C3, A5)
	3		Fittings to gutters 125 mm diam. X332	2 × stop ends + 1 × outlet.
	2.40		Downpipes 75 mm diam. X333	
	2		Fittings to downpipes 75 mm diam. X334	1 × swan neck + 1 × shoe.

WORKED EXAMPLE 8

Stone Faced Sea Wall

Cross-references

Explanatory Chapters

This worked example is primarily concerned with work affected by water and illustrates the requirements of paragraph 5.20 of CESMM3. Refer to Chapter 2 for a detailed discussion on compliance with paragraph 5.20 and the associated paragraphs 5.8 and 5.10.

With regard to the detailed work classifications, these include material which is explained in Chapter 5 CESMM3 – Class E: Earthwork; part of Chapter 6 CESMM3 – Classes F: *In Situ* Concrete and G: Concrete Ancillaries; part of Chapter 9 CESMM3 – Class P: Piling; and a small sample of work from Chapter 10 CESMM3 – Class R: Roads and Pavings. These sections of CESMM3 cover excavations and excavation ancillaries; provision and placement of *in situ* concrete, formwork and concrete accessories; steel sheet piling and light duty pavement.

Related Worked Examples

- WE2 Excavation and Filling (playing field levelling)
- WE3 Mass Concrete Retaining Wall (non-reinforced *in situ* concrete)
- WE5 Pumping Chamber (excavations and a straightforward example of reinforced *in situ* concrete)
- WE7 Pumphouse (excavations, simple concrete foundation and reinforced suspended slabs, structural brickwork)
- WE12 Timber Jetty (timber piling)
- WE13 Hybrid Piles (part bored, part driven *in situ* concrete piles)
- WE14 Quay with Concrete and Timber Piles (driven preformed concrete and timber piles)

WE15 Steel Sheet Piling (more advanced steel sheet piling)
WE17 Estate Road (more advanced excavations and paving)

Introduction

Worked Example 8 covers the measurement of a sea wall which will be affected to some extent by tidal water during construction. Therefore each group of items requires to be assessed as to whether it is affected by water or not. For example, the granite wall facing is affected by the tide for 7 out of 8 courses, thus generating separate items. In this respect some bill compilers would split the work up in an even more detailed way by additionally separating the work wholly below low tide from work between tides. In contrast, others might not separate any of the items by relationship to the tides, as they would comply with paragraph 5.20 merely by a note drawing attention to the water and referring to the drawings. The guiding principles which bill compilers should consider when deciding on the amount of detail to provide are covered by paragraphs 5.8 and 5.10 of CESMM3. The amount of detail provided should be consistent with the nature, location, importance, access, sequence or any other special consideration of cost of the proposed works.

DRAWING WE8: STONE FACED SEA WALL
is overleaf

STONE FACED SEA WALL

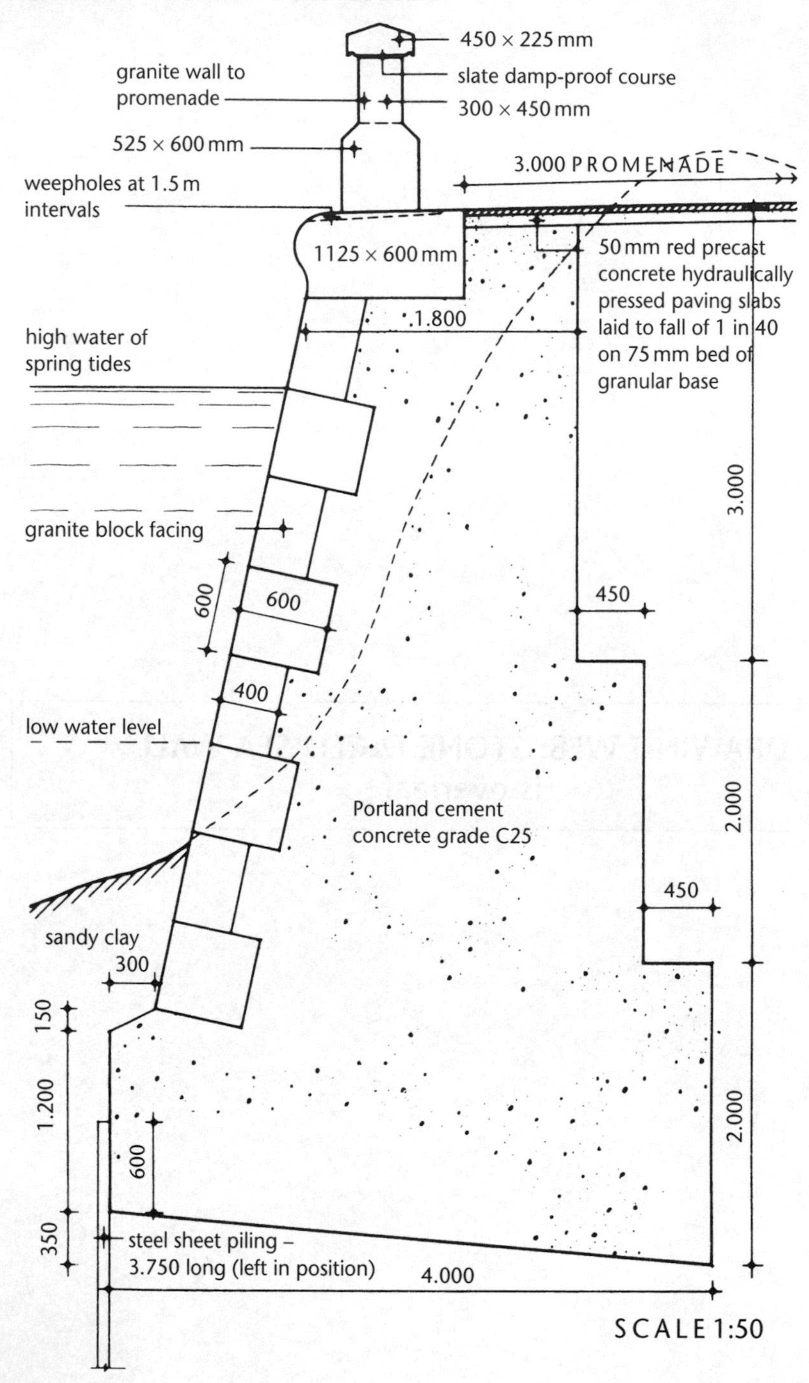

STONE FACED SEA WALL (60 m length)

Note: The dimensions in this example have been squared ready for transfer to the abstract in Chapter 3.

Earthworks

Dimensions	Squared	Description	Waste
			width
		grd. surf.	300
		hwl	1.650
			2 | 1.950
			975
60.00		Gen. excavn., max.	
0.98		depth: 1–2 m. excavated	
1.55	91.1	surf. hwl.	E424
			depth
			1.800
			2.000
			2.000
			5.800
			width
		hwl	2.150
		excvtd. surf.	4.080
			2 | 6.230
			3.115
60.00		Gen. excavn., max.	
3.12		depth: 5–10 m;	
5.80	1085.8	Commg. hwl.	
			E426

Note method of obtaining mean widths by means of waste calculations or side casts. The first section is taken down to the high water level, as excavation below this level could be under water (the depth is scaled). The width of the second section includes the thickness of the steel sheet piling, and the front face of the excavation takes the form of a give and take line. It is necessary to separate work to be carried out below high water level (rules M7 and A2 of Class E). CESMM3 5.20 requires identification of the water levels in the preamble to the Bill of Quantities and on the drawings. Note the use of the terms 'Commencing Surface' and 'Excavated Surface' (CESMM3 5.21). The Commencing Surface shall be identified in the description of the work where it is other than the Original Surface, and the Excavated Surface requires identification if it is not the Final Surface (rule A4 of Class E).

The Contractor will need to cover the cost of all temporary works in General Items or in the billed rates for earthworks, concrete and masonry.

Separate items are not required for upholding sides of excavation, additional excavation to provide working space and removal of dead services (rule Cl of Class E).

STONE FACED SEA WALL (Contd)

		Description		Notes
		Excavn. ancillaries		It is necessary to measure the volume of excavated material which will be removed from the site and the quantity which will be required for filling to the void behind the sea wall.
60.00 0.98 1.55	91.1	Disposal of excavtd. mat.	E532	
60.00 3.12 5.80	1085.8			The volume of disposal of excavated material is the difference between the total net volume of excavation and the net volume of excavated material used for filling (rule M12 of Class E).
		1176.9		
			Fillg. upper sectn. depth 3.000 250 3.250 width 450 450 900	The disposal of excavated material is deemed to be disposal off site unless otherwise stated in item descriptions (rule D4). The excavation quantities are taken as disposal and then adjustments made for the filling of the void. Filling material is deemed to be non-selected excavated material other than topsoil or rock, unless otherwise stated (rule D6). Items for filling are deemed to include compaction (rule C3).
60.00 0.90 3.25	175.5	Ddt. Disposal of excvtd. mat.	(rear upper sectn. E532	
		&		
60.00 0.45 2.00	54.0	add Fillg. to structures	(rear lower sectn. E613	Filling is behind completed wall and not affected by tidal water.
60.00 0.40 1.00	24.0		(frt. face	
		253.5		
60.00 4.00	240.0	Prepn. of excvtd. surfs. below hwl.	E522.1	The preparation of the excavated surface to receive the base of the wall is measured separately (rule M11).

STONE FACED SEA WALL (Contd)

			Filling ancillaries	
	60.00		Prepn. of filled surfs.	
	0.90	54.0		E722
				Piles
			Interlocking steel piles,	
			type 2N, section modulus	
			1150 cm^3/m, grade 43A to	
	60.00		BS 4360	
	3.75	225.0	Driven area.	
				P832
			&	
			Area of piles of len: n.e. 14 m;	
			treated w. 2cts. bit. paint.	
				P833
				In situ concrete
				width
				2.750
				3.170
				2	5.920
	60.00			2.960
	4.00		Provsn. of conc.	(base
	2.00	480.0	designed mix, grade	
			C25, ct. to BS 12, 40 mm	
	60.00		agg. to BS 882.	F224
	2.96			(middle
	2.00	355.2	&	(sectn.
			Placg. of conc. mass walls	
	60.00		thickness: ex. 500 mm; backg.,	
	2.10		to masonry below hwl.	(upper
	1.80	226.8	1062.0	(sectn.
				F544.1
½/	60.00		Ddt. both last	
	4.00			
	0.35	42.0		(tapg. base
	60.00			
	0.35			
	0.35	7.4	49.4	(top of toe,
			1012.6	fair average

(Rules M23, D9)
Preparation measured as pavement is to be laid on filling.

Two items are required for the interlocking steel sheet piling – the driven area and the area classified according to the length categories in the Third Division of Class P. Rule A11 permits treatment to be included in description.

The concrete is subdivided into provision and placing, and the placing is further subdivided into work above and below high water level in accordance with CESMM3 5.10 and the footnote on page 41 of CESMM3, whereby the location of concrete members in the works may be stated in item descriptions for placing of concrete where special characteristics may affect the method and rate of placing concrete. Some may feel that this subdivision of the work is unnecessary, provided the appropriate information with regard to water levels is shown on the drawing and referred to in the preambles to the Bill of Quantities.

The measurements include the volume occupied by the masonry which will need to be adjusted later. A suffix is added to the code reference on account of the additional description items.

It is often easier to measure the total enclosing rectangle and then deduct the voids from it.

STONE FACED SEA WALL (Contd)

Dimensions	Squaring	Description
		width 1.800 1.900 2 | 3.700 1.850
60.00 1.85 0.60	66.6	Provsn. of conc. abd. (upper sectn. F224
		&
60.00 0.75 0.48	21.6	Placg. of conc. abd. above hwl. F544.2
		88.2
		Conc. ancillaries ht. 2.000 2.000 1.800 5.800
60.00 5.80	348.0	Fwk. ro. fin. vert; below hwl. (rear face G145
60.00 0.60	36.0	Fwk. ro. fin. vert. width: 0.4–1.22 m; below hwl. (frt. face above piling G144.1
60.00 0.35	21.0	Fwk. ro. fin. slopg; width: 0.2–0.4 m; below hwl. G123 (frt. face toe

Finally, the concrete above high water level is measured. It is unnecessary to repeat the previous descriptions when by using the expression abd (as before described), it is possible to refer back to the earlier items for the full descriptions.

Note the use of waste for preliminary calculations – recording in this way permits checking of the calculations as well as showing the build-up of dimensions.

A second suffix is added to the reference code for the placing item, because of the varied description.

The volume of the coping stone has been omitted from the dimensions. The concrete items are followed with the supporting formwork.

It is assumed that no formwork will be required to the stone face (the masonry serving as the formwork).

Formwork is deemed to be to plane areas exceeding 1.22 m unless otherwise stated (rule D2).

Formwork to horizontal, sloping, battered and vertical surfaces are each kept separate and widths exceeding 200 mm are measured in m^2.

STONE FACED SEA WALL (Contd)

	Dimensions	Squaring	Description	Notes
			600	
			500	It is considered desirable to state the width range in this case as the width does not exceed 1.22 m, even although it is part of a larger area in the same plane. However, some may feel that this separation is unnecessary.
			1.100	
	60.00		Fwk. ro. fin. vert. width:	
	1.10	66.0	0.4–1.22 m; above hwl.	
			G144.2	
			Masonry	The masonry is measured in m^2 as battered facing to concrete and stating the nominal thickness as rule A1 of Class U.
			Ashlar masonry, granite, flush ptd. w. mortar type M3	
			weighted av. width	
			4/600 2.400	
			3/400 1.200	
			7 ⌊ 3.600	The masonry has been subdivided between that above and below high water level, but the use of these classifications could be regarded as optional.
			514	
	60.00		Battered fcg. to conc;	
	4.20	252.0	nom. 600 & 400 in alt. cos., av. 514 mm, below hwl.	
			U746	Items for masonry are deemed to include fair facing (rule C1).
				The cutting to form the splayed top edge is not measured separately and the Contractor must allow for cutting in the masonry rates.
	60.00		Ditto; thickness; nom.	
	0.70	42.0	400 mm above hwl.	
			U736	
			In situ concrete	
	60.00		Ddt. provsn. of conc. abd. F224	Deduction of concrete (provision and placing) for the volume occupied by the masonry.
	0.51		&	
	4.20	128.5	Ddt. placg. of conc. abd. below hwl. F554.1	
	60.00		Ddt. provsn. of conc. abd. F224	The use of code numbers will assist in identifying the items and quantities from which the deductions are to be made, and permit abbreviated descriptions.
	0.40		&	
	0.60	14.4	Ddt. placg. of conc. abd. above hwl. F544.2	Ashlar only deducted as cope was excluded from volume of item F544.2.

STONE FACED SEA WALL (Contd)

		Description	Notes
		Granite Masonry flush ptd., mortar type M3.	The copings and plinths are measured as linear surface features, stating the cross-sectional dimensions, where the area exceeds 0.05 m^2. Reference to a drawing is usually necessary to provide adequate information for pricing (rules A6 and A7).
60.00	60.0	Copg. 1125 × 600 mm rdd. w. sinkgs. as Dwg. WE8. U771.1	
60.00	60.0	Plinth 525 × 600 mm 2ce splyd. as Dwg. WE8. U777	
60.00 0.45	27.0	Vert. st. wall; thickness: 300 mm, fair faced b.s. U731	The promenade wall is measured in m^2 stating the thickness and including fair face on both sides.
60.00	60.0	Copg. 450 × 225 mm 2ce wethd. & 2ce thro. as Dwg. WE8. U771.2	The coping stones may be connected by cramps and the plinth stones by dowels but these are not measured separately.
60.00	60.0	Dpc; width: 300 mm of 2 cos. of slates, ld. bkg. jt. in mortar type M3. U782	Damp – proof courses are covered in ancillaries and are measured as linear items stating the material and the dimensions (rule A8 of Class U). Additional material in laps is not measured (rule M5).
		Promenade	
60.00 1.30 0.30	23.4	Gen. excavn. max. depth: 0.25–0.5 m. E422 & Disposal of excvtd. mat. E532	Even shallow excavation is measured by volume, stating the depth classification in the Third Division. This is followed by the appropriate disposal item.

8.6

STONE FACED SEA WALL (Contd)

	Dimensions	Quantity	Description	Notes
			Excavn. ancillaries	(Rules M11, D5)
	60.00		Prepn. of excvtd. surfs.	Preparation measured as
	1.30	78.0	above hwl. E522.2	pavement is to be laid on excavation.
			Light duty Pavement	
	60.00		Red precast conc. flags to	The promenade pavement is
	3.00	180.0	BS 7263 type D; thickness 50 mm. R782	measured in accordance with the rules for Class R (Roads and Pavings), which requires
			&	the separation of the concrete flags and the
			Granular base, depth: 75 mm. R713	underlying granular base.

WORKED EXAMPLE 9

Sewer

Cross-references

Explanatory Chapter

This worked example includes material which is explained within Chapter 7 CESMM3 – Classes I–L: Pipework. These sections of CESMM3 cover pipes, fittings and valves, manholes and pipework ancillaries and supports, protection, ancillaries to laying and excavation. The rules are the same as those for measuring all other pipelines such as water mains or district heating pipes.

Related Worked Examples

WE5 Pumping Chamber (example of chamber measured in detail rather than under Class K)
WE6 Sewage Holding Tank (simple brick-built manholes incorporated on top of a large chamber measured in detail)
WE10 Water Main (another type of pipework measured under the same rules)
WE17 Estate Road (surface water drainage in connection with road works)
WE20 Sewer Renovation (specialist remedial works)
WE21 Water Main Renovation (specialist remedial works)

Introduction

Worked Example 9 covers the measurement of a typical sewer installation at a variety of depths and excavated through various surfaces.

It is worth reiterating that the depths stated for trenches are the invert depths of the respective pipes (Class I; rule D3) and for manholes, either the invert or the top of the base whichever is lower (Class K; rule D2). These requirements are most convenient for the taker-off as such depths are normally easy to calculate. Estimators, on the other hand, need to be aware of the additional excavations required below invert level necessary to install pipes and chambers.

DRAWING WE9: SEWER
is overleaf

is overleaf

SEWER

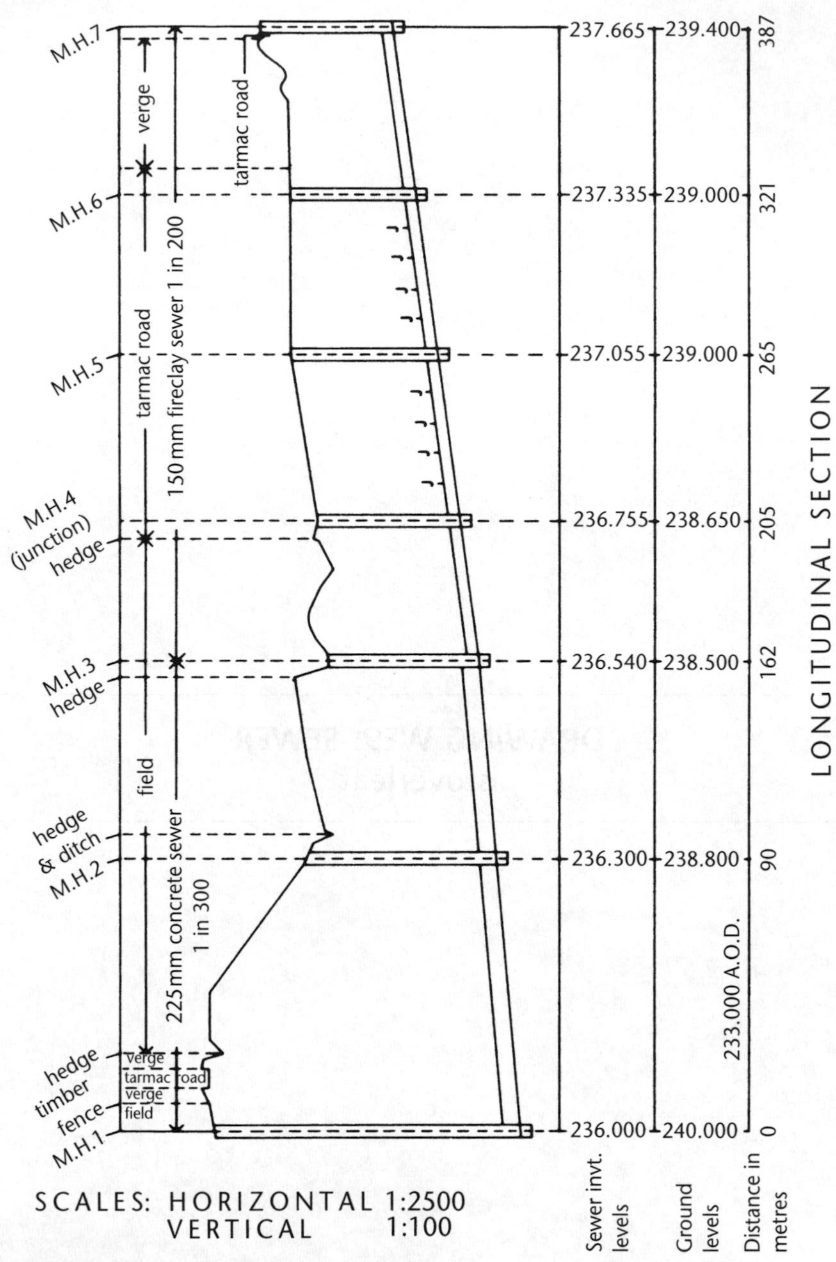

SCALES: HORIZONTAL 1:2500
VERTICAL 1:100

Sewer invt. levels | Ground levels | Distance in metres

SEWER MANHOLE DETAILS

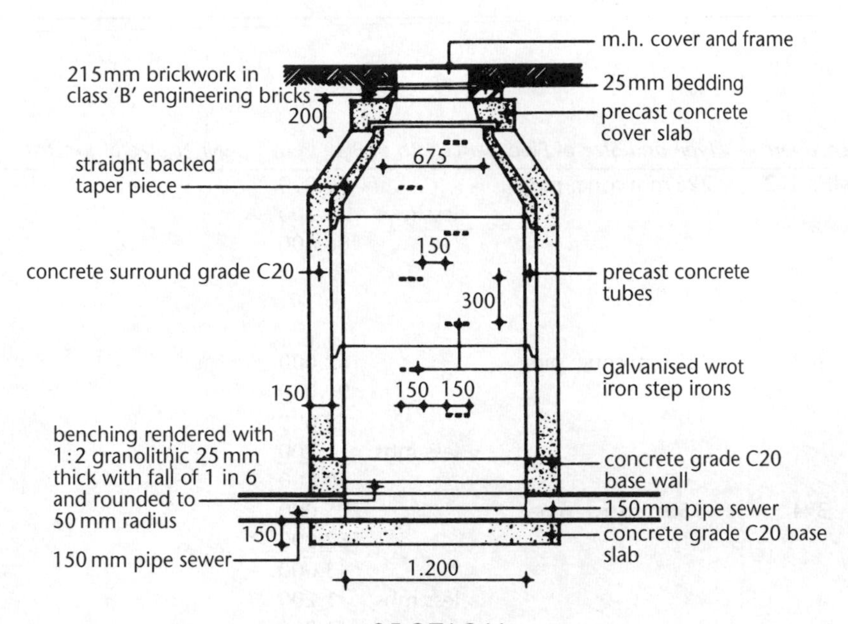

SECTION

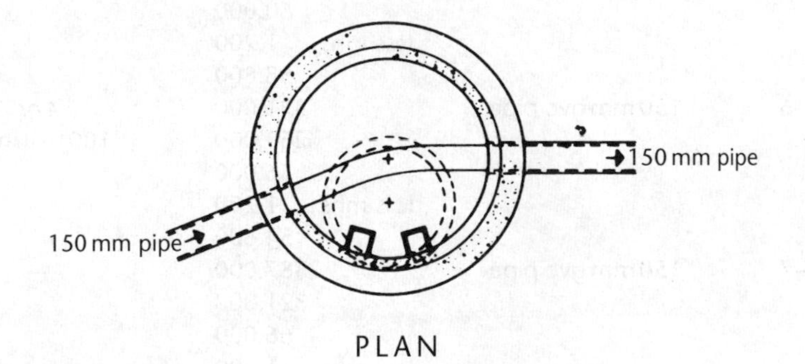

PLAN

SCALE 1 : 50

Sewer Schedule

Location	*Type and Size of Pipe*	*Length of Pipe in m*		*Nr & Size of Junctns.*
MHs 1–2	225 mm conc. pipe		90.000	—
		less mhs	1.200	
			88.800	
2–3	225 mm conc. pipe		162.000	—
			90.000	
			72.000	
		less mhs	1.200	
			70.800	
3–4	150 mm gvc pipe		205.000	—
			162.000	
			43.000	
		less mhs	1.200	
			41.800	
4–5	150 mm gvc pipe		265.000	4 nr
			205.000	100/150 mm
			60.000	
		less mhs	1.200	
			58.800	
5–6	150 mm gvc pipe		321.000	4 nr
			265.000	100/150 mm
			56.000	
		less mhs	1.200	
			54.800	
6–7	150 mm gvc pipe		387.000	—
			321.000	
			66.000	
		less mhs	1.200	
			64.800	

Length of Trench 1.5–2 m (Total Depth)	*Length of Trench 2–2.5 m (Total Depth)*	*Length of Trench 2.5–3 m (Total Depth)*	*Length of Trench 3–3.5 m (Total Depth)*	*Length of Trench 3.5–4 m (Total Depth)*	*Nr of Hedge and Fence Crossings*
—	—	16.300 (field)	14.000 (field)	6.500 (road) 10.000 (verge) 42.000 (field)	1 fence 1 hedge
—	70.800 (field)	—	—	—	2 hedges
35.800 (field) 6.000 (road)	—	—	—	—	1 hedge
58.800 (road)	—	—	—	—	—
54.800 (road)	—	—	—	—	—
13.000 (road) 51.800 (verge)	—	—	—	—	—

Manhole Schedule

Manhole nr	*Ground Level*	*Invert Level*	*Total Depth*	*Depth of 1200 mm Rings*	*Depth of 1200–675 mm Taper*	*Depth of 675 mm Rings*
1	240.000	236.000	4.000	1.500	600	1.000
2	238.800	236.300	2.500	750	600	300
3	238.500	236.540	1.960	600	600	—
4	238.650	236.755	1.895	450	600	—
5	239.000	237.055	1.945	600	600	—
6	239.000	237.335	1.665	300	600	—
7	239.400	237.665	1.735	300	600	—
Totals	—	—	15.700	4.500	7 nr (4.200)	1.300

Depth of 215 mm bwk.	Type of m.h. Cover	Sewer Sizes	Junctions Size & nr	Type of Channel	Nr of Step Irons (all in precast units)	Combined depth of Cover, Cover Slab & Base Wall	Location
150	Medium	2/225	—	225 straight	10	750	field
100	Medium	2/225	—	225 curved	5	750	field
—	Medium	1/225 1/150	—	225–150 straight	4	750	field
95	Heavy	3/150	1/150	150 curved with junctn.	4	750	road
—	Heavy	2/150	—	150 curved	4	750	road
15	Heavy	2/150	—	150 curved	3	750	road
85	Heavy	2/150	—	150 straight	3	750	road
445	3 Med. 4 Heavy	5/225 10/150	1/150	—	33 nr	—	

SEWER

Timesing	Dimensions	Squaring	Description	Notes
			PIPEWORK – PIPES	
			Conc. pipes of Class M to BS 5911 w. s&s flexible jts., nom.bore: 225mm in trenches. Between manholes 1&3	The description of the pipes shall include materials, joint types, nominal bores and lining requirements, with references to British Standards where appropriate (rule A2 of Class I).
	70.80		Depth: 2–2.5m in field. (mhs 2–3 I224.1	The locations of pipe runs shall also be given for identification purposes (rule A1) and differing working conditions resulting in different costs shall also be identified.
	16.30		Depth: 2.5–3m in field. (mhs 1–2 I225.1	Pipes in trenches are subdivided into the total depth ranges entered in the Third Division of Class I.
	14.00		Depth: 3–3.5m in field. (mhs 1–2 I226.1	The pipe items include excavation, preparation of sufaces, disposal of excavated material, upholding sides of excavation, backfilling and removal of dead services (rule C2).
	6.50		Depth: 3.5–4m in road. (mhs 1–2 I227.1	Lengths are measured up to the inside surfaces of manhole walls (rule M5).
	10.00		Depth: 3.5–4m in verge. (mhs 1–2 I227.2	Any concrete or other protection to pipes would be measured under Class L.
	42.00		Depth: 3.5–4m in field. (mhs 1–2 I227.3	The change of pipe material and bore entails a new heading, followed by the appropriate locational reference.
			Clay pipes of normal quality to BS 65 w. s&s flexible jts., nom.bore: 150mm in trenches. Between manholes 3&7	All the necessary particulars can be extracted direct from the sewer schedule.
	35.80		Depth: 1.5–2m in field. (mhs 3–4 I113.1	

9.1

SEWER (Contd)

Quantity	Description	Ref.	Notes
			Continue with the measurement of the pipes and fittings until all have been entered. Double check against the schedule entries and cross out each item as transferred to the dimensions sheets. Similar provisions apply to fitting descriptions as for pipes (rules C1, C2 and Al of Class J).
6.00	Depth: 1.5–2m in road.	(mhs 3–4	
58.80		(mhs 4–5	
54.80		(mhs 5–6	
13.00		(mhs 6–7 I113.2	
51.80	Depth: 1.5–2m in verge.	(mhs 6–7 I113.3	
	PIPEWORK – FITTINGS & VALVES		
	Clay pipe fittings to BS 65 w. s&s flex. jts.		The actual bores of clay pipe fittings should be stated, as prescribed by rule A1 of Class J. Where fittings comprise pipes of different nominal bores, they shall be classified in the third division by the nominal bore of the largest pipe (rule D1 of Class J).
4	Junctions & branches nom.bore: 150mm.	(mhs 4–5 J121	
	&		
4		(mhs 5–6	
	Stoppers; nom.bore: 150mm.	J191	
	PIPEWORK – MANHOLES AND PIPEWORK ANCILLARIES		Manhole types or mark numbers are to be included in item descriptions and the constructional particulars are obtained from the detailed drawings (rule A1).
	Manholes Precast conc. manholes with in situ conc. surrounds all as Dwg WE 9		
1	Manhole depth: 1.5–2m; w. c.i. medium wt. cover to BS 497 (MH3).	K152.1 (mh 3	Separate items are required for manholes of different materials, in different depth ranges and with different covers, but manhole items are deemed to include all items of metalwork and pipework, other than valves (rule C3 of Class K).
1	Manhole as last; depth 2–2.5m (MH2).	K153 (mh 2	

SEWER (Contd)			
1		Manhole as last; depth 3.5–4 m (MH1). K156 (mh 1	
4		Manhole depth: 1.5–2 m; w. c.i. heavy wt. cover to BS 497 (MHs 4, 5, 6 & 7). K152.2 (mhs 4, 5, 6, 7	The manhole schedule will assist the tenderer in pricing.
		Crossings	The ditch crossing is not taken as it is assumed not to exceed 1 m wide (rule M5 of Class K).
4		Hedges; pipe nom.bore: n.e. 300 mm. (mhs 1–4 K641	It is not necessary to classify separately pipes of differing nominal bores if within the same pipe bore range in the Third Division, as they will have little effect on price.
1		Fence; pipe nom.bore: n.e. 300 mm. (mhs 1–2 K661	
		Reinstatement	A combined item of breaking up and reinstatement is required for paved surfaces measured in metres on the lines of the pipe trenches. The type and maximum depth of surface is stated in the description, but no item is required for removal and reinstatement of kerbs (rule C8 of Class K). An additional length is given to pick up reinstatement over the manholes, which is excluded from the pipe lengths.
6.00		Breakg. up & tempy. reinstatement of rds.; pipe nom. bore: n.e. 300 mm; flexible rd. constn. max. depth: 75 mm w. 200 mm sub-base. (mhs 3–4	
58.80		(mhs 4–5	
54.80		(mhs 5–6	
13.00		(mhs 6–7	
6.50		(mhs 1–2	
4/ 1.20		(mhs 4, 5, 6 & 7 K711	

SEWER (Contd)

Timesing	Dimensions	Squaring	Description	Side notes
	35.80		Reinstatement of grassland; pipe nom.bore: n.e. 300 mm. (mhs 3-4	Reinstatement of roadside verges has been kept separate from grassland to allow the tenderer to price it differently, and as this is not listed in the Second Division, the digit 9 is inserted in the code. Testing of pipes would be covered by a General Item (A260).
	16.30		(mhs 1-2	
	14.00		(mhs 1-2	
	42.00		(mhs 1-2	
	70.80		(mhs 2-3	
3/	1.20		(mhs 1, 2 & 3 K751.1	
	51.80		Reinstatement of roadside verge; pipe nom.bore: n.e. 300 mm. (mhs 6-7	Check the sewer schedule to ensure that all lengths have been taken. The omission of quantities is a serious matter.
	10.00		(mhs 1-2 K791	
	4		Marker posts; 50 × 50 × 600 mm oak set in conc. base. (mhs 4-5	The marker posts are needed to indicate the positions of the junctions. Item descriptions are to include sizes and types of posts (rule A11 of Class K).
	4		(mhs 5-6 K820	

PIPEWORK - SUPPORTS AND PROTECTION, ANCILLARIES TO LAYING AND EXCAVATION

Timesing	Dimensions	Squaring	Description	Side notes
			Extras to excavn. and backfillg.	
	12.00 0.73 0.90		In pipe tr. excavn. in rock. L111 (mh 1-2	(Rules D1, M4) Assume site investigation reveals rock between MH 1-2.
	1.00 1.00 1.00		In manholes, excavn. in rock. L121 (mh 2	(Rule M5) Assumed quantity from above.

SEWER (Contd)

		Haunches	
		Imported granular material type C2 pipe nom.bore n.e. 200 mm; bed depth 200 mm.	Assume specification requires haunches where pipes laid in roads. (Rules M11, D2, D3, A3)
		L431	
6.00		(mh 3–4	Quantities from pipe item I 113.2.
58.80		(mh 4–5	
54.80		(mh 5–6	
13.00		(mh 6–7	
		Imported granular material type C2 pipe nom.bore 200–300 mm; bed depth 200 mm.	
		L432	
6.50		(mh 1–2	Quantity from pipe item I 227.1.

WORKED EXAMPLE 10

Water Main

Cross-references

Explanatory Chapter

This worked example includes material which is explained within Chapter 7 CESMM3 – Classes I–L: Pipework. These sections of CESMM3 cover pipes, fittings and valves, access chambers and pipework ancillaries and supports, protection, ancillaries to laying and excavation. The rules are the same as those for measuring all other pipelines such as sewers or district heating pipes.

Related Worked Examples

WE5 Pumping Chamber (example of chamber measured in detail rather than under Class K)
WE6 Sewage Holding Tank (simple brick-built manholes incorporated on top of a large chamber measured in detail)
WE9 Sewer (another type of pipework measured under the same rules)
WE20 Sewer Renovation (specialist remedial works)
WE21 Water Main Renovation (specialist remedial works)

Introduction

Worked Example 10 covers the measurement of a typical water main installation laid below grass verges which have been excavated to formation level by others. The reinstatement of the verges is also assumed to be carried out by others as general landscaping and is not measured here. However should reinstatement be required in water main work it would be measured in exactly the same way as for those items in Worked Example 9 Sewer.

It should be noted that more information than is demanded by CESMM3 for spun iron pipe fittings under 300 mm bore has been given in this example as additional information to tendering contractors (see the second page of take off).

WATER MAIN

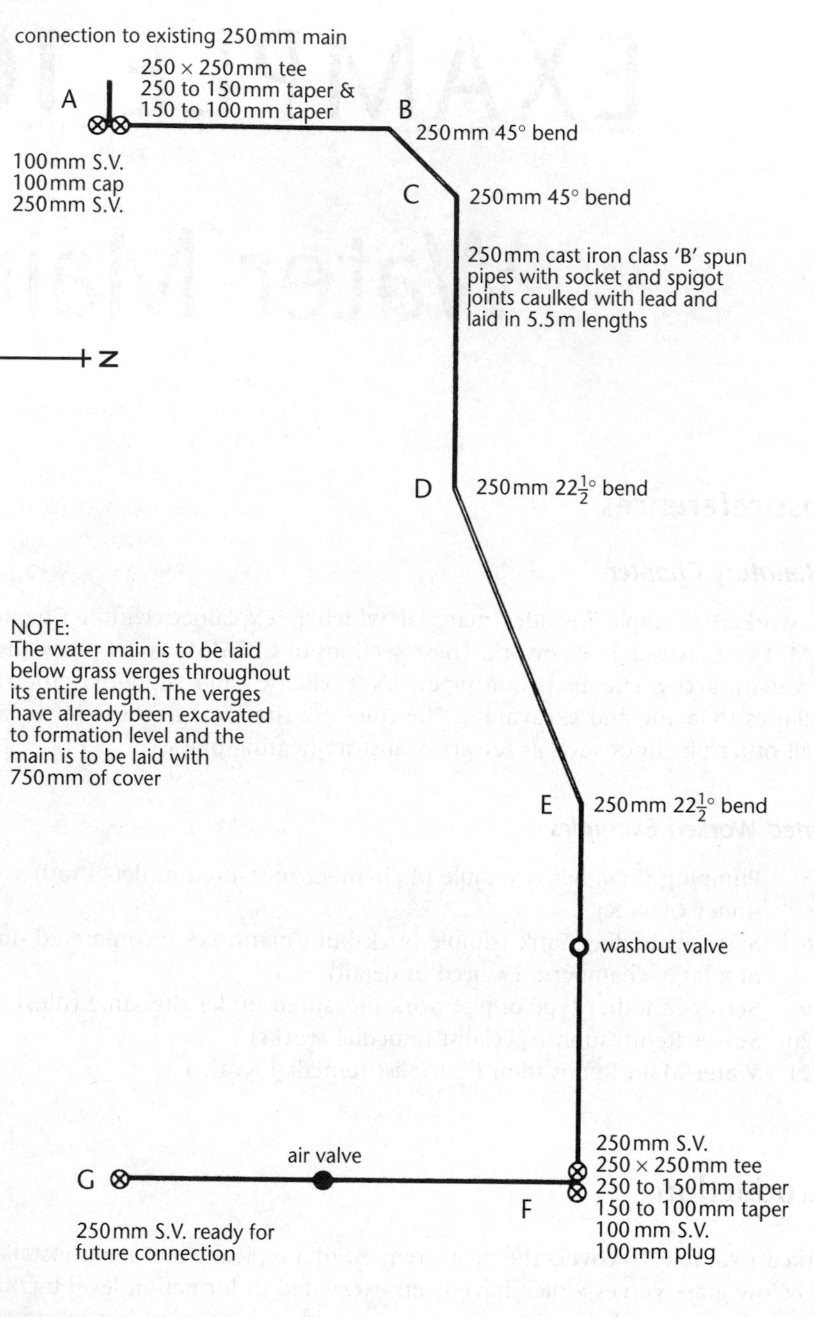
connection to existing 250 mm main
250 × 250 mm tee
250 to 150 mm taper &
150 to 100 mm taper
A
B
250 mm 45° bend
100 mm S.V.
100 mm cap
250 mm S.V.
C
250 mm 45° bend
250 mm cast iron class 'B' spun pipes with socket and spigot joints caulked with lead and laid in 5.5 m lengths
N
D
250 mm 22½° bend
NOTE:
The water main is to be laid below grass verges throughout its entire length. The verges have already been excavated to formation level and the main is to be laid with 750 mm of cover
E
250 mm 22½° bend
washout valve
air valve
G
F
250 mm S.V.
250 × 250 mm tee
250 to 150 mm taper
150 to 100 mm taper
100 mm S.V.
100 mm plug
250 mm S.V. ready for future connection
SCALE 1 : 1250

WATER MAIN

Timesing	Dimension	Squaring	Description		Side notes
			PIPEWORK - PIPES		The material, joint type and nominal bore shall be given with references to British Standards where appropriate (rule A2 of Class I).
			Cast (spun) iron s&s pipes to BS 1211 (Class B) with caulked lead jts.; nom. bore: 250 mm (A–G on Dwg. WEIO)		The location of each item or group of similar items is to be given, so that the pipe runs can be identified by reference to the drawings (rule A1).
	7.50		In trenches, depth: n.e. 1.5 m.	(to A	
	47.50			(A–B	Lengths of pipes are measured on their centre lines, including the lengths occupied by fittings and valves (rule M3).
	16.00			(B–C	
	48.50			(C–D	This item includes the provision, laying and jointing of pipes in trenches and excavating, preparing surfaces, disposal of excavated material, upholding sides of excavation, backfilling and removal of dead services (rule C2).
	56.50			(D–E	
	63.50			(E–F	
	75.00			(F–G I322	Trench depth ranges are measured from Commencing Surface to inverts of pipes (rule D3).
	PIPEWORK FITTINGS & VALVES				
			Cast (spun) iron s&s pipe fittgs. to BS 1211 (Class B) with caulked lead jts.		Fittings are enumerated giving similar particulars as for pipes.
2/	1		Taper; nom.bore: 150–250 mm.	(A&F J332	Arranging all the items under appropriate headings reduces the length of entries and groups items ready for billing.
2/	1		Taper; nom.bore: 100–150 mm.	(A&F J331	Location references are given in waste for identification purposes.

WATER MAIN (Contd)

Timesing	Quantity	Description	Notes
2/	1	Junctions & branches; nom.bore: 250 × 250 ×250 mm. (A&F J322.1	The fittings items are really 'extra over' items as the pipes, with their accompanying excavation and backfill have already been measured for the lengths occupied by fittings.
	1	Junctions & branches; nom.bore: 250 × 250 ×63 mm w. flanged branch. (wo E–F J322.2	Vertical bends in metal pipework exceeding 300 mm bore have to be so described (rule A3 of Class J). In strict compliance with CESMM3, the angles of bends and effective lengths would be given where the nominal bore exceeds 300 mm. Hence the addition of angles in these items is not a requirement of the CESMM, but is included as being of assistance to the estimator.
2/	1	Bends; nom.bore: 250 mm, 45°. (B&C J312.1	
2/	1	Bends; nom.bore: 250 mm, $22\frac{1}{2}$°. (D&E J312.2	Note use of suffixes to cover additional descriptions.
3/	1	Flanged spigots; nom.bore: 250 mm. J352.1 & Flanged socs; nom.bore: 250 mm. (A.F&G J352.2	Flanged spigots and sockets are needed to connect spigot and socket pipes to the flanged valves. It is generally considered advisable to use sluice valves with flanged joints as they can withstand more effectively the pressures resulting from the opening and closing of the valves.
2/	1	Flanged spigots; nom.bore: 100 mm. J351.1 & Flanged socs; nom.bore: 100 mm. (A&F J351.2	These items have been coded under adaptors (category 5 in Second Division). Alternatively they might be given the independent classification of 9, i.e. J391.
	1	Plug nom.bore: 100 mm. (F J391.1 & Cap nom.bore: 100 mm. (A J391.2	These fittings are not listed in the Second Division of Class J and hence the digit 9 is used in the coding (Second Division).

WATER MAIN (Contd)

Timesing	Dimension	Squaring	Description	Notes
			Cast iron gate valves hand operated to BS 5150, class 125, clamp patt., w; extensn. spindles, flanged jts., & T keys.	The descriptions of gate valves shall include such particulars as materials, nominal bores, joints and extension spindles, and provide references to applicable British Standards and specified qualities (rule A6 of Class J).
3/	1		250 mm nom.bore. (A.F&G J812.1	
2/	1		100 mm nom.bore. (A&F J811.1	
			Cast iron air valve, small single orifice as X catalogue Nr. 2416.	The remaining valves are enumerated with essential particulars listed in accordance with rule A6.
	1		250 mm nom.bore.	
	1		J861 (F–G	
			Cast iron hydrant as washout, spindle type as X catalogue Nr. 347C.	The supplier's catalogue reference can be given as an alternative to a British Standard.
	1		63 mm w. flange.	
	1		J891 (E–F	

PIPEWORK – VALVE CHAMBERS AND PIPEWORK ANCILLARIES

Timesing	Dimension	Squaring	Description	Notes
			Valve chambers brick depth: n.e. 1.50 m; type VCI	It is considered more appropriate to describe these as valve chambers, as they come within the other stated chambers category. A drawing will show the detailed construction for a type VCI chamber and it does not therefore require repeating in the item description.
5/	1		w. c.i. SV cover as X catalogue Nr. 47A. K211.1	
	1		w. c.i. W.O. cover as X catalogue Nr. 51B K211.2 & w. c.i. A.V. cover as X catalogue Nr. 52C. K211.3	The suffixes are added to the code numbers relating to the valve chamber items, to signify the different covers.

WATER MAIN (Contd)

Timesing	Dimension	Squaring	Description	Side notes
				The measurement of the water main finishes with the relevant items of other pipework ancillaries in KB.
			Other pipework ancillaries	
7/	1		Marker posts; r. conc. (p.c. £12.50ea.), bolting on plate supplied by Water Authority & settg. in conc. as detail E, Dwg. WS 26. K820	Valve markers require additional particulars to enable them to be priced, involving where appropriate references to Drawings and/or Specification.
	1		Connectn. of pipe to xtg. pipe, nom.bore 250 mm, inc. excavn. to locate pipe & burning out plug. K862	Enumerated connection item incorporating any additional particulars considered necessary. The testing of the pipeline should be included in the General Items (Class A) under classification A260, stating the length and nominal bore of pipe, test pressure and period of test.

WORKED EXAMPLE 11

Steel-Framed Gantry

Cross-references

Explanatory Chapters

This worked example is largely concerned with material which is explained within part of Chapter 8 CESMM3 – Class M: Stuctural Metalwork, with a single item from Class N: Miscellaneous Metalwork. In addition there are associated items for painting the metalwork which are explained in part of Chapter 11 CESMM3 – Class V: Painting.

Related Worked Examples

WE12 Timber Jetty (structural steel associated with timber construction and associated painting)

WE16 Navigation Lamp Platform (miscellaneous metalwork in handrails and ladder)

Introduction

Worked Example 11 covers the measurement of typical structural steel frame. The drawing details one bay of the construction but represents ten bays, which feature requires careful assessment of the total quantities. For example in ten bays there are eleven times the centre-line cross members but only ten times all longitudinal members.

Note that a more detailed take off is measured here than is necessary to comply with the less detailed requirements of the CESMM3 rules. However this approach allows the take off to be checked more readily for accuracy and completeness. In this example when all the quantities for items M311 and M321 are appropriately combined, there will only be three items in the fabrication section of the final bill.

DRAWING WE11: STEEL-FRAMED GANTRY
is overleaf

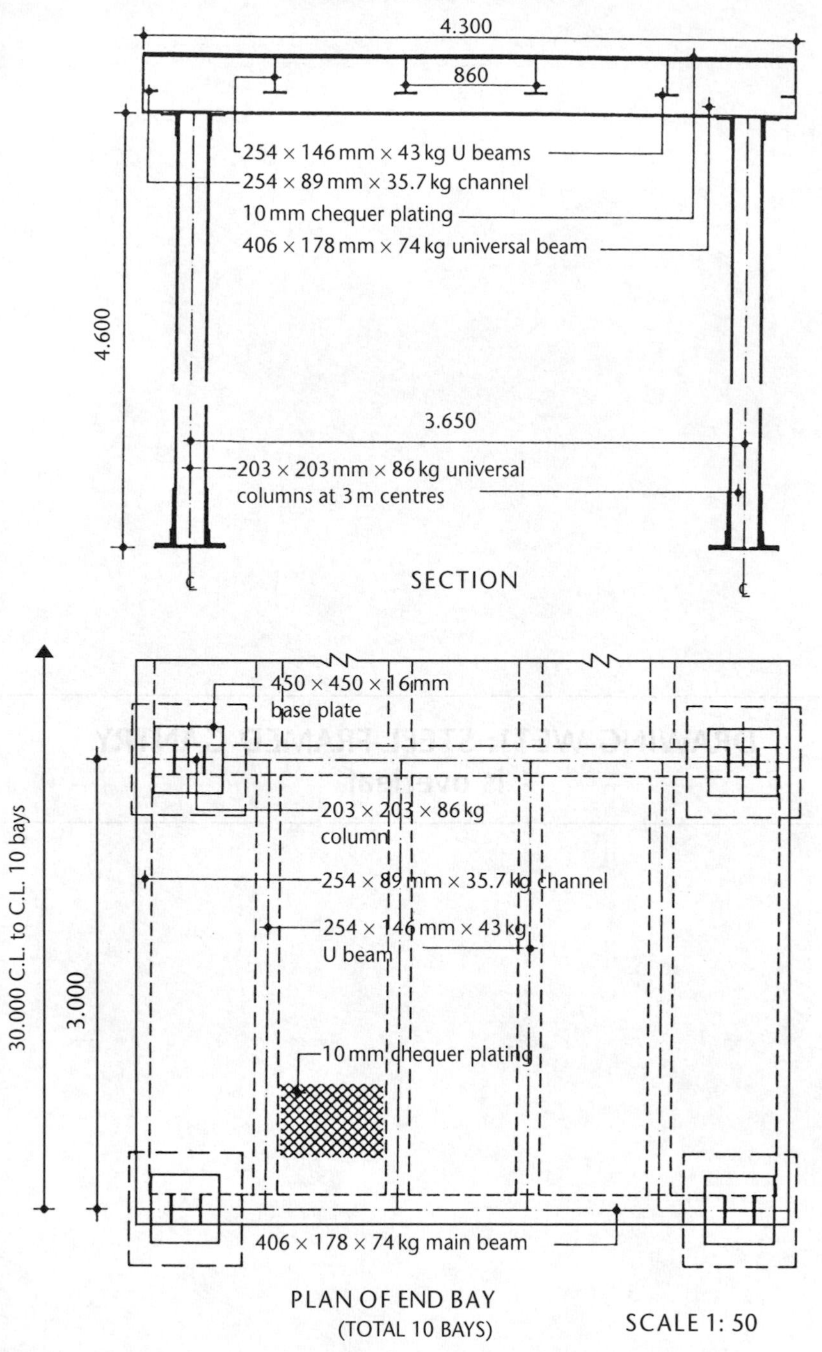
STEEL-FRAMED GANTRY
4.300
860
254 × 146 mm × 43 kg U beams
254 × 89 mm × 35.7 kg channel
10 mm chequer plating
406 × 178 mm × 74 kg universal beam
4.600
3.650
203 × 203 mm × 86 kg universal columns at 3 m centres
SECTION
450 × 450 × 16 mm base plate
203 × 203 × 86 kg column
254 × 89 mm × 35.7 kg channel
254 × 146 mm × 43 kg U beam
10 mm chequer plating
30.000 C.L. to C.L. 10 bays
3.000
406 × 178 × 74 kg main beam
PLAN OF END BAY
(TOTAL 10 BAYS)
SCALE 1: 50

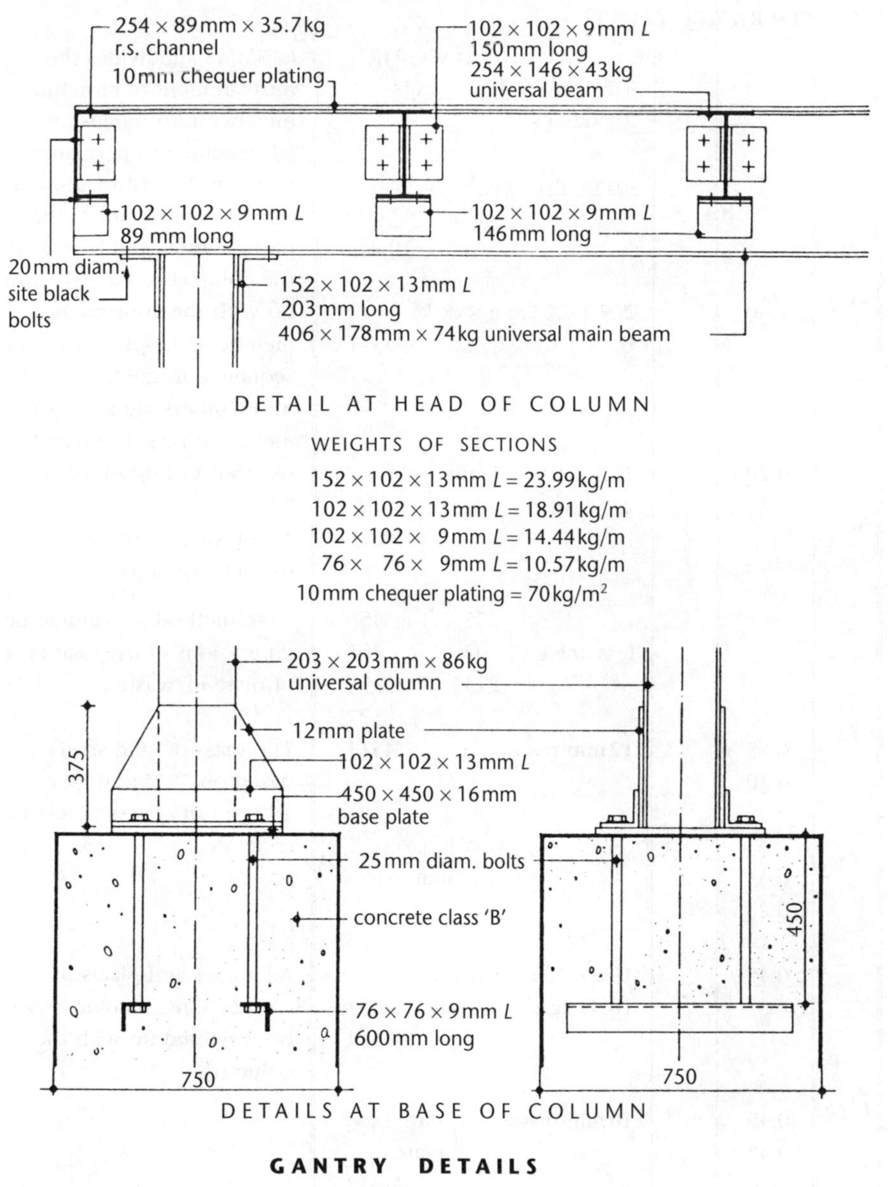

GANTRY DETAILS
SCALE 1:20

STEEL-FRAMED GANTRY

Timesing	Dimensions	Squaring	Description	Side notes
			STRUCTURAL METALWORK	CESMM3 subdivides the measurement of structural metalwork in frames into fabrication and permanent erection. The fabrication in this example is subdivided into columns and beams and the connections are weighted up with the appropriate members; adopting a logical sequence in the taking off. All members are taken off in metres to be subsequently reduced to tonnes, prior to billing.
			Fabrication of members for frames	
			Columns, straight on plan 3.000)30.000 10 + 1	
11/2/	4.60		203 × 203 mm × 86 kg U.C. M311	
11/2/2/	0.20		152 × 102 × 13 mm × 23.99 kg ∠ (stan. conns. M311	At top of column (2 brackets to each column).
			375 450 less angle 102 203 273 2)653 327	Note method of building up dimensions of irregular area of plate in 'waste'.
11/2/2/	0.45 0.10		12 mm plate. M311	The mass of mild steel is based on 785 kg/m² per 100 mm thickness (7.85 t/m³) (rule M6).
11/2/2/	0.33 0.27		(stan. bases	
11/2/2/	0.45		102 × 102 × 13 mm × 18.91 kg ∠. (stan. bases M311	All angles and plates in connections to columns will be weighted up with the columns.
11/2/	0.45 0.45		16 mm plate. (stan. base plates M311	
			Fabrication of members for frames Beams, straight on plan	No allowance is made for the mass of weld fillets, bolts, nuts, washers, rivets and protective coatings (rule M4).
11/	4.30		406 × 178 mm × 74 kg UB. (main beams M321	
10/2/	3.00		254 × 89 mm × 35.7 kg Channel. (subsid. beams M321	10 bays with 2 lengths of channel to each bay.

STEEL-FRAMED GANTRY (Contd)

Timesing	Dimensions	Squaring	Description	Side notes
10/4/	3.00		254 × 146 mm × 43 kg UB. (subsid. beams M321	It is unnecessary to deduct the very small thickness of the web in the main beam when determining the length of the subsidiary beams.
10/10/2	0.15		102 × 102 × 9 mm × 14.44 kg∠. M321	Side cleats to ends of beams and channels (both sides of main beams).
10/4/2/	0.15			brackets to beams
10/2/2/	0.09		(beam conns.	brackets to channels
			Fabrication of members for frames holding down bolt assemblies	
11/2/	1		Holding down bolt assemblies comprising 4 × 25 mm bolts 575 mm long and 2 × 76 × 76 × 9 mm angles 600 mm long M380	(Rules A5, M7) Complete assemblies enumerated.
			Erection of members for frames	(Rules A6, C2)
	total tonnes from fabricatn		Permanent erection M620	A single item for all members of this frame including cleats etc. is given in tonnes for erection. Note the holding down assemblies are normally handed to concretor and therefore excluded from this item.
			Site bolts: black, diam. 20 mm. M632	(Rule C3) Lengths of bolts usually ignored as normally not cost significant.
11/2/	4		(cols. to main beams	
10/2/	2		(channel to shelf angle	
11/4/	4		(254 beams to shelf angle	
11/	4		(channel to main beams	
11/	16		(254 beams to main beams	
			MISCELLANEOUS METALWORK	
	30.18 4.30		Chequer plate floorg; thickness: 10 mm, mass: 70 kg/m^2. N170	The item description for the plate flooring shall state the specification and thickness of metal used (rule A1 of Class N).

STEEL-FRAMED GANTRY (Contd.)

Timesing	Dimensions		Description	Side notes
	PAINTING		Site Painting Zinc phosphate primer on metal sections after erection & V170 3 coats oil paint on ditto. V370	Site painting after erection is measured in m^2 in accordance with Class V.
			Columns 203 × 203 2/203 406 4/203 812 1.218 (cols.	Girth of column = twice the depth + 4 times the width. Most of the area of connecting brackets will be included in the area of beams.
11/2/	4.60 1.22			
11/2/2/	0.45 0.10		Primer (angles	
11/2/2/	0.33 0.27		& ③ 450 (outside of plates 203 247	Alternatively, the surface area of universal columns and beams, and channels can be extracted from Steelwork Tables.
11/2/	0.25 0.10		(part of insides of angles	
11/2/	0.45 0.45		(base plates V170 and V370	Location notes are inserted in waste to help in identifying the particular items.
			Beams 406 × 178 2/406 812 4/178 712 1.524 254 × 89 2/254 508 4/89 356 864 254 × 146 2/254 508 4/146 584 1.092	Same approach to calculation of girth of beams as for columns. Surface treatment of structural metalwork prior to erection is also measured in m^2.
11/	4.30 1.52		Primer (main beams	Item descriptions for painting shall state the material used and either the number of coats or the film thickness (rule A1 of Class V).
10/2/	3.00 0.86		& (channs.	
10/4/	3.00 1.09		③ (sub-beams V170 and V370	

11.3

WORKED EXAMPLE 12

Timber Jetty

Cross-references

Explanatory Chapters

This worked example is primarily concerned with work affected by water and illustrates the requirements of paragraph 5.20 of CESMM3. Refer to Chapter 2 for a detailed discussion on compliance with paragraph 5.20 and the associated paragraphs 5.8 and 5.10.

With regard to the detailed work classifications, these include material which is explained in part of Chapter 8 CESMM3 – Classes M: Structural Metalwork and O: Timber; Chapter 9 CESMM3 – Classes P: Piles and Q: Piling Ancillaries; and part of Chapter 11 CESMM3 – Class V: Painting.

Related Worked Examples

WE7 Pumphouse (examples of joinery timber work measured under Class Z)
WE11 Steel-Framed Gantry (structural steel and associated painting)
WE13 Hybrid Piles (part bored, part driven concrete piles)
WE14 Quay with Concrete and Timber Piles (further examples of piling work affected by water)
WE15 Steel Sheet Piling (sheet piling affected by water)
WE16 Navigation Lamp Platform (example of preformed concrete piling affected by water)

Introduction

Worked Example 12 represents a typical jetty for small boats constructed in tidal waters comprising timber piles supporting a structural steel frame which in turn supports timber decking with timber balustrades. Associated fittings and fastenings to the timber work and painting of the steel sections are also covered. The drawing shows one typical bay but there are 20 bays in total and care should be taken in calculating the true quantity of components at centres in such circumstances.

The location in tidal waters initiates the requirements of paragraph 5.20 of CESMM3. In this example the requirements are accommodated by incorporating appropriate headings within the bill drawing attention to the effect of the tidal waters on those items of work.

An interesting anomaly occurs in the measurement of the jetty decking, where in the worked example, rule M2 of Class O is correctly applied in that the drainage gaps in the planking are deducted (see the 4th and 5th pages of the take off). The total deduction size of each gap is 12.5 mm × 92 m = 1.15 m^2 which of course exceeds the minimum deduction size of 0.5 m^2 in rule M2. Many bill compilers would prefer to measure the whole area of decking gross with a suitably worded item as to the spacing of the planks. Estimators can readily calculate a rate for such work and this approach may seem more practical. Should this method be adopted, an appropriately worded note should be inserted in the bill to draw attention to the divergence from rule M2.

DRAWING WE12: TIMBER JETTY
is overleaf

TIMBER JETTY

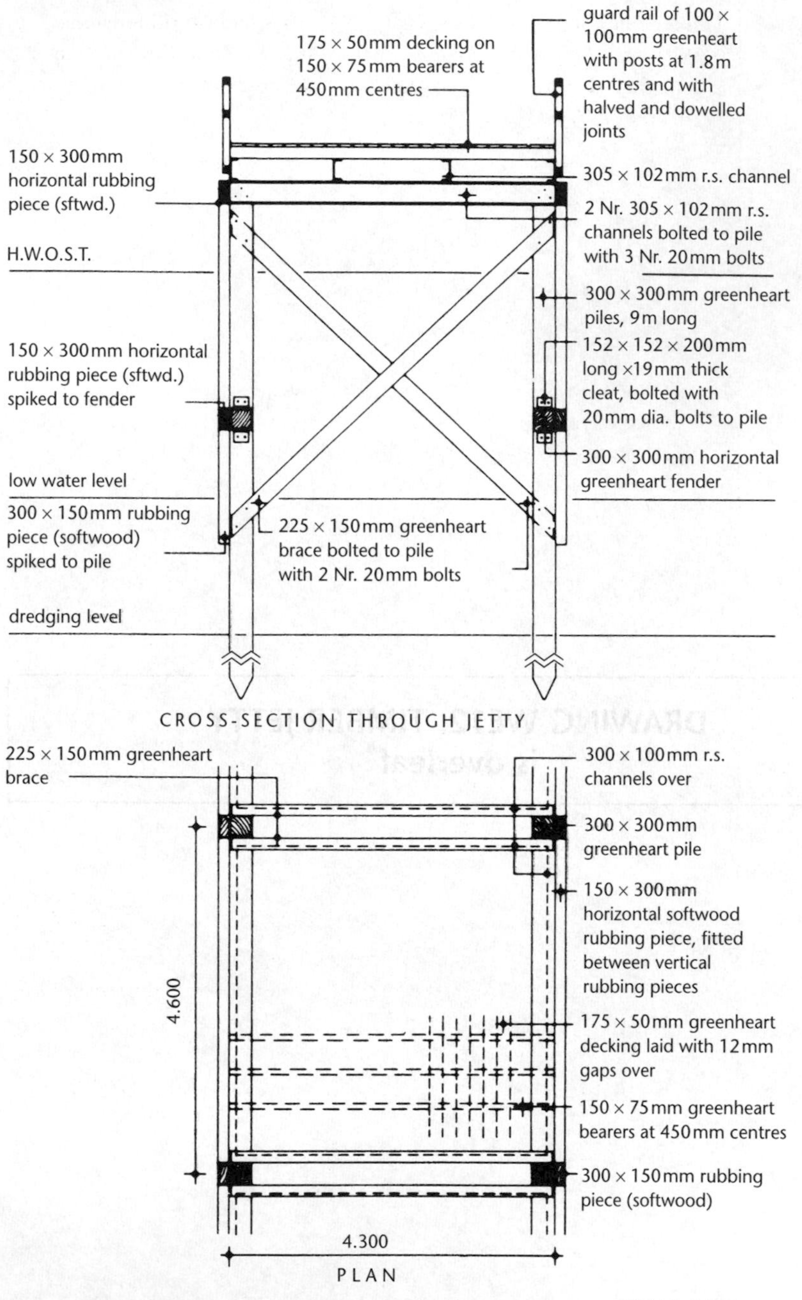

TIMBER JETTY (92 m length)

Timesing	Dimensions	Description	Notes
		PILES Timber piles supportg. jetty, csa 0.05–0.1 m^2; 300 × 300 mm greenheart, driven into dredged sea bed about 4.75 m below HWOST.	The cross-section type and cross-section dimensions shall be stated in the item description (rule A6 of Class P). Paragraph 5.20.
		4.600)92.000 20 + 1 9.000 add len. for ringing & removal after driving. 600 9.600	Add 1 to allow for a pair of piles at each end of the jetty.
21/	2	Nr. of piles, len: 9.6 m, gms drivg. hd. & shoe as detail C Dwg. RJ/5/1. P631	Two separate items are required for each group of timber piles: (1) number of piles of stated length (2) depth driven.
21/2/	3.00	Depth driven. P632	The lengths of timber piles include heads and shoes (rule D3 of Class P).
21/2/	0.60	Pilg. ancillaries Cuttg. off surplus lens; 300 × 300 mm. Q473	Follow with the work to the tops of piles. No separate items are required for pointed ends or ringing heads.
21/	2	Preparg. heads; 300 × 300 mm. Q483	
		TIMBER Work in this section may be affected by tidal water; ref. Dwg. WE12. Hardwood components, csa 0.04–0.1 m^2; wrought finish. fenders 4.600 less piles 2/150 300 4.300	Paragraph 5.20. Descriptions of timber components shall state gross cross-sectional dimensions, grade or species, any impregnation requirements or special surface finishes (rule A1 of Class O).
20/2/	4.30	300 × 300 mm greenheart, len: 3–5 m; hor. fender. 0143	The description includes gross (unplaned) dimensions, species of timber, length range and function.
		Hardwood components, csa 0.02–0.04 m^2; wrought finish.	The cross-sectional area of each brace is 0.034 m^2 and hence it falls in the 0.02–0.04 m^2 range. The splayed ends are included in the timber rates (rule C1 of Class O).
21/2/	6.05	225 × 150 mm greenheart, len: 5–8 m; braces. 0134	

12.1

TIMBER JETTY (Contd)

Timesing	Dimension	Description	Side notes
		Fittgs & Fastengs. galvd. mild steel.	Cleats would come within the fittings and fastenings classification but there is no specific mention of them in the Second Division; hence the use of the digit 9.
20/2/4/	1	Cleats; 152 × 152 × 19 mm ∠, len: 200 mm. (fenders/piles 0590 fender 300 cleats 38 clearance 40 378	Materials, types and sizes of fittings and fastenings shall be stated in item descriptions (rule A4 of Class O).
20/2/4/	1	Bolts; len: 380 mm, (fenders diam: 20 mm 0540.1	
21/2/4/	1	Bolts ab. (piles 0540.1 & Plates: 50 × 50 mm, thickness 6 mm. 0550 piles 300 brace 150 clearance 40 490	Plates are measured separately from the bolts as prescribed in the Second Division. 21 pairs of braces with 4 bolts to each brace.
21/2/4/	1	Bolts: len: 500 mm; diam: 20 mm. 0540.2 & (braces/piles Plates; 50 × 50 mm, thickness 6 mm 0550	
		Softwood components; csa 0.04–0.1 m^2, wrought finish, pressure creosoted.	The cross-sectional area is 0.045 m^2 and it thus comes within the range 0.04–0.1 m^2. The location of the component and any labours should be included in the item description.
2/	92.00	150 × 300 mm len: 3–5 m; hor. rubbg. piece w.rdd edge. 0243.1	
20/2/2/	2	Spikes gms, len: 225 mm. 0520	Horizontal rubbing piece is spiked to heads of piles (2 spikes at each end of each piece).
20/2/	4.30	150 × 300 mm, len: 3–5 m; hor. rubbg. piece. 0243.2	The lower horizontal rubbing pieces rum between the vertical rubbing pieces (20 lengths on each side).
20/2/2/	2	Spikes, gms, len: 225 mm. 0520	Spikes are enumerated, stating the material and size (rule A4 of Class O).

12.2

TIMBER JETTY (Contd)

Timesing	Dimension	Squaring	Description	Notes
21/2/	4.50		300 × 150 mm, len: 3–5 m; vert. rubbg. piece. 0243.3	There are 21 pairs of piles and vertical rubbing pieces. The vertical rubbing pieces are spiked to the piles.
21/	8		Spikes, gms, len: 225 mm. 0520	Alternatively, all the spikes could be taken together under a heading of fittings and fastenings.
			STRUCTURAL METALWORK Steel grade 43A Work above HWOST.	Paragraph 5.20.
21/2/	4.30		Fabrication of members for frames, beams, st. on plan; channel 305 × 102 mm × 46.14 kg. (deckg. brrs. M321 & Erection of members for frs, perm. erectn, ditto. M620 len. pile 300 2 channels 20 clearance 40 360	The steel members are taken as linear items, stating the weight in kg/m. They are subsequently weighted up and entered in the Bill in tonnes as fabrication and erection items. Drilling holes are not enumerated as they are included in the steelwork rates.
21/2/3/	1		Site bolts: black; len: 360 mm, diam: 20 mm. M632.1	Bolts through webs on 2 channels and head of pile. Items for site bolts are deemed to include supply and delivery to site (rule C3 of Class M).
4/	92.00		Fabricatn. of members for frames, beams, st. on plan; channel 305 × 102 mm × 46.14 kg. M321 & Erection of members for frs. perm. erectn, ditto. M620 len. 2 channel flamges 30 clearance 40 70	Channels running the full length of the jetty. Proceed in a logical sequence with the fabrication and erection of the structural metalwork, using the descriptions prescribed in Class M.
21/4/2/	1		Site bolts: black; len. 70 mm, diam: 20 mm. M632.2	One bolt taken at each connection.

TIMBER JETTY (Contd)

Timesing	Dimension	Description	Notes
		TIMBER Work above HWOST. Hardwood components csa 0.01–0.02 m^2, unwrought finish.	Paragraph 5.20.
		Deckg. 450|92.000 205 + 1	
206/	4.30	150 × 75 mm greenheart, len: 3–5 m; deckg. brrs. 0123	Bearers are fixed to channels with coach screws.
		Fittgs. & Fastengs. galvd. mild steel.	
206/	4	Coach screws 20 mm diam. 0530	
		width of deck 4.300 total width of gaps = $^1/_{15}$ × 4.300 = 287 (allowance for 12.5 mm gap between 175 mm decking members is 1 : 15 gap) 4.300 less gaps 287 4.013	The effective width of hardwood decking is obtained by deducting the gaps between the decking members, as each gap exceeds 0.5 m^2 in area (rule M2 of Class O). See Introduction to this Worked Example.
		Hardwood decking; thickness: 50 mm; wrought finish.	The description includes the timber species and surface finish. The actual thickness has been given instead of the range as only one thickness is involved. The gaps need mentioning as they will increase the fixing costs.
	92.00 4.01	Greenheart 175 mm widths septd. by 12.5 mm gaps (mesd. net). 0320	
		Hardwood components; csa n.e. 0.01 m^2; wrought finish.	There are three rails on each side of the quay. The number of posts is calculated in waste. The guardrail is broken down into component parts and measured as linear items.
		Guardrail 1.800|92.000 51 + 1	
2/3/	92.00	100 × 100 mm greenheart len: 1.5–3 m; guardrails.	The timber rates are deemed to include forming joints (rule C1 of Class O).
2/3/52/	0.10	(laps) 0112	

12.4

TIMBER JETTY (Contd)

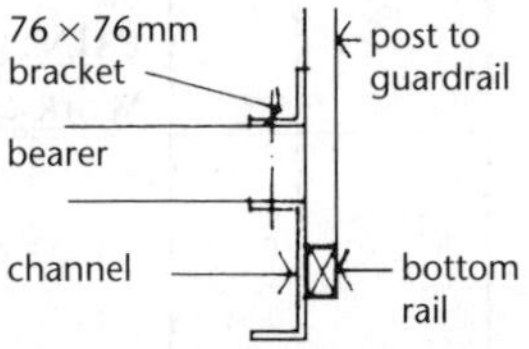

Timesing	Dimension	Squaring	Description	Side notes
2/52/	1.30		100 × 100 mm greenheart, len: ne 1.5 m; posts to guardrail. 0111	76 × 76 mm bracket; post to guardrail; bearer; channel; bottom rail
			Fittings & Fastenings galvd. mild steel.	
52/2/	1		Cleats; 76 × 76 × 9 mm ∠, len: 75 mm. 0590.2 post 100 angle 10 clearance 40 150	Double fixing of guardrail at 1.80 m centres: (1) bottom rail bolted to channel (2) post bolted to bracket which is bolted to 150 × 75 mm bearers.
52/2/	1		Bolts; len: 150 mm (to posts diam: 12 mm. 0504.3 bearer 150 angle 10 clearance 40 200	
52/2/	1		Bolts; len: 200 mm (to brrs. diam: 12 mm. 0540.4 bottom rail 100 channel web 10 clearance 40 150	
52/2/	1		Bolts; len: 150 mm, diam: 12 mm. (bolt rail to chann. 0540.3	A similar size of bolt to that measured earlier and so it carries the same code reference.

(*continued overleaf*)

TIMBER JETTY (Contd)

			PAINTING Work above HWOST. 305 2/102 204 2/509 1.018	Paragraph 5.20. The measurement of painting of steelwork follows. It is assumed that the steelwork is also to be painted by the main contractor after its erection, and is therefore measured in accordance with Class V.
4/	92.00 1.02		② bit. paint, met. sectns.	Girth of channel = twice height + 4 times width. Item descriptions state the materials used and either the number of coats or the film thickness (rule A1 of Class V).
21/2/	4.30 1.02		(channs. V870	

The painting of metal sections is deemed to include painting the surfaces of connecting plates, brackets, rivets, bolts, nuts and similar projections (rule C2 of Class V). Hence separate painting items are not required for cleats.
Preparation of surfaces before painting is deemed to be included unless there is more than one type of preparation, when they shall be described in the item description (rules C1 and A2 of Class V).

WORKED EXAMPLE 13

Hybrid Piles

Cross-references

Explanatory Chapter

This worked example includes material which is explained in Chapter 9 CESMM3 – Class P: Piles and Q: Piling Ancillaries. This example deals with construction which differs from standard as covered by the normal rules.

Related Worked Examples

WE12 Timber Jetty (timber piles driven into tidal water)
WE14 Quay with Concrete and Timber Piles (further examples of piling work affected by water)
WE15 Steel Sheet Piling (sheet piling affected by water)
WE16 Navigation Lamp Platform (example of preformed concrete piling affected by water)

Introduction

Worked Example 13 covers the measurement of part bored and part driven *in situ* concrete piles. The normal rules deal separately with bored and driven types of pile and thus some additional care in description and itemisation of these hybrid piles is necessary.

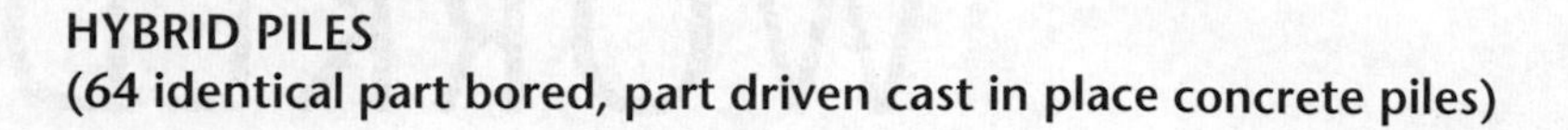

HYBRID PILES
(64 identical part bored, part driven cast in place concrete piles)

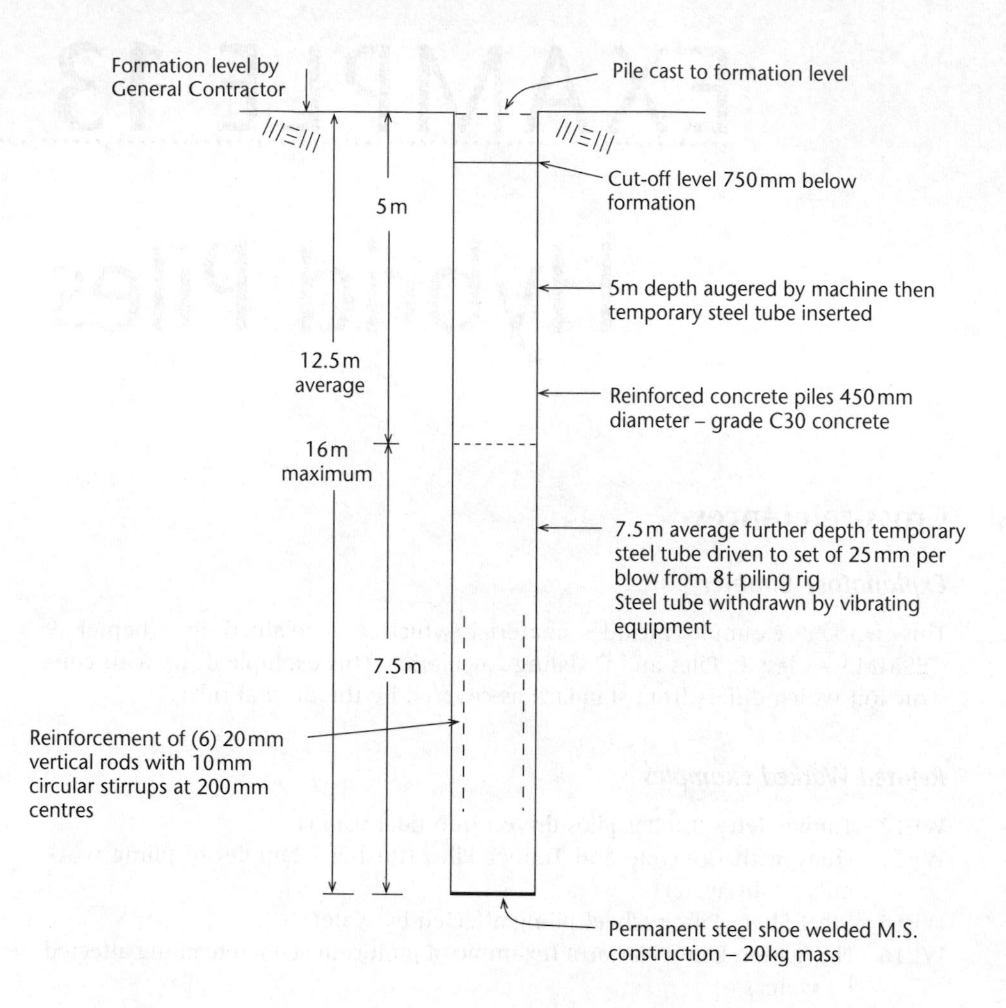

HYBRID PILES

Class P: Piles

Times	Dimension	Squared	Description	Side notes
			Part bored, part driven, cast in place concrete piles, 450 mm diameter, grade C30 concrete, commencing surface formation level. Note: Pre-boring measured under Class Q.	(Rule A4) Worth making this clear to tenderer.
	64		Diameter: 450 mm, number of piles (each including 20 kg m.s. shoes). P221	(Rules M1, M2, C1, D1) Worth drawing attention to permanent steel shoes. Coded as mainly driven.
64/	12.50		Concreted length. P222	(Rules M2, M3)
64/	7.50		Depth driven (driven from 5 m to max. of 16 m deep – first 5 m bored). P223	Average total depth = 12.5 m assume max. of 16 m.

Class Q: Piling Ancillaries

Times	Dimension	Squared	Description	Side notes
			Part bored, part driven, cast in place concrete piles, 450 mm diameter.	
64/	5.00		Pre-boring Q112	(Rules D1, M1, C1)
64/	0.75		Cutting of surplus lengths. Q172	(Rules M1, C1)
	64		Preparing heads. Q182	
64/6/	12.50 × 2.466 kg per m		Reinforcement, straight bars nom. size n.e. 25 mm. Q211	Measured by tonne, length converted to mass using tables. Actual diam = 20 mm.
64/63/	1.10 × 0.616 kg per m		Reinforcement, circular stirrups, 10 mm diam. Q219	Not strictly helical thus taken as 'rogue' item. Rein. cage is 350 mm diam at 200 mm centres = 63 per pile.
	4		Pile tests, maintained loading with various reactions, test load 50 t. Q811	(Rule A8) Actual load stated. Specification would give the various requirements in detail.

WORKED EXAMPLE 14

Quay with Concrete and Timber Piles

Cross-references

Explanatory Chapters

This worked example is primarily concerned with work affected by water and illustrates the requirements of paragraph 5.20 of CESMM3. Refer to Chapter 2 for a detailed discussion on compliance with paragraph 5.20 and the associated paragraphs 5.8 and 5.10.

With regard to the detailed work classifications, these include material which is explained in part of Chapter 6 CESMM3 – Classes F: *In Situ* Concrete and G: Concrete Ancillaries; part of Chapter 8 CESMM3 – Class O: Timber; Chapter 9 CESMM3 – Classes P: Piles and Q: Piling Ancillaries; and a small amount of work from Chapter 5 CESMM3 – Class E: Earthwork.

Related Worked Examples

- WE8 Stone Faced Sea Wall (excavation, concrete and sheet piling affected by tidal water)
- WE12 Timber Jetty (timber piling affected by tidal water)
- WE13 Hybrid Piles (part bored, part driven concrete piles)
- WE15 Steel Sheet Piling (sheet piling affected by water)
- WE16 Navigation Lamp Platform (example of preformed concrete piling affected by water)

Introduction

Worked Example 14 represents a typical quay for commercial shipping constructed in tidal waters, comprising preformed concrete piles supporting an *in situ* reinforced concrete deck with associated timber piles and timber work acting as fenders. The drawing shows one typical bay but there are 30 bays in total and care should be taken in calculating the true quantity of components at centres in such circumstances.

The location in tidal waters initiates the requirements of paragraph 5.20 of CESMM3. In this example the requirements are accommodated by incorporating appropriate headings within the bill drawing attention to affect of the tidal waters on those items of work.

There are three items of Class E: Earthwork at the end of this example involved in providing a uniform protected slope to the sea bed under the quay. This work comprises filling and pitching with imported rock. It is worth noting that although the pitching as shown on the drawing appears to be a finished surface, 'trimming' (as a filling ancillary) is measured whether or not it is expressly required. See Chapter 5 for further explanation on the measurement of trimming and preparation of surfaces in earthwork.

QUAY WITH CONCRETE AND TIMBER PILES

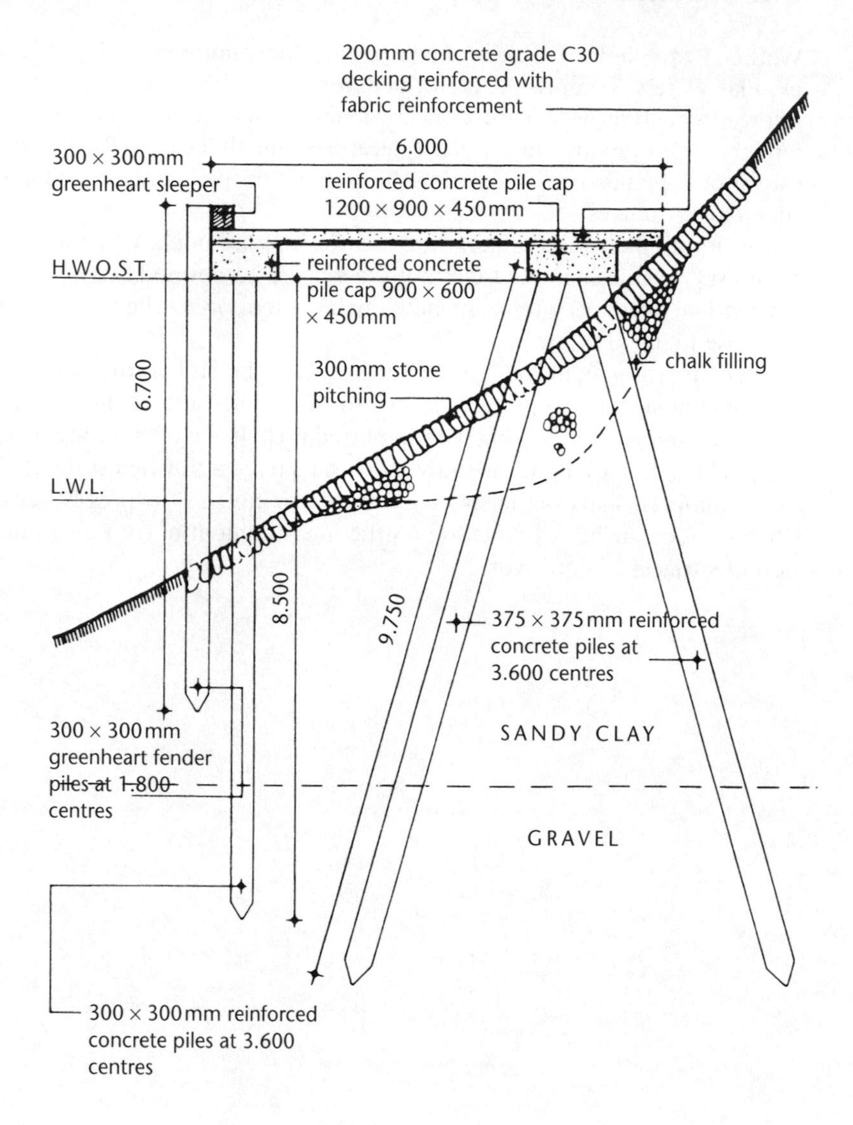

SECTION THROUGH QUAY
SCALE 1:100

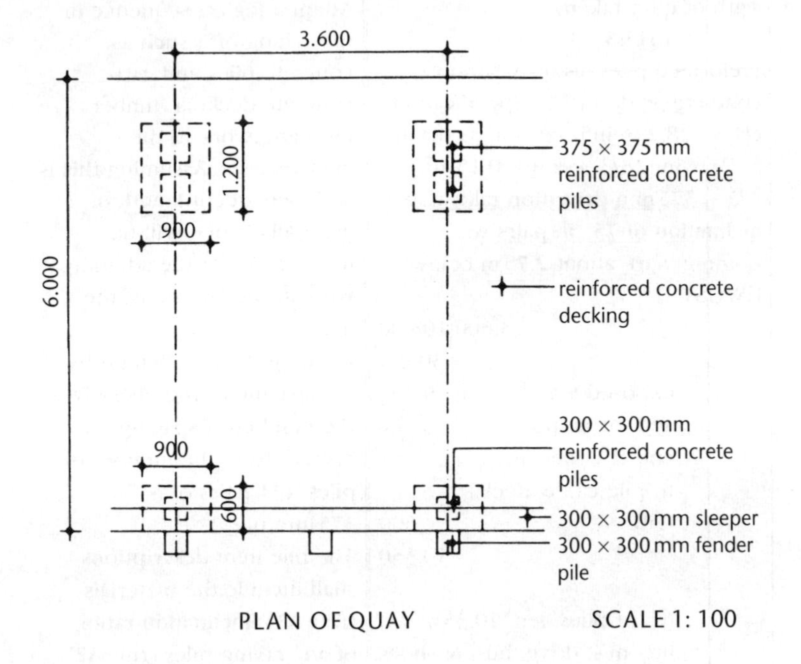

PLAN OF QUAY SCALE 1: 100

Timesing	Dimension	Squaring	Description	Side notes
			QUAY WITH CONCRETE AND TIMBER PILES (108 m length of quay taken)	Adopt a logical sequence in the 'taking off', such as concrete piles and caps, concrete decking, timber piles and work to the embankment. Assuming this is an independent length of quay, allowance will have to be made for the additional work at the far end of the quay.
			PILES	
			Preformed piles, as quay support, concrete grade C25 as Specification clause 28.2; reinforcement as detail 3, Drawing J8/3, csa 0.1–0.15 m^2, 375 × 375 mm driven on rake at an inclination of 75° in pairs w. Commg. Surf. about 2.75 m below HWOST.	
			3.600 ⌊108.00 30 + 1	Dividing the total length by the spacing of the piles gives the number of spacings, as distinct from the number of piles (31 pairs of 375 × 375 mm piles).
			exposed len. 9.750 add for strippg. end & connectg. to pile cap & deck slab. 600 10.350	The pile item descriptions shall include the materials (rule A1), inclination ratios of any raking piles (rule A2), structure to be supported and the Commencing Surface (rule A3). Preformed concrete pile prices include reinforcement, chamfered corners, tapered toes, moulds, shoes and related items. The description includes the cross-sectional dimensions or diameters of piles (rule A6), regardless of the cross-sectional area and diameter ranges given in the Second Division.
31/	2		Nr. of piles, len. 10.35 m inc. m.s. drivg. hds. & shoes. P341	
			8.500 9.250 2)17.750 8.875	
31/2/	8.88		Depth driven. P342	
			Piling Ancillaries	The cost of provision, use and removal of a driving rig will probably be covered by method-related charges. Follow with any piling ancillaries; in this example a linear item for cutting off surplus lengths and an enumerated item for preparing heads.
31/2/	0.30		Cuttg. off surplus lens; 375 × 375 mm. Q374	
31/	2		Prepg. heads; 375 × 375 mm. Q384	

14.1

QUAY WITH CONCRETE AND TIMBER PILES (Contd)

Ref.	Dimension	Squaring	Description	Notes
			Preformed piles, as quay support, concrete grade C25 as Specification clause 28.2; reinforcement as detail 4, Drawing J8/3, csa 0.05–0.1 m², 300 × 300 mm w. Commg. Surf. about 3.5 m below HWOST. 8.500 600 9.100	Start with a suitable heading encompassing all the particulars listed in Class P, including the cross-sectional area range and the cross-sectional dimensions.
31/	1		Nr. of piles, len. 9.1 m inc. m.s. drivg. hds. & shoes. P331	The 300 × 300 mm piles fall into a different cross-sectional area range than the 375 × 375 mm piles (the respective cross-sectional areas being 0.141 and 0.09 m²).
31/	5.10		Depth driven. P332	
			Pilg. Ancillaries	
31/	0.30		Cuttg. off surplus lens; 300 × 300 mm. Q373	Follow with piling ancillaries as with the 375 × 375 mm piles.
31/	1		Prepg. heads; 300 × 300 mm. Q383	
			IN SITU CONCRETE Work at or near HWOST Pile caps	
31/	1.20 0.90 0.45		Provsn. of conc; designed mix, grade C30, ct. to BS 12, 20 mm agg. to BS 882. F123	Provision and placing of concrete are separated.
31/	0.90 0.60 0.45		& Placg. of conc. reinfd. pile caps; thickness: 300–500 mm. F623	Pile caps are included in the same Second Division classification as bases and ground slabs, and the appropriate thickness range must be included in the item description.

QUAY WITH CONCRETE AND TIMBER PILES (Contd)

Timesing	Dimensions	Squaring	Description	Notes
			Conc. ancillaries	Wrought formwork has been
			Fwk. fair fin; pile caps	measured to the pile caps as
31/	1.20		Hor. width: 0.4–1.22 m.	they will be exposed.
	0.90		(soffs.	No adjustment has been made
			G214	for heads of piles or the
31/	0.90			cutting on formwork around
	0.60		1.200 900	them.
			900 600	Note build up of length of
			2/2.100 2/1.500	enclosing formwork in waste.
			4.200 3.000	The side forms are measured
31/	4.20		Vert. width: 0.4–1.22 m.	in m^2 as they exceed 200 mm
	0.45		(sides	wide.
31/	3.00			
	0.45		G244	
			Reinforcement	
			ms bars to BS 4449	
			less 1.200 900 600	4 nr. 25 mm reinforcing bars
			cover 2/40 80 80 80	have been taken in each
			1.120 820 520	direction to each pile cap.
31/4/				
31/4/	1.12		Diam. 25 mm.	Reinforcing bars are classified
31/4/	0.82			in the diameters listed in the
31/4/	0.82		G517	third division and measured
	0.52			in tonnes.
			R.c. decking	
	108.00		Provsn. of conc; designed	Follow with reinforced
	6.00		mix grade C30, ct. to BS 12,	concrete decking, adopting
	0.20		20 mm agg. to BS 882.	the same sequence as for the
			& F233	pile caps.
			Placg. of conc., reinfd. susp.	The placing item
			slab, thickness: 150–300 mm.	distinguishes between mass and reinforced concrete and
			F632	the relevant thickness range
			less 108.00 6.00	must be stated.
			cover 2/20 0.40 0.40	
			107.60 5.60	
			Reinft.	
	107.60		Fabric high yield reinft. to	Fabric reinforcement is
	5.60		BS 4483, nom. mass	measured in m^2, giving the
			2–3 kg/m^2, ref. A142.	fabric reference as rule A9 of
			G562	Class G.

14.3

QUAY WITH CONCRETE AND TIMBER PILES (Contd)

Timesing	Dimensions	Squaring	Description	Notes
			Conc. ancillaries Fwk. fair fin.	As the width of the decking exceeds 1.22 m it is unnecessary to state a width of formwork. Deductions are made for the area of pile caps as each exceeds 0.5 m^2 (rules M4 and D3). The formwork to the edges of the decking is measured as a linear item. Formwork to temporary surfaces, such as construction joints, at the discretion of the Contractor, is not measured separately (rule M2c).
	108.00 6.00		Hor. G215	
31/	1.20 0.90		Ddt. ditto.	
31/	0.90 0.60		(pile caps G215	
2/ 2/	108.00 6.00		Vert. width: 0.2 m. (edges. G242	
			Inserts	
91/	1		25 mm ragbolts 500 mm long, proj. from one surface. G832	Fixing bolts for fender, see below for calculation.
			TIMBER Work above HWOST Hwd. components, csa 0.04–0.1 m^2; wrought fin. & chfd. upper edges.	It is necessary to state the nominal gross cross-sectional dimensions, grade or species of timber and any impregnation requirements or special surface finish in the item description (rule A1 of Class O).
	108.00		300 × 300 mm greenheart, len: 3–5 m; sleeper. O143 1.200 | 108.000 90 + 1	Separate items are not required for fixing timber components, or for boring, cutting and jointing (rule C1 of Class O).
			Fittgs. & fastengs. galvd. mild steel.	
91/	1		Plates; 50 × 50 mm, thickness: 6 mm. O550	The sleeper is fixed at 1.2 m centres to bolts supplied as inserts under Class G. Only plates require to be taken here.
			PILES Fender piles add. len. to be ringed & removed after driving: 6.700 + 600 = 7.300 1.800 | 108.000 60 + 1	Calculation of length and number of timber piles in waste (two fender piles in each 3.6 m length of quay).

QUAY WITH CONCRETE AND TIMBER PILES (Contd)

Timesing	Dimensions	Squaring	Description	Notes
			Timber fender piles csa 0.05–0.1 m^2, 300 × 300 mm greenheart, w. Commg. Surf. about 4 m below HWOST.	
61/	1		Nr. of piles, len: 7.3 m; gms drivg. hd. & shoe as detail D Drvg. FQ/17/C. P631	The measurement of timber piles follows the same procedure as for preformed concrete piles. Details of driving heads and of shoes shall be stated in item descriptions for the number of piles (rule A8 of Class P).
61/	2.00		Depth driven. P632	
			Pilg. ancillaries	Follow with piling ancillaries.
61/	0.60		Cuttg. off surplus lens; 300 × 300 mm. Q473	
61/	1		Preparg. heads; 300 × 300 mm. Q483	
61/	1		Bolts gms; len: 600 mm, diam. 25 mm. 0540 & Plates gms; 50 × 50 mm, thickness: 6 mm. 0550	Assume each pile is bolted to the fender. The bolts are enumerated giving relevant particulars as rule A4 of Class O.
			EARTHWORKS Work to Embankment mainly below hwl.	
$\frac{1}{2}$/	108.00 5.70 1.35		Fillg. to embankment, imported rock. (chalk fillg. E627	This is assuming no great variation in the cross-sectional area of the filling. In practice the volume would normally be computed from a number of cross-sections. The triangular cross-sectional area is obtained from 'give and take' lines drawn across the boundaries.
	108.00 9.30		Pitching, imported rock; thickness: 300 mm, at ∠ of 10° to 45° to hor. E647 & Trimming of pitching, at ∠ of 10° to 45° to hor. E714	Rules A13, A14, D8. Trimming to be measured whether or not expressly required (rule M22).

WORKED EXAMPLE 15

Steel Sheet Piling

Cross-references

Explanatory Chapters

This worked example is primarily concerned with work affected by water and illustrates the requirements of paragraph 5.20 of CESMM3. Refer to Chapter 2 for a detailed discussion on compliance with paragraph 5.20 and thc associated paragraphs 5.8 and 5.10.

There is only one detailed work classification concerned in this example: steel sheet piling from part of Chapter 9 CESMM3 – Classes P: Piles. In this particular example there are no additional items required from Class Q: Piling Ancillaries.

Related Worked Examples

WE8 Stone Faced Sea Wall (simple sheet piling affected by tidal water)
WE12 Timber Jetty (timber piling affected by tidal water)
WE13 Hybrid Piles (part bored, part driven concrete piles)
WE14 Quay with Concrete and Timber Piles (two other piling types affected by water)
WE16 Navigation Lamp Platform (example of preformed concrete piling affected by water)

Introduction

Worked Example 15 represents a typical use of steel sheet piling as a cost-effective way of protecting a foreshore from erosion. As the sheet piling is driven in estuary mud to a pre-determined level, there are no likely requirements for cutting piles or providing extensions to them, hence there are no ancillaries items from Class Q.

The location in tidal waters initiates the requirements of paragraph 5.20 of CESMM3. In this example the straightforward requirement is accommodated by incorporating an appropriate heading within the bill drawing attention to effect of the tidal waters on those items of work.

DRAWING WE15: STEEL SHEET PILING
is overleaf

STEEL SHEET PILING

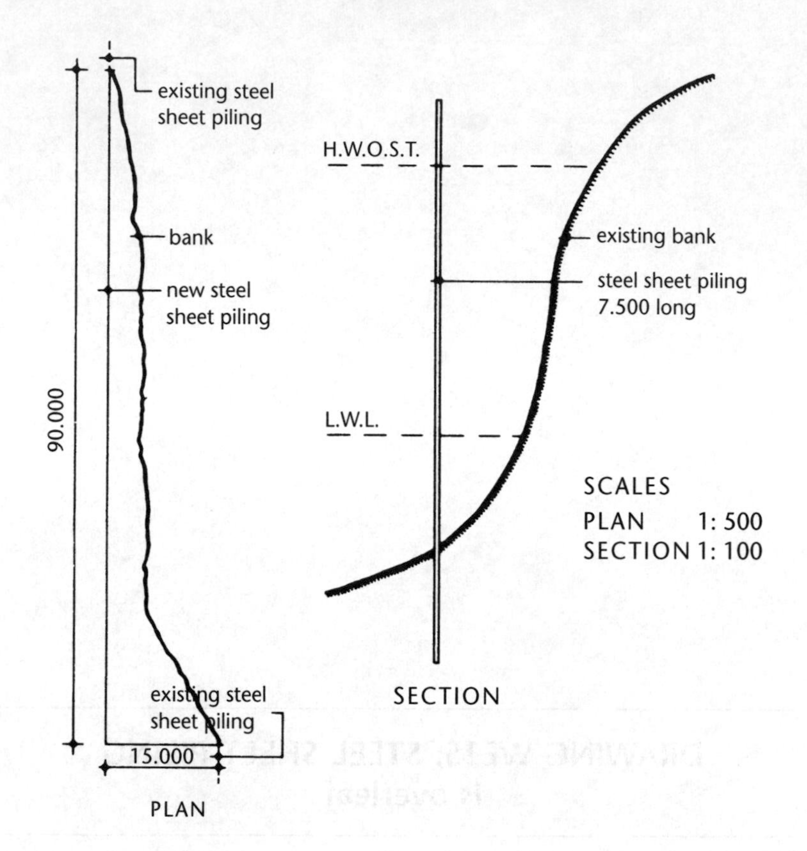

			Description	Notes
			STEEL SHEET PILING (permanent)	
			Interlockg. steel piles grade 43A type 2N, section modulus 1150 cm^3/m, Commg. Surf. about 5 m below HWOST.	The section reference or mass per metre and section modulus are required for interlocking steel piles (rule A10 of Class P). The Commencing Surface should also be stated (rule M1).
2/	7.50		Len. of junctn. piles; connectn. to xtg. P831.1	
	7.50		Len. of corner piles. P831.2 90.000 15.000 105.000	Corner, junction, closure and taper piles are classified as special piles and measured as linear items (rule D7). It is necessary to add suffixes to the codes in these cases.
	105.00 1.50		Driven area. P832	The driven area is measured separately from the total area of piling computed in accordance with rule M7.
	105.00 7.50		Area of piles of len: n.e. 14 m; treated w. 2 cts. of bitumen paint. P833	

WORKED EXAMPLE 16

Navigation Lamp Platform

Cross-references

Explanatory Chapters

This worked example is primarily concerned with work affected by water and illustrates the requirements of paragraph 5.20 of CESMM3. Refer to Chapter 2 for a detailed discussion on compliance with paragraph 5.20 and the associated paragraphs 5.8 and 5.10.

With regard to the detailed work classifications, these include material which is explained in part of Chapter 6 CESMM3 – Classes F: *In Situ* Concrete and G: Concrete Ancillaries; part of Chapter 8 CESMM3 – Class N: Miscellaneous Metalwork; and Chapter 9 CESMM3 – Classes P: Piles and Q: Piling Ancillaries.

Related Worked Examples

WE8 Stone Faced Sea Wall (excavation and concrete affected by tidal water)
WE12 Timber Jetty (timber piling affected by tidal water)
WE13 Hybrid Piles (part bored, part driven concrete piles)
WE14 Quay with Concrete and Timber Piles (preformed concrete and timber piling affected by tidal water)
WE15 Steel Sheet Piling (sheet piling affected by water)

Introduction

Worked Example 16 represents a navigation lamp platform constructed in a tidal estuary, comprising preformed concrete piles supporting a simple *in situ* reinforced concrete platform with metal handrail and access ladder.

The location in a tidal estuary initiates the requirements of paragraph 5.20 of CESMM3. Unlike all the other examples in this book, this work is well away from shore and thus working with plant based on dry land is not feasible. This part of the contract would require all work to use plant based on barges and all materials to be delivered by boat from the shore. The drawings and specification should make this locational difficulty quite clear but an appropriate heading must be incorporated into the bill. As this particular piece of construction is likely to be just one feature of a larger contract for dock or navigational improvements, it is important under CESMM3, paragraph 5.10, that such work is not incorporated with other work with differing locations and cost considerations.

In this example the requirements regarding the tidal water effects (CESMM3, paragraph 5.20) are accommodated by incorporating appropriate headings for each section or class of work according to the actual location within the works. This approach is considered the fairest way of indicating the cost significance of the tidal water on the various items of work.

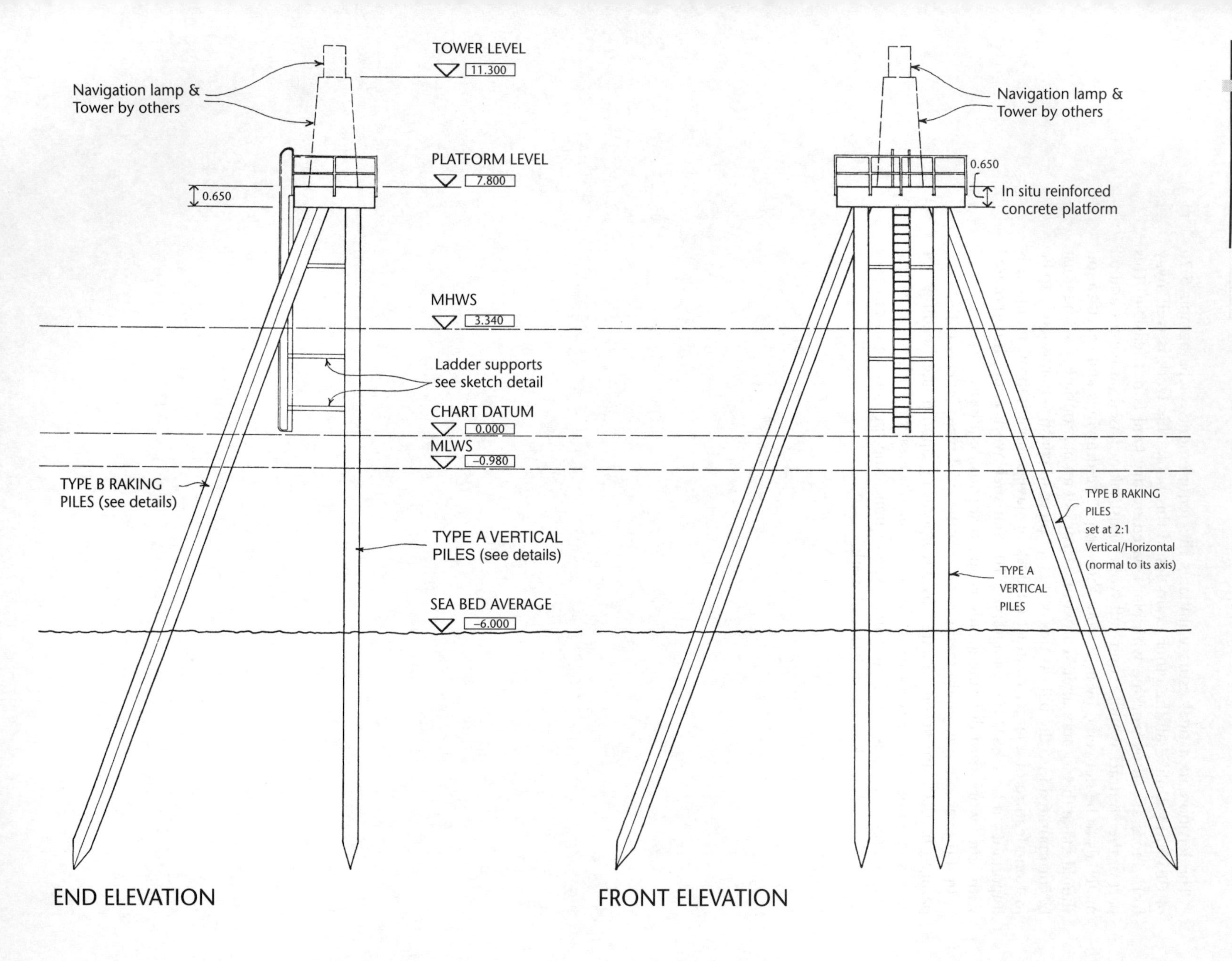

Navigation lamp &
Tower by others
TOWER LEVEL
11.300
PLATFORM LEVEL
7.800
0.650
MHWS
3.340
Ladder supports
see sketch detail
CHART DATUM
0.000
MLWS
–0.980
TYPE B RAKING
PILES (see details)
TYPE A VERTICAL
PILES (see details)
SEA BED AVERAGE
–6.000
END ELEVATION
Navigation lamp &
Tower by others
0.650
In situ reinforced
concrete platform
TYPE B RAKING
PILES
set at 2:1
Vertical/Horizontal
(normal to its axis)
TYPE A
VERTICAL
PILES
FRONT ELEVATION

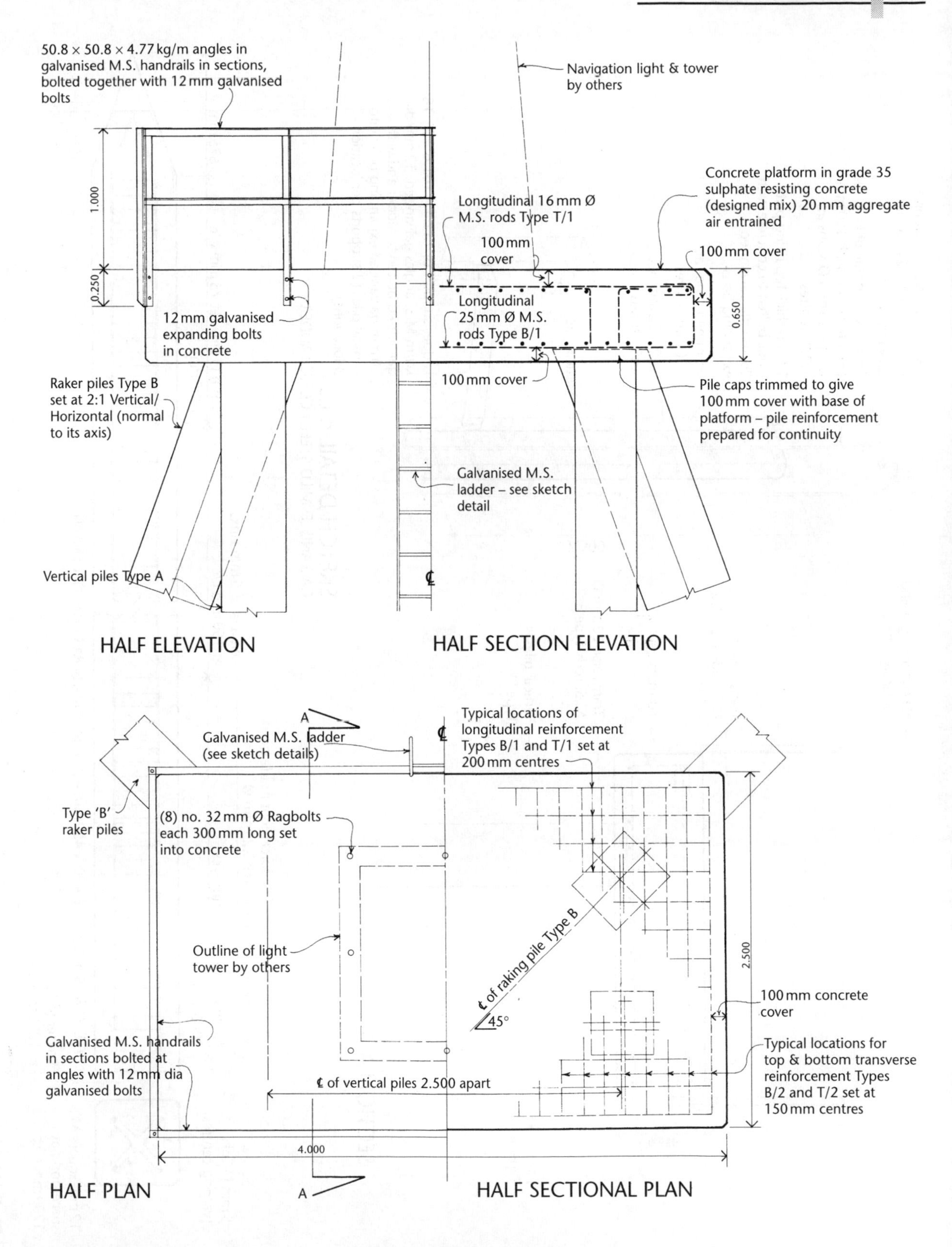
50.8 × 50.8 × 4.77 kg/m angles in galvanised M.S. handrails in sections, bolted together with 12 mm galvanised bolts
Navigation light & tower by others
1.000
0.250
Longitudinal 16 mm Ø M.S. rods Type T/1
100 mm cover
Concrete platform in grade 35 sulphate resisting concrete (designed mix) 20 mm aggregate air entrained
100 mm cover
Longitudinal 25 mm Ø M.S. rods Type B/1
0.650
12 mm galvanised expanding bolts in concrete
100 mm cover
Raker piles Type B set at 2:1 Vertical/ Horizontal (normal to its axis)
Pile caps trimmed to give 100 mm cover with base of platform – pile reinforcement prepared for continuity
Galvanised M.S. ladder – see sketch detail
Vertical piles Type A
℄
HALF ELEVATION
HALF SECTION ELEVATION
A
Galvanised M.S. ladder (see sketch details)
℄
Typical locations of longitudinal reinforcement Types B/1 and T/1 set at 200 mm centres
Type 'B' raker piles
(8) no. 32 mm Ø Ragbolts each 300 mm long set into concrete
℄ of raking pile Type B
Outline of light tower by others
2.500
45°
100 mm concrete cover
Galvanised M.S. handrails in sections bolted at angles with 12 mm dia galvanised bolts
Typical locations for top & bottom transverse reinforcement Types B/2 and T/2 set at 150 mm centres
℄ of vertical piles 2.500 apart
4.000
HALF PLAN
A
HALF SECTIONAL PLAN

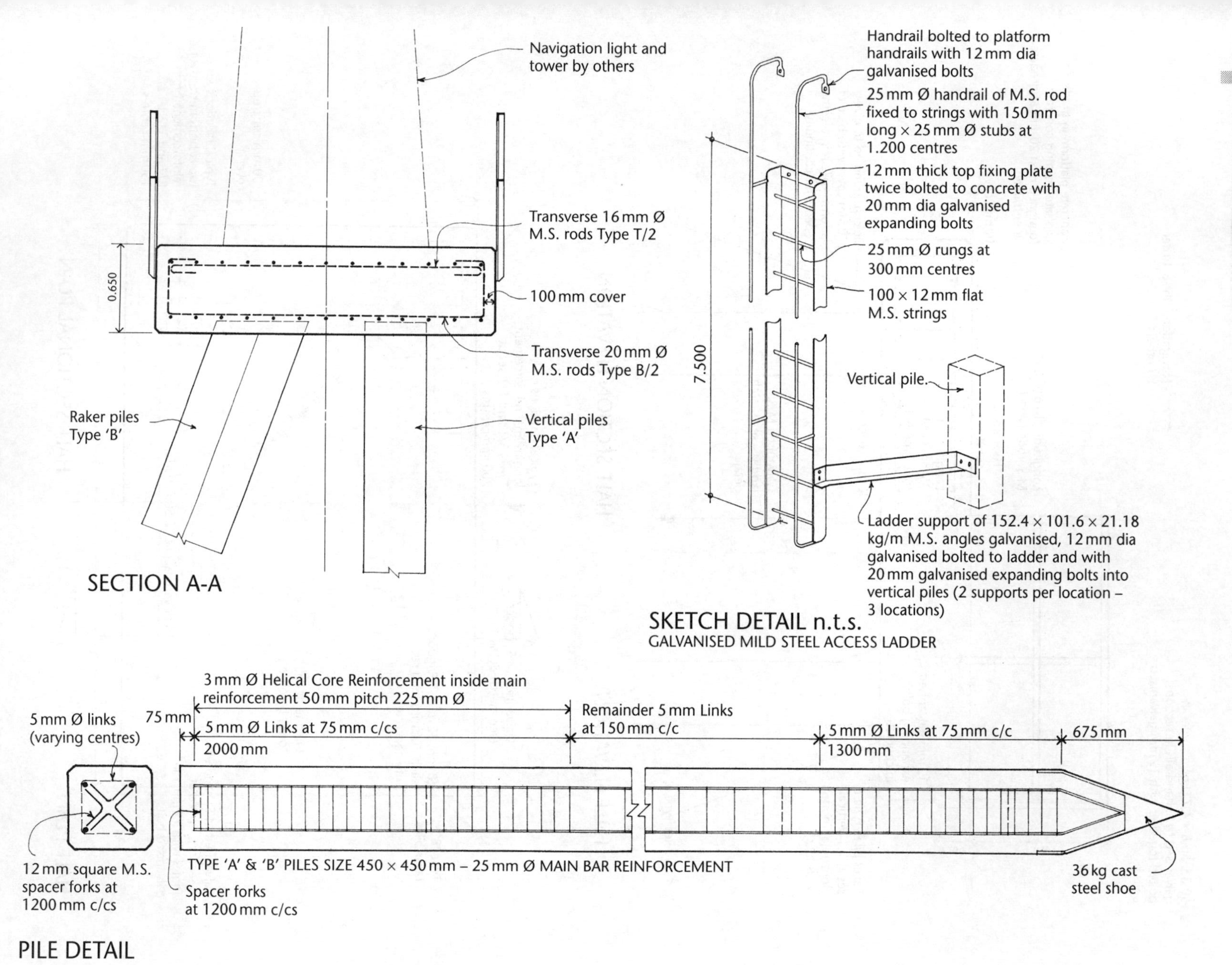
Navigation light and tower by others
Transverse 16 mm Ø M.S. rods Type T/2
0.650
100 mm cover
Transverse 20 mm Ø M.S. rods Type B/2
Raker piles Type 'B'
Vertical piles Type 'A'
SECTION A-A
Handrail bolted to platform handrails with 12 mm dia galvanised bolts
25 mm Ø handrail of M.S. rod fixed to strings with 150 mm long × 25 mm Ø stubs at 1.200 centres
12 mm thick top fixing plate twice bolted to concrete with 20 mm dia galvanised expanding bolts
25 mm Ø rungs at 300 mm centres
100 × 12 mm flat M.S. strings
7.500
Vertical pile.
Ladder support of 152.4 × 101.6 × 21.18 kg/m M.S. angles galvanised, 12 mm dia galvanised bolted to ladder and with 20 mm galvanised expanding bolts into vertical piles (2 supports per location – 3 locations)
SKETCH DETAIL n.t.s.
GALVANISED MILD STEEL ACCESS LADDER
3 mm Ø Helical Core Reinforcement inside main reinforcement 50 mm pitch 225 mm Ø
5 mm Ø links (varying centres)
75 mm
5 mm Ø Links at 75 mm c/cs
2000 mm
Remainder 5 mm Links at 150 mm c/c
5 mm Ø Links at 75 mm c/c
1300 mm
675 mm
12 mm square M.S. spacer forks at 1200 mm c/cs
TYPE 'A' & 'B' PILES SIZE 450 × 450 mm – 25 mm Ø MAIN BAR REINFORCEMENT
Spacer forks at 1200 mm c/cs
36 kg cast steel shoe
PILE DETAIL

GENERAL NOTES

REINFORCEMENT: All reinforcement to be mild steel rods to BS 4449. Minimum cover in platform to be 100 mm

MILD STEEL COMPONENTS: Handrails and ladder to be fabricated in mild steel sections and later to be hot dipped galvanised. Site connections to be galvanised bolts, nuts and washers throughout

CONCRETE: Platform of grade 35 sulphate resisting concrete (designed mix) cement to BS 4027, 20 mm aggregate, air entrained

REINFORCEMENT SCHEDULE

All mild steel reinforcement rods to BS 4449.
Main dimensions from detail drawings. 100 mm concrete cover throughout.

ROD REFERENCE	DIAMETER	OUTLINE	REMARKS
B1	25 mm	200; 450	Set at 200 mm centres longitudinal bottom reinforcement
B2	20 mm	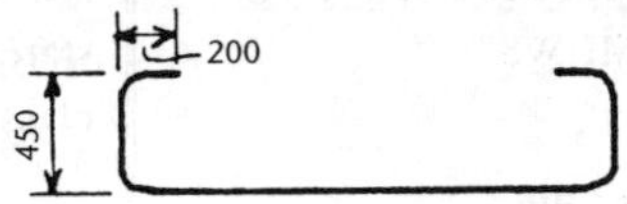 200; 450	Set at 150 mm centres transverse bottom reinforcement
T1	16 mm	200	Set at 200 mm centres longitudinal top reinforcement
T2	14 mm	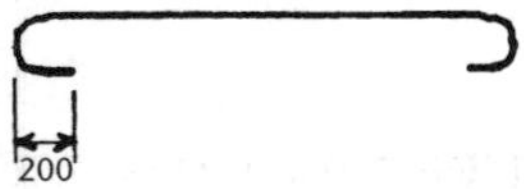 200	Set at 150mm centres transverse top reinforcement

PILES: Preformed concrete piles to be in Grade 35 steam cured concrete, 20 mm aggregate, sulphate resisting cement to BS 4027

REF.	SECTION	LOCATION	LENGTH	MINIMUM PENETRATION
TYPE 'A'	450 × 450	Vertical Front Piles	22.500	7.000
TYPE 'B'	450 × 450	Raking Rear Piles	25.500	8.000

All piles driven to set of 10 blows per 25 mm from 8 tonne rig.

One vertical and one raking pile to be subjected to a test load of 80 tonnes for 12 hours each.

NAVIGATION LAMP PLATFORM

Class F: In situ Concrete

Timesing	Dimensions	Squaring	Description	Side notes
			Work approximately 4.4 m above MHWS	(Paragraph 5.20)
	4.00 2.50 0.65		Provsn. of conc. designed mix grade C35, ct. to BS 4027, air entrained, 20 mm agg. F277	(Rules M1 and M2) Stated cement and admixture. *Note*: No deductions for pile tops or splays as rules M1c and M1d.
			&	
			Placg. of conc. reinforced, pile cap forming lamp platform, thickness exc. 500 mm. F628	(Rule A4) Other concrete forms component identified.

Class G: Concrete Ancillaries

Timesing	Dimensions	Squaring	Description	Side notes
			Work approximately 4.4 m above MHWS	(Paragraph 5.10) Location stated again as separate work class.
	4.00 2.50		Fwk. fair fin. Horizontal, (platform soffit). G215	(Rules M1, M6, D1, D2) Piles not deducted nor labour for working around same given in spirit of rule M6. Extra description in item informs Contractor of location.
2/ 2/	4.00 0.65 2.00 0.65		Vertical, width 0.4–1.22 m. G244	(Rules M1, M2, D1, D2)
2/ 2/ 4/	4.00 2.00 0.65		Conc. comp. of constant cross-section, intrusions. G286.1 (vert. corners	(Rules D5, A5) Internal splays formed with fillets.

NAVIGATION LAMP PLATFORM (Contd)

Timesing	Dimensions	Squaring	Description	Side notes
			Conc. comp. of constant cross-section, intrusions, upper surfaces.	(Rules M3, A2)
2/	4.00			Splays to top surface. Some QS may not trouble to
2/	2.00		G286.2	separate these splays from those in last item.
			Reinforcement, M.S. bars to BS 4449	(Rules D6, C1, M8)
			Diam. 16 mm.	Measured by tonne, lengths
			G515	multiplied by mass/metre
13/	4.32		(T1	from tables. 16 mm =
27/	2.80		(T2	1.579 kg/m.
			Diam. 20 mm.	20 mm = 2.466 kg/m.
			G516	
27/	3.60		(B2	
			Diam. 25 mm.	25 mm = 3.854 kg/m.
			G517	
13/	5.10		(B1	
	4.00 2.50		Conc. accessories, finishg. of top surfs., wood float. G811	(Rule M13) Smooth top surface required.
	8		Conc. accessories, other inserts 32 mm galv. rag bolts 300 mm long, proj. frm. one surf. of conc. G832	(Rules D11, A14, A15, A16)

Class N: Miscellaneous Metalwork

Timesing	Dimensions	Squaring	Description	Side notes
			Work approx. 4.5–5.5 m above MHWS	(Paragraph 5.20)
			M.S. welded fabrication, hot dipped galv. after fabrication, site bolted connections	(Rules A1, C1)
			Handrails 1250 mm total ht. as detail dwg.	
2/	4.00			
	2.50		N140	
	2.05		(net of opening	

16.2

NAVIGATION LAMP PLATFORM (Contd)

			Description	Notes
			Work approx. 1.3 m above MLWS to approx. 4.5 m above MHWS M.S. welded fabrication, hot dipped galv. after fabrication	(Paragraph 5.20) Different location from handrails. (Rules A1, C1)
	7.50		Ladder with handrail to both sides, incl. supports all as detail dwg. N130	(Rule A2) All inclusive item as tenderers will price this work from the detailed drawings.
Class P: Piles				
			Preformed conc. piles as platform support, grade C35 conc. reinforced and with cast steel shoes as detail dwg.	(Rules A1, A3, M1, A8) Structure being supported stated.
			Driven between MHWS and MLWS, commg. surf. sea bed av. sounding 6.00 m below O.D.	(Paragraph 5.20)
	2		Piles 450 × 450 mm, cross-sect. area 0.15–0.25 m², nr. of piles length 22.50 m. P351.1	(Rules A6, D3, M4)
	2		Piles 450 × 450 mm, cross-sect. area 0.15–0.25 m², nr. of piles length 25.50 m. P351.2	
2/	7.00		Depth driven. P352.1	Assuming min. penetration in bill as work will be remeasured.
2/	8.00		Depth driven raking, inclination ratio 1 horiz. to 2 vert. P352.2	(Rule A2)

NAVIGATION LAMP PLATFORM (Contd)

Class Q: Piling Ancillaries

			Preformed concrete piles, cross-sectional area 0.15–0.25 m^2 450 × 450 mm section. Work at approx. 3.8 m above MHWS.	Paragraph 5.20.
4/	1.80		Cuttg. off surplus lens. Q375	No real cost difference between vert. and raking.
	2		Prepg. heads. Q385.1	As raking preparation is a bit more difficult than vert. these have been separated.
	2		Prepg. heads of raking piles. Q385.2	
	1		Pile test, maintained loadg. with various reactions, test load 80 t. Q811.1	(Rule A8) Actual load to be stated.
	1		Pile test all as last but to raking pile. Q811.2	(Rule A8) Raking piles stated.

16.4

WORKED EXAMPLE 17

Estate Road

Cross-references

Explanatory Chapters

This worked example includes material which is explained in Chapter 5 CESMM3 – Class E: Earthworks; Chapter 7 CESMM3 – Classes I–L: Pipework; and part of Chapter 10 CESMM3 – Class R: Roads and Pavings.

Related Worked Examples

WE1 Demolition and Site Clearance (prior considerations before commencing excavation work)
WE2 Excavation and Filling (example of cut and fill measurements)
WE6 Sewage Holding Tank (straightforward excavations)
WE8 Stone Faced Sea Wall (simple light-duty paving)
WE9 Sewer (larger scale example of drainage items)

Introduction

Worked Example 17 includes the measurement of excavation and filling to create the road and footpath formation. The work involves creating sloping side banks to the excavations and the filling to suit the contours, with the banks specified to be set to a slope of 1 in 2. Side bankings create a problem in assessing the horizontal component of the banks because of the compounding effect of the existing natural ground slopes. To make the task more straightforward the existing ground is often assumed to slope evenly throughout and fair approximations are made. It should be remembered that all quantities in civil contracts are subject to remeasurement and that the quantities in the bills are 'estimated', thus reasonable accuracy is required rather than adopting pedantic and laborious approaches to such work. (Graphical methods of solving sloping bank quantities are fully covered in WE2 Excavation and Filling.)

In addition to the excavation and filling, some landscaping work is included. An important point should be noted, where landscaping occurs within Class E: Earthworks then neither 'trimming' nor 'preparation' is measured to these excavated or filled surfaces, as landscaping is deemed to include these tasks (rule C4). This also ties in with the exclusions mentioned in rules M11 and M23.

The roads and pavings comprise an *in situ* concrete carriageway with bituminous macadam footpaths and associated kerbs and edgings. It is worth noting that roads or pavings comprising several built-up layers require separate items for each layer under CESMM3 – Class: R.

Lastly the relatively straightforward surface water drainage requirements are measured under CESMM3 – Classes I–L.

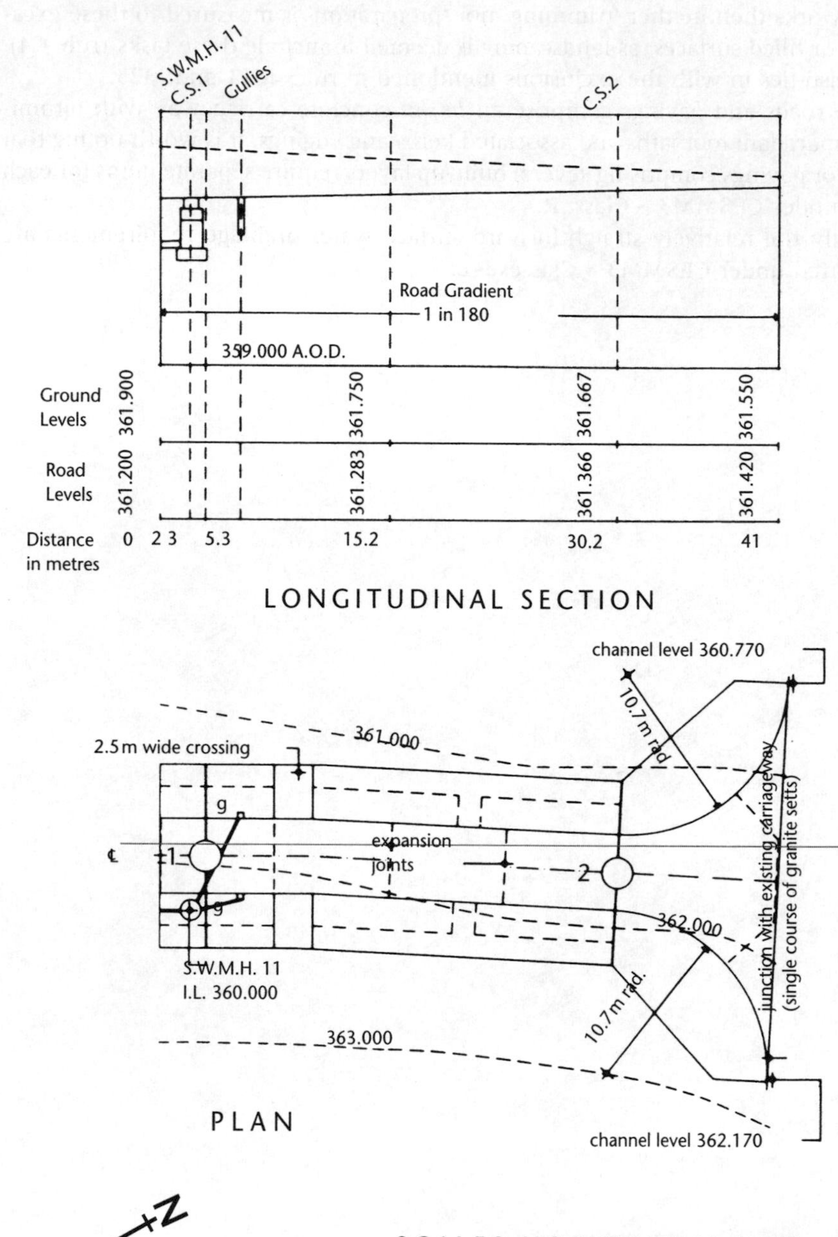
ESTATE ROAD
S.W.M.H. 11
C.S.1
Gullies
C.S.2
Road Gradient
1 in 180
359.000 A.O.D.
Ground Levels
361.900
361.750
361.667
361.550
Road Levels
361.200
361.283
361.366
361.420
Distance in metres
0 2 3 5.3 15.2 30.2 41
LONGITUDINAL SECTION
channel level 360.770
10.7 m rad.
361.000
2.5 m wide crossing
g
expansion joints
1
2
362.000
S.W.M.H. 11
I.L. 360.000
10.7 m rad.
junction with existing carriageway
(single course of granite setts)
363.000
PLAN
channel level 362.170
N
SCALES: HORIZONTAL 1:500
VERTICAL 1:100

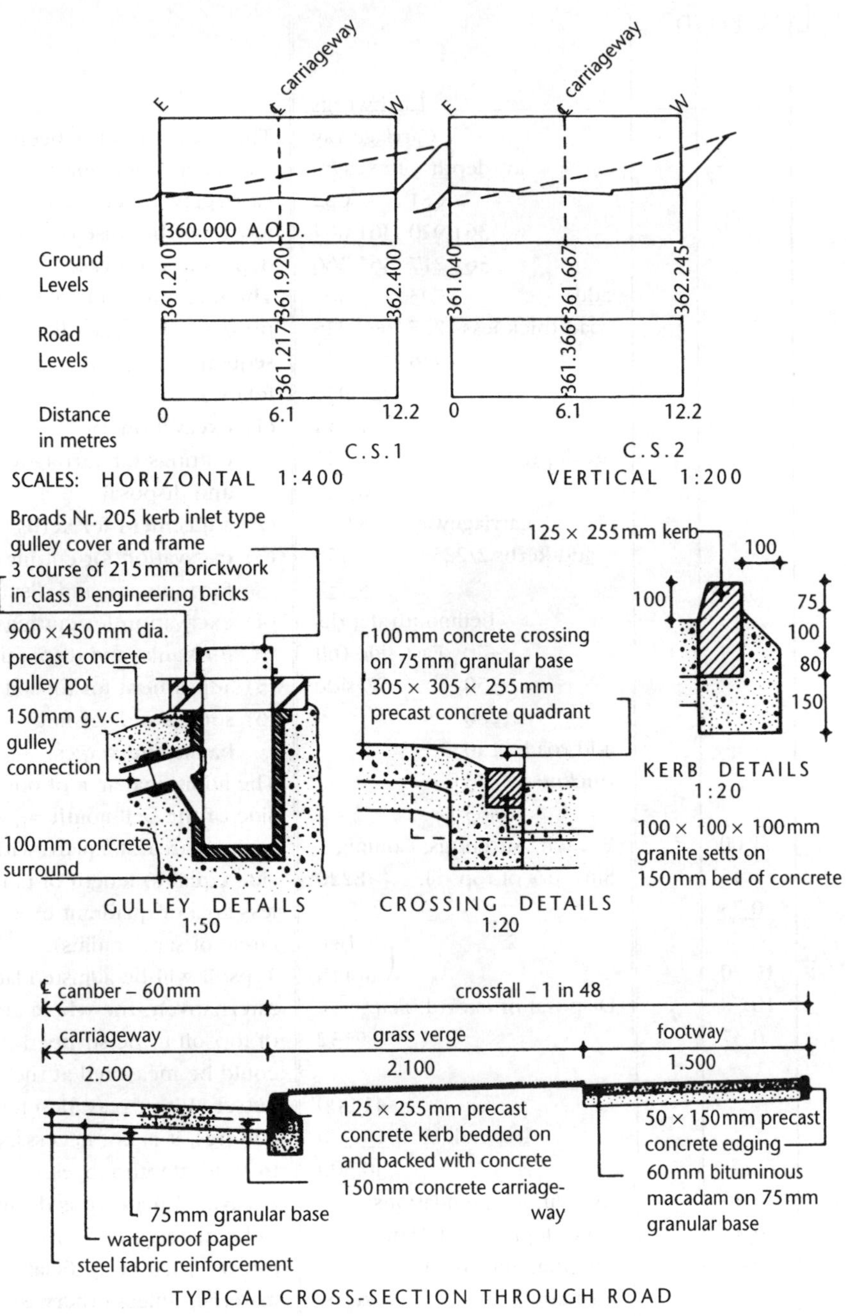

TYPICAL CROSS-SECTION THROUGH ROAD
SCALE 1:50

ESTATE ROAD

Timesing	Dimensions	Squaring	Description
			Earthworks
			Carriageway
			av. depth. of excavn.
			CS1 CS2
			361.920 361.667
			361.217 361.366
			add 703 301
			road thickness 225 225
			928 526
			928
			2⌊1.454
			av. depth of excavn. 727
			width
			carriageway 5.000
			add kerbs 2/225 = 450
			5.450
			bellmouth depths
			−70 East side (fill
			350 W. side
			2⌊280
			add road 140
			thickness 225
			365
	41.00		Excavn. for cuttgs; Commg.
	5.45		Surf. u/s of topsoil. E220
	0.73		
			& (bell mouth
2/$\frac{3}{14}$/	10.70		
	10.70		Disposal of excvtd. mat
	0.37		E532
			41.000
			less rad. kerb 10.700
			30.300
2/	30.30		Excavn. for foundations;
	0.23		max. depth: ne 0.25 m;
	0.08		Commg. Surf. road
			formatn. (kerbs
			E321.1
2/$\frac{1}{2}$/$\frac{22}{7}$	10.70		& (bell mouth
	0.23		
	0.08		Disposal of excvtd. mat.
			E532

The excavation has been taken separately for carriageway, kerbs and footways, because of varying depths in each case.
The measurement rules are prescribed in Class E and the sequence adopted is as follows:
(1) excavation for cuttings for carriageway and disposal
(2) adjustment for kerbs
(3) excavation for cuttings for footways and disposal
(4) excavation for cuttings for banks and disposal
(5) adjustment for topsoil
(6) soiling and seeding banks and verges.
The additional area of one side of the bellmouth $= \frac{3}{14} \times$ radius^2 (area of square with side equal to length of radius less area of quadrant or $\frac{1}{4}$ circle of same radius).
Topsoil will be adjusted later. Alternatively, the whole area of topsoil to be stripped could be measured at the outset. With excavation for cuttings, it is not necessary to state depth ranges.
Excavated material is deemed to be material other than topsoil, rock or artificial material, unless otherwise described (rule D1).
Fill is a separate item.
The additional excavation for kerb foundations below road formation is kept separate from excavation for cuttings as it will be a more expensive item, possibly involving hand excavation.

ESTATE ROAD (Contd)

			Footways E. side W. side av. depth at CS1 60 900 add thickness of path or verge 135 195 av. depth at CS2–250 (fill 700 less thickness of path or verge 135 –115 (fill 2⌊1.600 800 add thickness of 135 path or verge 939 E. side CS1 195 CS2 topsoil 150 2⌊345 172 width path 1.500 verge 2.100 3.600 less kerb & backg 225 3.375	The fill required under footways and verges on the east side will be made up of non-selected excavated material. The whole of the area of paths and verges is normally stripped of topsoil, so that some excavation is required even in places which will subsequently receive fill. Excavation for kerbs and backing has already been taken with the carriageway and so needs deducting from the overall width of path and verge. All excavated material for disposal is taken as material other than topsoil, rock or other hard material in the first instance, and the necessary adjustments will be made later.
30.30 3.38 0.94 30.00 3.38 0.17			Excavn. for cuttgs; (W. side Commg. Surf. u/s of topsoil. E220 & (E. side Disposal of excvtd. mat. E532	The depths to surface of paving at extreme ends of paths are calculated thus:
			Footways at bellmouth E. side W. side CS2 –250 700 extremity –407 543 2⌊–657 2⌊1.243 –328 622 add thickness of path or 135 135 verge –193 (fill) 757	E. side W. side channel 360.770 362.170 lev. add depth of kerb + $\frac{1}{2}$ fall 137 137 on path 360.907 362.307 ground lev. at centre of path (interpolated) less finished 360.500 362.850 level 360.907 362.307 depth –.407 (fill) .543

17.2

ESTATE ROAD (Contd)

Timesing	Dimensions	Description	Notes
	12.60	Excavn. for cuttgs; Commg. Surf. u/s of topsoil E220	The additional 40 mm depth of excavation over the areas of the two crossings is not large enough to justify separate measurement.
	5.20 0.76	& (paths at bellmouth	Similarly the extra excavation for quadrants over that required for kerbs would be largely offset by the smaller quantity of excavation required for the granite setts – a sense of proportion must be maintained.
	12.60 5.20 0.15	Disposal of excvtd. mat. E532 (topsoil on E. side	
		Banks	
		Width of banks (inc. 150 mm additnl. excavn. for topsoil) E. side W. side CS1 150 2.650 CS2 850 2.850 2⌊1.000 2⌊5.500 av. width 500 (fill) 2.750	The build-up of dimensions for the bank excavation is inserted in waste, to obtain the average widths and heights.
		bellmouth 850 2.850 1.750 750 2⌊2.600 2⌊3.600 1.300 (fill) 1.800	The topsoil component will require subsequent adjustment. Disposal of excavated material is deemed to be disposal off the site unless otherwise stated in the item description (rule D4).
		height of banks E. side W. side CS1 150 1.050 CS2 450 950 2⌊600 2⌊2.000 300 1.000	
		bellmouth 450 950 1.000 750 2⌊1.450 2⌊1.700 725 850	
½/	30.30 2.75 1.00	Excavn. for cuttgs; Commg. Surf. u/s of topsoil E220 (w. side	Slopes of 1 in 2 to banks hove been assumed.
½/	10.00 1.80 0.85	& (bellmouth w. side	The volume of bank excavation = length × average width × average depth.
		Disposal of excvtd. mat. E532	

ESTATE ROAD (Contd)

Timesing	Dimensions	Description	Notes
½/	30.30 0.50 0.30	Fillg. embankments; selected excvtd. mat. other than topsoil or rock. (E. side E624	Filling to embankments is kept separate from general fill. The description must contain the appropriate Third Division classification.
½/	10.00 1.30 0.73	(bellmth E. side	
	41.00 5.00 0.15	Ddt. Excavn. for cuttgs; Commg. Surf. u/s of topsoil. (carrgwy. E220 &	Adjustment of topsoil excavation over area of carriageway, paths and verges The depositing and spreading of the topsoil will be picked up in subsequent verge and bank slope items. The small surplus quantity of topsoil can remain on the site and make up surface irregularities.
2/$\frac{3}{14}$/	10.70 10.70 0.15	Ddt. Disposal of excvtd. mat. (bellmth. E532	
2/	30.30 3.60 0.15	& (paths & verges	
2/	12.60 5.20 0.15	Add Excavn. for cuttings; topsoil. E210 (bellmth.	
		Verges 30.300 less crossings 2.500, 1.500 = 4.000 26.300	The total lengths of verges are adjusted for the lengths of the crossings.
2/	26.30 1.98	Fillg. thickness: 150 mm, excvtd. topsoil. E641.1 &	The soiling of verges is kept separate from grass seeding
		Landscapg., grass seedg. E830.1	Trimming and preparation deemed included (rule C4).

ESTATE ROAD (Contd)

Timesing	Dimensions	Squaring	Description	Side notes
			Banks	Two items arise in connection with the banks: 1 soiling of slopes 2 grass seeding.
	27.70 2.85		Fillg. thickness: 150 mm, excvtd. topsoil; to surfs. unclined at an ∠ of 10° to 45° to the hor. E641.2	The filling item is measured in m^2 as it is to a stated depth or thickness; stating the appropriate inclination category from rule A14.
	10.00 1.90			
			&	
			Landscapg., grass seedg. to surfs. inclined at an ∠ ex. 10° to the hor. E830.2	The grass seeding on banks has a separate classification to that of the verges, as it falls into the inclined category under rule A18.
	27.70 0.65		(E. side	
	10.00 1.00		(bellmth. E. side	Rule C4 states that items for landscaping shall be deemed to include fertilizing, trimming and preparation of surfaces. Thus neither trimming nor preparation is measured where grass seeding applies. However any excavation or filling which receives roads or pavings requires preparation to be given as rules M11 and M23.
			Roads and Pavings	
	41.00 5.00		Base granular mat. DTp Specfd. type 1, depth: 75 mm. R113	Many details of road construction can be obtained from the Department of Transport 'Specification for Highway Works', to which reference can be made in the item descriptions. The actual thicknesses of slabs and courses should be given instead of the Third Division depth ranges in accordance with rule A1 of Class R.
			&	
2/3/14/	10.70 10.70		Carriageway slab of (bellmth. DTp specifd. pavg. qual. conc., depth; 150 mm. R414	

ESTATE ROAD (Contd)

Timesing	Dimensions	Description	Notes
	41.00 5.00	Steel fabric reinft. to BS 4483, nom. mass 3–4 kg/m^2; type A252. R443	
2/$\frac{3}{14}$/	10.70 10.70	&	
		Waterproof membrane below conc. pavement; waterproof paper to BS 1521 class BIF. R480	The waterproof membrane is likely to be of waterproof paper or impermeable plastic sheeting (250 or 500 grade).
		&	Preparation of excavated or filled surfaces to receive permanent works is measured under Class E (rules M11 and M23).
		Excavn. ancillaries, prepn. of excvtd. surfaces. E522	
		Joints in conc. pavements	
5/	5.00	Expansion jts. depth: 150 mm; as detail J, Drawing WE17. (transverse jts.	Expansion joints are always measured but construction joints only when they are expressly required (rule M7). No formwork is measured (rule C1).
	10.80	(bellmth.	
2/	4.40	(do.	
	5.00	(do. R524	
		Kerbs, channels & edgings less 30.200 setts 2.500 quads. 2/300 = 600 3.100 27.100	The length of kerb is adjusted in 'waste' for the crossings on both sides of the road.
2/	27.10	Precast conc. kerb to BS 7263 Pt. 1, fig. 1(d), st. or curved to rad. ex. 12 m; bedded and backed w. conc. grade C10 as detail X; Dwg WE17. R611	The kerb section is identified by reference to BS 7263. Kerbs laid to a radius exceeding 12 m are included with those laid straight. Details of concrete beds and backings to kerbs are included in the kerb descriptions (rule C3).
2/$\frac{1}{2}$/$\frac{22}{7}$/	10.70	Precast conc. kerb to BS 7263 Pt. 1, fig. 1(d), curved to rad. n.e. 12 m; bedded & backed a.b. R612	The kerbs to the bellmouth are kept separate as they are laid to less than 12 m radius.

ESTATE ROAD (Contd)

Timesing	Dimensions	Squaring	Description	Side notes
			Granite setts	
2/	2.50		Granite sett edgings (2 crossgs.) 100 × 100 mm, st. or curved to rad. ex 12 m; bedded on conc. grade C10 as detail Y, Dwg. WE17. R691	This item is not listed in Class R and hence the figure 9 is used in the Second Division to represent a non-standard item.
2/	10.70		junctn. w xtg. road	
	5.00		do.	
2/	10.70		Take up and remove xtg. precast conc. kerbs.	Kerbs at junction of new and existing roads; another non-standard item.
	5.00		R900	
2/	2		Precast conc. quadrant, 305 × 305 × 255 mm type QHB to BS 7263, fig. 1(q) bedded & backed w. conc. grade C10 as detail Q, Dwg. WE17. R693	To crossings (one each side at junction of kerbs and setts). Enumerated item but following the same approach as for kerbs. Excavation was dealt with previously.
			Light Duty Pavements Crossings 3.600 less setts 100 3.500	Vehicular crossings traversing paths and verges.
2/	3.50 2.50		Gran. base DTp Specfd. type 1, depth: 75 mm. R713	Similar base to that for carriageway.
			&	
			In situ conc. to BS 5328 mix grade C25 depth: 100 mm; w. tamped non-skid fin. R773	The description of the concrete slab follows the approach prescribed for light duty pavements, but substituting the grade of concrete in accordance with BS 5328.
			&	
			Waterproof membrane below conc. pavement; w.p. paper to BS 1521 class BIF. R480	

17.7

ESTATE ROAD (Contd)

Timesing	Dimensions	Squaring	Description	Notes
2/	3.50 2.50		Excavn. ancillaries, prepn. of excvtd. surfs. E522	
			Footways 30.200 less crossgs. 2.500 27.700	
			verge crossgs. verge 2.100 less kerb 125 1.975	Each course constitutes a separate item and the particulars are obtained from the Department of Transport 'Specification for Highway Works', with the thickness given in each case.
2/	27.70 1.50		Gran. base, DTp Specfd. type 1., depth: 75 mm. R713	
2/	1.98 1.50		& (verge crossgs.	Locational notes are given in waste for identification purposes. All preliminary calculations are also inserted to prevent errors and provide the facility for checking.
2/	12.60 5.20		Dense bit. macadam base-course DTp specfd. clause 906, depth: 50 mm. R752 (bellmth.	
			&	
			Dense bit. macadam wearg. course DTp specfd. clause 912, depth: 10 mm. R751	
			&	
			Excavn. ancillaries, prepn. of excvtd. surfs. E522	
			Edgings	
2/	27.70		Precast conc. edging to BS 7263 PT. 1, fig. 1(m), 50× 150 mm; st. or curved to rad. ex. 12 m, bedded & backed w. conc. grade C10 as detail E, Dwg. WE17 R651	Precast concrete flag descriptions include the types of slab in BS 7263 and the thickness. Precast concrete edging is measured and described in a similar manner to precast concrete kerbs. Figure 1(m) of BS 7263 shows three sets of dimensions for the round top variety and so dimensions have to be included in the description.
2/	10.00			First calculate the average depth of the surface water gully connections.

17.8

ESTATE ROAD (Contd)

Timesing	Dimension	Squaring	Description	Notes
			Surface Water Drainage Depths (inc. 150 mm conc. bed) gully 900 MH 1.287 2 | 2.187 av. depth 1.094	
	3.00 6.50		Clay pipes of S W qual. to BS 65 w. s & s flex. jts., nom. bore: 150 mm in trs., depth: ne 1.5 m., in rd. gully connectns. I112 &	The descriptions of pipes include materials, joint types and nominal bores with references to British Standards where appropriate (rule A2 of Class I)
			Surround, mass conc. grade C10, pipe nom. bore: 150 mm; thickness: 150 mm. L541	Materials and thicknesses of beds, haunches and surrounds are stated in item descriptions (rule A3 of Class L).
2/	1		Clay pipe fittgs. SW qual. to BS 65 w. s & s flex. jts., bends, nom. bore: 150 mm. J111	Pipe fittings are enumerated giving similar particulars as for pipes (rule A1 of Class J).
2/	1		Gullies, precast conc. trapped; to BS 5911, fig. 2(a) as detail 2 Dwg. WE17, w. Broads Nr. 205 kerb inlet gully cover. K360	Gullies are enumerated with adequate references for detailed particulars and stating the type of cover (rules A1 and A2 of Class K).

WORKED EXAMPLE 18

Rail Track

Cross-references

Explanatory Chapter

This worked example includes material which is explained within part of Chapter 10 CESMM3 – Class S: Rail Track. This section of CESMM3 covers the laying of new rail track and certain alterations and upgrading of existing track work. Note that any work required for earthworks, pipework, structures and the like would be measured in detail under the appropriate CESMM3 classes. Class S is solely concerned with track work above formation level.

Related Worked Examples

WE17 Estate Road (example of measurement of excavation and filling similar to that required for railway practice)
WE19 Tunnel (example similar to tunnelling in railway practice)

Introduction

Worked Example 18 covers the measurement of a typical upgrading contract for rail trackwork. A new passing loop is to be provided in place of an existing siding on a colliery branch. Associated slewing of the existing running track, point-work and ballasting is also included.

Rail Track

Proposed passing loop and associated works at Flatrigg Cutting on the Broadheath Open Cast Colliery Branch

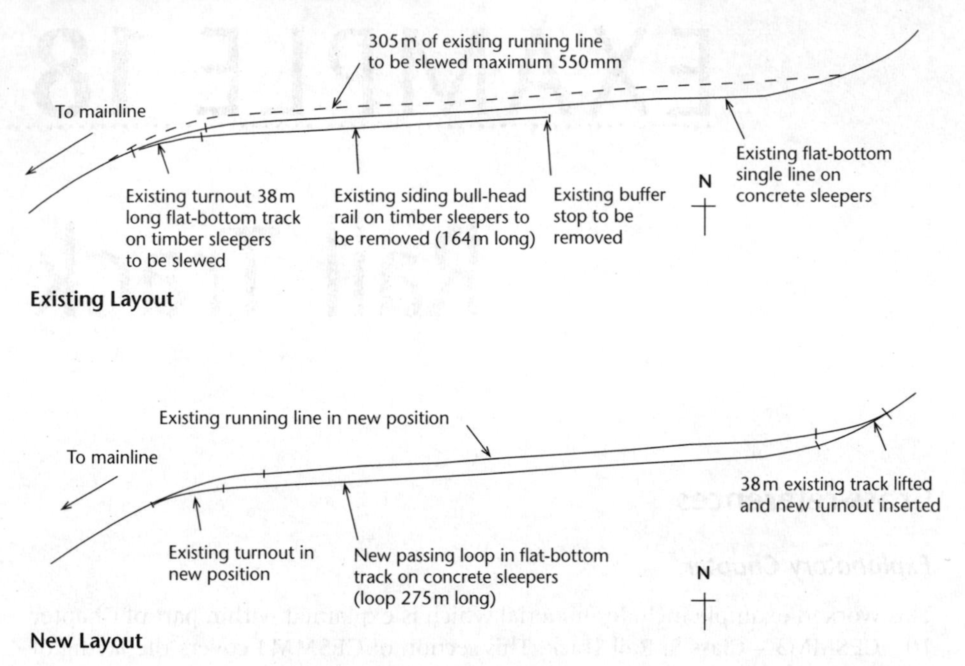

RAIL TRACK

Proposed passing loop at Flatrigg Cutting on the Broadheath Colliery Branch

Class S: Rail Track

The following work is concerned with standard gauge trackwork as detailed on Drawing WE18.

Dimensions	Description	Notes
	Track foundations	
	Crushed stone ballast as Specification Clauses S5–S7	
289.00	Bottom ballast.	(Rules D1, A1)
3.50	S110	
0.40	plain track 275.00	Full length of new loop taken
	extra @ new turnout 14.00	as old siding ballast in poor
	289.00	condition.
327.00	Top ballast.	(Rules M1, D2, A1)
3.15	S120	
0.20	as last item 284.00	Assume new top ballast for
	new turnout on old line 38.00	whole of new turnout.
	327.00	
	Taking up track	
	Lifting existing bull head track with fish plate joints on timber sleepers and chairs, fully dismantled and placed in employer's store	
164.00	Bull head rail, plain track. S211	(Rule A3)
1	Sundries, buffer stop, about 2 tonnes, steel rail construction. S281	(Rule A4)
	Lifting existing flat bottom welded track on concrete sleepers, fully dismantled etc as above	
38.00	Flat bottom rail, plain track. S221	Length removed for new turnout.

RAIL TRACK (Contd)

Timesing	Dimensions	Squaring	Description	Notes
			Lifting, packing and slewing	
	1		Flat bottom track with concrete sleepers of original running line net length 267 m (either side of next item), maximum slew 550 mm and maximum lift 150 mm with extra ballast as specified. S330	(Rules D3, C2, A5, A6)
	1		Flat bottom track with turnout on timber sleepers length 38 m otherwise as last item. S340	(Rule D3)
			Supplying	Supply items taken first followed by track laying measured separately.
2/	275.00 × 56 kg/m		Flat bottom rail, reference 113A, 56 kg/m. S425	(Rules C3, A9)
	394		Concrete sleepers 2600 mm long, with attached fittings as specified. S472	(Rules C4, A8) Sleepers set at 700 mm centres (275 m divided by 0.7 m ctrs + 1).
4/	394		Pandrol rail fastnings. S483	(Rule C5) 4 fastnings per sleeper.
2/	9		Plain fishplates (pairs) S484	(Rule M6) Rails supplied in 18 m lengths and welded into 36 m lengths, thus nr of fishplates = 275/36 + 1 = 9 per rail.
	1		Turnout, flat bottom track on timber sleepers as per Drawing WE18/?, maximum length 38 m S510	(Rules C3, A10)

18.2

RAIL TRACK (Contd)

Timesing	Dimension	Squaring	Description	Side notes
			Laying	
			Flat bottom track reference 113A, 56 kg/m	
			Plain track, part welded, part fish-plated joints on concrete sleepers. S621	(Rules M8, A15) Rule M8 requires a centre line measurement including all lengths occupied by turnouts.
	275.00			
	38.00		(turnout main	
	15.00		(turnout branch	
	30.00		Form curve on plain track, radius exceeding 300 m. S623	(Rule M8, in effect extra over plain track.)
	1		Turnout on timber sleepers as Drawing WE18/?, fishplated joints, length 38 m. S624	(Rule M8, in effect extra over plain track to lay turnout.)
2/	8		Welded joints, thermit process. S627	(Rule A17) Rails supplied in 18 m lengths and welded into 36 m lengths, thus nr of welds = 275/36 = 8 per rail.

WORKED EXAMPLE 19

Tunnel

Cross-references

Explanatory Chapter

This worked example includes material which is explained within part of Chapter 10 CESMM3 – Class T: Tunnels. This section of CESMM3 covers all the work involved in constructing a tunnel including excavation, lining, support and stabilisation.

Related Worked Examples

There are no other directly related Worked Examples.

Introduction

Worked Example 19 covers the measurement of a relatively small-diameter tunnel for a sewer diversion scheme. The tunnel is of cast iron segment construction and items are included for the possibility of pressure grout stabilisation, should that be specified by the Engineer. Tunnels of much larger diameters are commonly required for road and rail schemes but the principles of measuring such work are the same.

DRAWING WE19: TUNNEL
is overleaf

TUNNEL

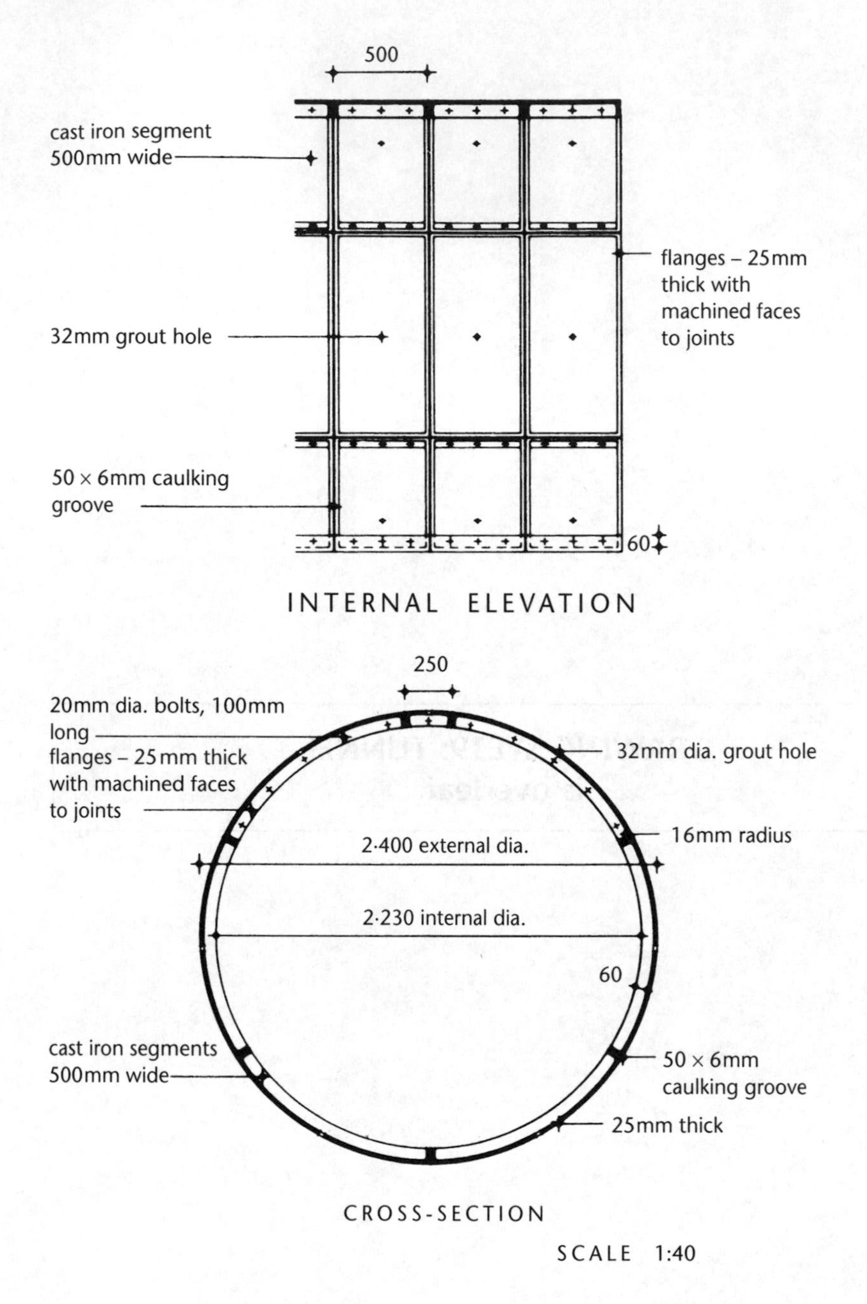
500
cast iron segment
500mm wide
flanges – 25mm
thick with
machined faces
to joints
32mm grout hole
50 × 6mm caulking
groove
60
INTERNAL ELEVATION
250
20mm dia. bolts, 100mm
long
flanges – 25mm thick
with machined faces
to joints
32mm dia. grout hole
16mm radius
2·400 external dia.
2·230 internal dia.
60
cast iron segments
500mm wide
50 × 6mm
caulking groove
25mm thick
CROSS-SECTION
SCALE 1:40

Timesing	Dimensions	Squaring	Description	Notes
	TUNNEL			
	BRADWELL SEWER TUNNEL			
			350 m length	A locational heading is
			Tunnel excavation	needed for purposes of
			ext. diameter 2.40 m	identification. The diameter
$\frac{22}{7}$/	350.00		In med. dense gravel	stated is the external
	1.20		& sand; st. T122	diameter of the tunnel lining.
	1.20			The material through which
				the tunnel is to be driven is
				stated. If the work was under
				compressed air this would be
$\frac{22}{7}$/	350.00		Excavated surfs. in med. dense	stated in a heading, with the
	2.40		gravel & sand; voids filled w.	operative gauge pressure
			ct. grout as Spec. Clause 184.	range (rule A1 of Class T).
			T180	As no payment lines are
			Segmental lings.	shown on the Drawing, the
			500|350.000	excavated surface is
			700	measured to the area
			bolts/ring	enclosing the permanent
			circumf. 6 × 5 + 1 31	work (net void). The
			long. 7 × 3 21	Contractor will price the
			52	over-break (excess
				excavation) and subsequent
				grouting in this item (rule M4).
700/	1		Preformed segmental tunnel	Number of bolts per ring are
			lings. of c.i. bolted rings, ext.	calculated in waste, to ensure
			diameter 2.40 m; ring nom.	accuracy and permit
			width 500 mm, comprisg. 7	checking. Preformed
			segments, max. piece wt.	segmental linings are
			144 kg, 52 bolts & grummets	enumerated by rings, giving
			& 104 washers. T532	the nominal ring width,
				number of segments, bolts,
			&	grummets and washers, and
				maximum piece weight (rule
				A9).
			Parallel circumferential packg.	The measurement unit for
			for preformed segmental	packing shall be the number
			tunnel lings; bit. impregnated.	of rings of segments packed
			fibrebd., thickness: 8 mm.	(rule M7).
			T571	
			caulkg. jts.	
			ling. thickness 25	Build up of caulking
			$\frac{1}{2}$ flange depth − $\frac{1}{2}$/60 30	dimensions in waste, to
			55	arrive at the mean
			ext. diam. of ling. 2.400	length to be caulked.
			less 2 × outer face of ling.	
			to centre of caulkg.	
			groove. 2/55 110	
			mean diam of groove 2.290	

19.1

TUNNEL (Contd)

Timesing	Dimensions	Squaring	Description	Notes
700/$\frac{22}{7}$/	2.29		Lead fibre caulkg. for preformed segmental tunnel lings. (circum.	Caulking of grooves between segments to ensure watertight joints is measured as a linear item.
700/7/	0.50		(long- T574	
			If pressure grouting is required it will be measured in the following manner:	This may be required to support and stabilise the ground surrounding the tunnel.
			Pressure grouting	
	1		Sets of drillg. & groutg. plant. T831	An enumerated item for drilling and grouting plant.
700/	7		Face packers. T832	There is one grout hole to each segment.
700/	4.00		Drillg. & flushg., hole diam. 32 mm, len. ne 5 m. T834	The lengths of holes are stated in stages of 5 m in item descriptions for drilling and re-drilling holes for pressure grouting (rule A17).
700/	2.00		Re-drillg. & flushg. holes, len. ne 5 m. T835	
	450 t		Injectn. of ct. grout as Spec. clause 215. T836	The quantity of cement grout has been calculated on the basis of 75 mm average thickness around the lining. Mass of mixing water ignored (rule M11).
			The following additional support and stabilisation item might be needed:	
	200.00		Fwd. probg., len.: 5–10 m. T840	A linear item with lengths of holes stated in 5 m stages (rule A17).

19.2

WORKED EXAMPLE 20

Sewer Renovation

Cross-references

Explanatory Chapter

This worked example includes material which is explained within part of Chapter 12 CESMM3 – Class Y: Sewer and Water Main Renovation and Ancillary Works. This section of CESMM3 covers the various specialist works involved with the renovation of existing sewers, comprising preparation, stabilisation and renovation of sewers and associated laterals.

Related Worked Examples

WE21 Water Main Renovation (further work measured under Class Y)

Introduction

Worked Example 20 is concerned with typical remedial work to be carried out on an existing sewer. Although no drawing has been provided in this case, the intentions and requirements of the renovation will be apparent from the measured items.

Note the differences between external grouting and annulus grouting which are explained in Chapter 12.

SEWER RENOVATION

Dimensions	Description	Notes
	RODNEY STREET MANHOLES 8–12 XTG. BK. SEWER, NOM. SIZE: 1050 × 750 mm, EGG SHAPED	The location of the work is stated to permit identification by reference to Drawings (rule Al of Class Y). Principal dimensions and profiles of sewers are to be given (rule A2).
	Prepn. of xtg. sewer	
130.00	Cleaning. Y110	Cleaning item is deemed to include making good resultant damage (rule C2).
16	Removg. intrusns; lateral, bore n.e. 150 mm; clay. Y121	Intrusions into bores of existing sewers to be removed prior to renovation (rule D1).
60.00	CCTV surveys. Y130	A popular technique, giving excellent guidance as to condition.
2	Plugging laterals w. grout to specfn. clause 24.3, bore n.e. 300 mm. Y141	Plugging laterals not exceeding 300 mm bore taken as an enumerated item, stating the materials.
1.00 0.40 0.30	Fillg. lateral w. grout to Specfn. clause 24.3, int. c.s. dims, 400 × 300 mm U-shaped. Y152	Filling laterals and other pipes measured in m^3, stating the materials used and the stated profile and size.
3	Local intl. repairs; area: 0.1–0.25 m^2. Y162	The area stated in item descriptions is the finished surface area (rule D2) and the item is deemed to include cutting out and repointing (rule C4).

20.1

SEWER RENOVATION (Contd)

Timesing	Dimensions	Squaring	Description	Notes
			XTG. BK. SEWER, NOM. SIZE: 1050 × 750 mm, EGG SHAPED	
			Stabilisation of xtg. sewers.	Measured in m^2 stating the materials used. No deduction is made for openings or voids not exceeding 0.5 m^2 in area (rule M3).
	15.00 1.80		Pointg. bwk. in c.m. (1:3). Y210	
	9		Sealg. pipe jts., n.e. 300 mm bore, under pressure w. epoxy mortar. Y220	Pipe joint sealing is deemed to include preparation of joints (rule C5).
			Extl. groutg.	External grouting is measured only where grouting is expressly required to be carried out as a separate operation from annulus grouting (rule M4).
	6		Nr. of holes Y231	Where the external grouting is to be carried out through pipe joints, item descriptions for number of holes shall state this (rule A7).
	16.00 3.20 0.25		Injection of ct. grt. to Specfn. clause 24.3. Y232	External grouting consists of the grouting of voids outside the existing sewer, other than voids grouted in the course of annulus grouting (rule D3).
			Renovatn. of xtg. sewers	
			Slipling.	
	66.00		Butt fusion welded (HDPE) conventln. slipling; design II, min. thickness 4 mm, to egg shaped sewer, nom. size 1050 × 750 mm. Y311	The item description is to include the type of lining. minimum finished internal size and thickness or grade (rule A8).

SEWER RENOVATION (Contd)

Timesing	Dimensions	Squaring	Description	Notes
			XTG. BRICK SEWER, NOM. SIZE: 1050 × 750 mm, EGG SHAPED	Note main headings to each section.
			Renovatn. of xtg. sewers Segmental lings.	
	47.00		GRP single piece ling., design type III to Specfn. clause 28.3, min. int. c.s. dims. 900 × 600 mm, egg shaped. Y333	Item descriptions of segmental linings shall state the type of lining, its minimum finished internal size and its thickness or grade (rule A8).
	52.00		GRC design type I to Specfn. clause 29.4, 15 mm th., min. intl. c.s. dims. 900 × 600 mm, egg shaped. Y334.1	
	4.00		GRC, ditto., int. c.s. dims. 1170 × 700 mm, curved to offset of 80 mm/m. Y334.2	The offset shall be stated where the lining is curved to an offset which exceeds 35 mm/m (rule A9).
			Annulus groutg.	The volume does not include external grouting (rule M5) and consists of the annular voids between new linings and existing sewers and associated work (rule D4).
	103.00 2.80 0.13		Ct. grt. as Specfn. clause 24.4 Y360	
			Laterals to renovated sewers Jointing	Item descriptions shall state the type of lining to which the laterals are to be connected and identifying those laterals which are to be regraded (rule A10), and are deemed to include work involved in connecting to the lining within 1 m from inside face of lined sewer (rule C6).
	4		Bore 150–300 mm to HDPE slipling., design II, thickness 4 mm, regraded. Y412	

SEWER RENOVATION (Contd)

			XTG. BRICK SEWER, NOM. SIZE: 1050 × 750 mm, EGG SHAPED	Main headings are inserted in capitals to give greater emphasis.
			Flap valves	
	3		Remove xtg; nom. diam. 300 mm. Y421	Removing, replacing and provision of new flap valves are each enumerated, stating the size in each case.
	2		Replace xtg., nom. diam. 225 mm. Y422	
			New mhs, replacg. xtg. mhs.	The item description follows the procedure prescribed in Class K. Item descriptions shall separately identify new manholes which replace existing manholes and they are deemed to include breaking out and disposal of existing manholes (rules A14 and C11). Item descriptions for the abandonment or alteration of existing manholes supply the contractor with all the basic information required for pricing and are usually supported by relevant drawings which detail the works involved.
	2		Brick w. backdrop type 1B; depth 2.5–3 m, type CMH3, w.c.i. cover to BS 497, ref. B4-22. Y624	
			xtg. mhs. Abandonment as Dwg. WE20(F)	
	1		Depth 2.5–3 m, inc. removg. cover slab, demolishg. shaft & backfillg. w. sel. fillg. Y714	
			Alteratns.	
	1		Wk. to benchg. & invts. as Dwg. WE20(E), inc. breakg out, re-haunchg & dealg. w. flows. Y720	
			Interruptns.	Interruptions are measured only where a minimum pumping capacity is expressly required for periods of time during normal working hours, when the flow in the sewer exceeds the installed pumping capacity and work is interrupted (rule M7).
	12h		Prepn. of xtg. sewers. Y810	
	12h		Stabilistn of xtg. sewers. Y820	
	15h		Renovatn. of xtg. sewers; segmental lings. Y833	

20.4

WORKED EXAMPLE 21

Water Main Renovation

Cross-references

Explanatory Chapter

This worked example includes material which is explained within part of Chapter 12 CESMM3 – Class Y: Sewer and Water Main Renovation and Ancillary Works. This section of CESMM3 covers the specialist works involved with the renovation of existing water mains and ancillary works. Water main renovation is only one sub-section of Class Y (Y5**) but may also include access requirements covered under manholes (Y6** and Y7**).

Related Worked Example

WE20 Sewer Renovation (further work measured under Class Y)

Introduction

Worked Example 21 is concerned with typical remedial work to be carried out on an existing water main. Although no drawing has been provided in this case, the intentions and requirements of the renovation will be apparent from the measured items.

WATER MAIN RENOVATION

Dimensions	Description	Commentary
	VALVES SV5–18 XTG. C.I. MAINS, NOM BORE n.e. 200–300 mm	Commence with a suitable heading giving the location of the water mains to be treated. As they all come within the same nominal bore range, they can be arranged under a single heading. The procedure follows closely that adopted for renovating sewers.
220.00	Cleaning. Y512	Starting with cleaning measured in metres, measured along centre lines of mains, and including lengths occupied by fittings and values (rule M6 of Class Y).
6	Removg. intrusns. Y522	Removing intrusions and pipe sample inspections are enumerated, and the latter include replacing the length removed by new pipework (rule C7).
8	Pipe sample inspectns. Y532	
220.00	CCTV surveys. Y542	Closed-circuit television surveys are a linear item.
220.00	Epoxy ling. as specfn. clause 26.8 Y562	Item descriptions for lining shall state the materials, nominal bores and thicknesses of the lining (rule A11). In this item the additional information is obtained from the specification.

21.1

Bibliography

Institution of Civil Engineers, *Civil Engineering Standard Method of Measurement*, Third Edition (CESMM3), Telford (1991).

Martin Barnes, *CESMM3 Handbook*, Telford (1992).

Royal Institution of Chartered Surveyors and Construction Confederation, *Standard Method of Measurement of Building Works*, Seventh Edition Revised 1998 (SMM7).

Ivor H. Seeley and Roger Winfield, *Building Quantities Explained*, Macmillan – now Palgrave (1998).

Appendix 1 – Abbreviations

a.b. *as before*
a.b.d. *as before described*
additnl. *additional*
adj. *adjoining*
a.f. *after fixing*
agg. *aggregate*
alt. *alternate*
ancills. *ancillaries*
appd. *approved*
ard. *around*
art. *artificial*
asp. *asphalt*
attchd. *attached*
av. *average*
A.V. *air valve*

backg. *backing*
battg. or batterg. *battering*
bd. *board*
bdg. *boarding*
bearg. *bearing*
beddg. *bedding*
bellmth. *bellmouth*
benchg. *benching*
b.f. *before fixing*
b.i. *build in*
bit. *bitumen* or *bitumastic*
bk. *brick*
bkg. *breaking*
bldg. *building*
b.o.e. *brick on end*
borg. *boring*
bott. *bottom*
b. & p. *bed and point*
br. *branch*
brr. *bearer*
b.s. *both sides*
BS *British Standard*
bwk. *brickwork*

cal. plumb. *calcium plumbate*
calkg. *caulking*
cap. *capacity*
cast. *casement*
cat. *catalogue*
ccs. *centres*
c. & f. *cut and fit*
chan. *channel*
chbr. *chamber*
chfd. *chamfered*
chn-lk. *chain link*
chy. *chimney*
c.i. *cast iron*
circ. *circular*
circum. *circumference*
c.m. *cement mortar*
commg. or commncg. *commencing*
comp. *composite*
compactn. *compaction*
conc. *concrete*
conn. *connection*
constn. *construction*
c.o.p. *circular on plan*
copg. *coping*
cos. *course(s)*
covg. *covering*
c. & p. *cut and pin*
Cr. *Contractor*
c.s. *cross-section*
csa *cross-sectional area*
csg *clear sheet glass*
ct. *cement* or *coat*
cu *cubic*

ddt. *deduct*
deckg. *decking*
delvd. *delivered*
dep. *deposit*
dia. or diam. *diameter*
diag. *diagonally*
dim. or dimng. *diminishing*
dist. *distance*
do. *ditto. (that which has been said before)*
dp. *deep*

d.p.c. *damp-proof course*
dr. *door*
drvg. *driving*
dt. *deduct*
DTp *Department of Transport*
dwg. *drawing*

ea. *each*
embankt. *embankment*
eng. *engineering*
Eng. *English*
Engr. *Engineer*
ent. *entrance*
e.o. *extra over*
ex. *exceeding* or *extra*
exc. *excavate*
excavn. *excavation*
ext. *external* or *externally*

facewk. *facework*
fcg. or facg. *facing*
fdn. *foundation*
f.f. *fair face*
fillg. *filling*
fin. *finish*
fittg. *fitting*
f.l. *floor level*
Flem. *Flemish*
flex. *flexible*
floatg. *floating*
flr. *floor*
F.O. *fix only*
follg. *following*
form. *formation*
fr. *frame*
frd. *framed*
frg. *framing*
frt. *front*
ftg. *footing*
fwd. *forward*
fwk. *formwork*
fxd. *fixed*
fxg. *fixing*

galvd. *galvanised*
gen. *general*
g.i. *galvanised iron*
g.l. *ground level*
glzg. *glazing*
g.m. *gauged mortar*
g.m.s. *galvanised mild steel*
grano. *granolithic*
grd. *ground*
grdg. *grading*
greenht. *greenheart*
grtd. *grouted*
g.s. *general surfaces*
gtg. *grating*
gth. *girth*

H.A. *highway authority*
ha *hectare*
h.b. *half brick*
h.c. *hardcore*
hi. *high*
holl. *hollowed*
hor. *horizontal*
h.r. *half-round*
ht. *height*
hwd. *hardwood*
h.w.l. *high water level*
H.W.O.S.T. *high water of spring tides*

inc. *including*
int. *internal* or *internally*
intl. *internal*
invt. *invert*
irreg. *irregular*

jt. *joint*
jtd. *jointed*
junctn. *junction*

kg. *kilogramme(s)*
km *kilometre(s)*
k.p. & s. *knot, prime and stop*

l. *labour*
la. *large*
L.A. *local authority*
layg. *laying*
len. *length*
lev. *level*
lg. *long*
lin. *linear*
ling. *lining*
l.m. *lime mortar*
long. *longitudinal*
l.w.l. *low water level*
L.W.O.S.T. *low water of spring tide*

m *metre(s)*
matl. or mat. *material*
max. *maximum*
mech. *mechanically*
med. *medium*
memb. *membrane*
mesd. *measured*
met. *metal*
m.g. *make good*
m.h. *manhole*
MHWS *mean high water spring*
min. *minimum*
MLWS *mean low water spring*
mm *millimetre(s)*
mo. *mortar*
mors. *mortice*
m.s. *mild steel*
m/s. *measured separately*

nat. *natural*
n.e. *not exceeding*
nec. *necessary*
nom. *nominal*
nr. *number*
n. & w. *nut and washer*
n.w. *narrow widths*

o/a *overall*
O.D. *Ordnance Datum*
o'hg. *overhang*
opg. *opening*
ord. *ordinary*
orig. *original*
oslg. *oversailing*
ov'll *overall* (alternative *to o/a*)

patt. *pattern*
pavg. *paving*
p.c. *prime cost*
P.ct. *Portland cement*
perm. *permanent*
p.hse. *pumphouse*
pilg. *piling*
p.m. *purpose made*
ppt. *parapet*
pr. *pair*
prepd. *prepared*
prepn. *preparation*
proj. *projection*
provsnl. *provisional*
psn. *position*
p.s. *pressed steel*
P.st. *Portland stone*
pt. *paint*
ptd. *pointed*
ptg. *pointing*
ptn. *partition*
pumpg. *pumping*

qual. *quality*

rad. *radius*
rakg. *raking*
r.c. or r. conc. *reinforced concrete*
rd. *road*
rdd. *rounded*
reb. *rebate*
rec. *receive*
red. *reduced*
ref. *reference*
reinfd. *reinforced*
reinft. *reinforcement*
reqd. *required*
ret. *retaining*
retd. *retained* or *returned*
retn. *return*
r. & g. *rubbed and gauged*
r.h. *rivet head*
r.l. *red lead*
rly. *railway*
ro. *rough*
r.s. *rolled steel*
r.s.j. *rolled steel joist*
r.w. *rainwater*

scrd. *screwed*
sec. or sectn. *section*
seedg. *seeding*
settg. *setting*
sk. *sunk*
s.l. *short length*
sli. slight
slopg. *sloping*
sm. *small*
smth. *smooth*
soc. *socket*
soff. *soffit*
spec. *specification*
specd. or specfd. *specified*

spld. *splayed*
sq. *square*
s.q. *small quantities*
s. & s. *spigot and socket*
st. *stone or straight*
stan. *stanchion*
stand. *standard*
stl. *steel*
stlwk. *steelwork*
strt. *straight*
struct. *structure*
surf. *surface*
surrd. *surround*
susp. *suspended*
S.V. *sluice valve*
S.W. *surface water*
swd. *softwood*

t *tonne*
tankg. *tanking*
tapd. *tapered*
tarmac. *tarmacadam*
tbr. *timber*
tempy. *temporary*
t. & g. *tongued and grooved*
th. *thick*
thro. *through* or *throated*
timbg. or timberg. *timbering*
tr. *trench*
trimmg. *trimming*
trowld. *trowelled*

UB *Universal beam*
UC *Universal column*
u/c *undercoat*
u/s *underside*

vert. *vertical*
vol. *volume*

w. *with*
W.A. *water authority*
walg. *waling*
wd. *wood*
wdw. *window*
wethd. *weathered*
w.i. *wrought iron*
wk. *work*
W.O. *wash-out*
workg. *working*
w.p. *waterproof*
wrot. *wrought*
wt. *weight*

xtg. *existing*

Y.st. *York stone*

Note: The abbreviation CESMM3 has been used extensively throughout this book and refers to the *Civil Engineering Standard Method of Measurement, Third Edition*.

Appendix 2 – Mensuration Formulae

Figure	*Area*
Square	$(\text{side})^2$
Rectangle	length × breadth
Triangle	$\frac{1}{2} \times$ base × height or $\sqrt{[s(s-a)(s-b)(s-c)]}$ where $s = \frac{1}{2} \times$ sum of the three sides, and a, b and c are the lengths of the three sides
Hexagon	$2.6 \times (\text{side})^2$
Octagon	$4.83 \times (\text{side})^2$
Parallelogram	base × height
Trapezoid	height $\times \frac{1}{2}$(base + top)
Circle	$\frac{22}{7} \times \text{radius}^2$ or $\frac{22}{7} \times \frac{1}{4}\ \text{diameter}^2$ (πr^2) $\left(\frac{\pi D^2}{4}\right)$ circumference = $2 \times \frac{22}{7} \times$ radius or $(2\pi r)$ $\frac{22}{7} \times$ diameter (πD)
Sector of circle	$\frac{1}{2}$ length of arc × radius
Segment of circle	area of sector – area of triangle or for practical purposes, a useful approximation is $\frac{2}{3} \times$ base × height

Figure	*Volume*	*Surface Area*
Prism	area of base × height	circumference of base × height
Cube	$(\text{side})^3$	$6 \times (\text{side})^2$
Cylinder	$\frac{22}{7} \times \text{radius}^2 \times \text{length}$ $(\pi r^2 h)$	$2 \times \frac{22}{7} \times \text{radius} \times (\text{length} + \text{radius})$ $[2\pi r(h + r)]$
Sphere	$\frac{4}{3} \times \frac{22}{7} \times \text{radius}^3$ $(\frac{4}{3}\pi r^3)$	$4 \times \frac{22}{7} \times \text{radius}^2$ $(4\pi r^2)$
Segment of sphere	$\frac{22}{7} \times \frac{\text{height}}{6} \times (3\ \text{radius}^2 + \text{height}^2)$ $[(\pi h/6) \times (3r^2 + h^2)]$	curved surface $= 2 \times \frac{22}{7} \times \text{radius} \times \text{height}$ $(2\pi rh)$
Pyramid	$\frac{1}{3}$ area of base × height	$\frac{1}{2}$ circumference of base × slant height
Cone	$\frac{1}{3} \times \frac{22}{7} \times \text{radius}^2 \times \text{height}$ $(\frac{1}{3}\pi r^2 h)$	$\frac{22}{7} \times$ radius × slant height (l) (πrl)
Frustum of pyramid	$\frac{1}{3}$ height $[A + B + \sqrt{(AB)}]$ where A is area of large end and B is area of small end.	$\frac{1}{2}$ mean circumference × slant height
Frustum of cone	$\frac{22}{7} \times \frac{1}{3}$ height $(R^2 + r^2 + Rr)$ where R is radius of large end and r is radius of small end. $[\frac{1}{3}\pi h(R^2 + r^2 + Rr)]$	$\frac{22}{7} \times$ slant height $(R + r)$ $[\pi l(R + r)]$ where l is slant height

For Simpson's rule and prismoidal formula see Chapter 5.

Index